enVisionMATH ★ 2.0

Volume 1 Topics 1-8

Authors

Randall I. Charles
Professor Emeritus
Department of Mathematics
San Jose State University
San Jose, California

Janet H. Caldwell
Professor of Mathematics
Rowan University
Glassboro, New Jersey

Juanita Copley
Professor Emerita, College of Education
University of Houston
Houston, Texas

Warren Crown
Professor Emeritus of Mathematics
Education
Graduate School of Education
Rutgers University
New Brunswick, New Jersey

Francis (Skip) Fennell
L. Stanley Bowlsbey Professor
of Education and Graduate and
Professional Studies
McDaniel College
Westminster, Maryland

Stuart J. Murphy
Visual Learning Specialist
Boston, Massachusetts

Kay B. Sammons
Coordinator of Elementary Mathematics
Howard County Public Schools
Ellicott City, Maryland

Jane F. Schielack
Professor of Mathematics
Associate Dean for Assessment and
Pre K-12 Education, College of Science
Texas A&M University
College Station, Texas

Mathematicians

Roger Howe
Professor of Mathematics
Yale University
New Haven, Connecticut

Gary Lippman
Professor of Mathematics and Computer
Science
California State University East Bay
Hayward, California

SAVVAS
LEARNING COMPANY

Contributing Authors

Zachary Champagne
District Facilitator, Duval County Public Schools
Florida Center for Research in Science,
Technology, Engineering, and Mathematics
(FCR-STEM)
Jacksonville, Florida

Jonathan A. Wray
Mathematics Instructional Facilitator
Howard County Public Schools
Ellicott City, Maryland

ELL Consultants

Janice Corona
Retired Administrator
Dallas ISD, Multi-Lingual Department
Dallas, Texas

Jim Cummins
Professor
The University of Toronto
Toronto, Canada

Texas Reviewers

Theresa Bathe
Teacher
Fort Bend ISD

Chrissy Beltran
School Wide Project Coordinator
Ysleta ISD

Renee Cutright
Teacher
Amarillo ISD

Sharon Grimm
Teacher
Houston ISD

Esmeralda Herrera
Teacher
San Antonio ISD

Sherry Johnson
Teacher
Round Rock ISD

Elvia Lopez
Teacher
Denton ISD

Antoinese Pride
Instructional Coach
Dallas ISD

Joanna Ratliff
Teacher
Keller ISD

Courtney Jo Ridehuber
Teacher
Mansfield ISD

Nannie D. Scurlock-McKnight
Mathematics Specialist
A.W. Brown Fellowship-Leadership Academy
Dallas, TX

Brian Sinclair
Math Instructional Specialist
Fort Worth ISD

ISBN-13: 978-0-328-76721-2
ISBN-10:   0-328-76721-2
16 2021

Look for these digital resources in every lesson!

Digital Resources

 Go to SavvasTexas.com

 Solve
Solve & Share problems plus math tools

 Learn
Visual Learning Animation Plus with animation, interaction, and math tools

 Glossary
Animated Glossary in English and Spanish

 Tools
Math Tools to help you understand

 Check
Quick Check for each lesson

 Games
Math Games to help you learn

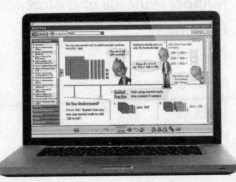

eText
The pages in your book online

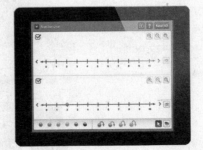

SavvasTexas.com
Everything you need for math anytime, anywhere

Key

Number and Operations

Algebraic Reasoning

Geometry and Measurement

Data Analysis

Personal Financial Literacy

Mathematical Process Standards are found in all lessons.

Digital Resources at SavvasTexas.com

Solve

Learn

Glossary

A-Z

Check

Tools

Games

And remember, the pages in your book are also online!

Contents

⊕ Topics

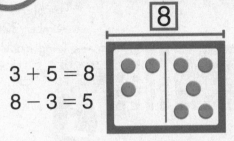

Volume 1

Addition Strategies

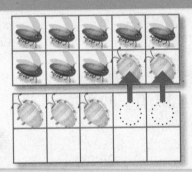

Hi, I'm Marta. This shows how you can use ten-frames to make a 10.

⭐ TEKS 2.1A, 2.1B, 2.1C, 2.1D, 2.1E, 2.1F, 2.1G, 2.4, 2.4A

Subtraction Strategies

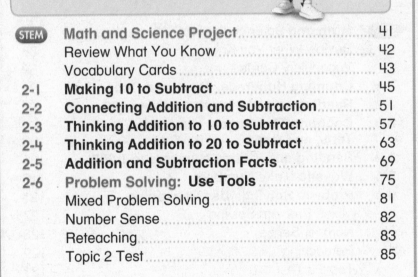

$$3 + 5 = 8$$
$$8 - 3 = 5$$

Hi, I'm Jackson. This shows a way to use counters to solve 8 − 3.

⭐ TEKS 2.1A, 2.1B, 2.1C, 2.1D, 2.1E, 2.1F, 2.1G, 2.4, 2.4A, 2.7, 2.7C

Volume 1

TOPIC 3 — Numbers to 1,200

Hi, I'm Emily. This shows the number 328 using models.

TEKS 2.1A, 2.1B, 2.1C, 2.1D, 2.1E, 2.1F, 2.1G, 2.2, 2.2A, 2.2B

TOPIC 4 — Comparing and Ordering to 1,200

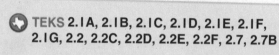

least , , 407 greatest

Hi, I'm Carlos. This shows how to compare and order numbers using place value.

TEKS 2.1A, 2.1B, 2.1C, 2.1D, 2.1E, 2.1F, 2.1G, 2.2, 2.2C, 2.2D, 2.2E, 2.2F, 2.7, 2.7B

TOPIC 5 — Exploring Addition and Subtraction

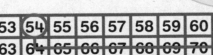

$$54 + 18 = 72$$

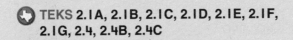

Hi, I'm Jada. This shows how you can add on a hundred chart.

TEKS 2.1A, 2.1B, 2.1C, 2.1D, 2.1E, 2.1F, 2.1G, 2.4, 2.4B, 2.4C

TOPIC 6 — Adding 2-Digit Numbers

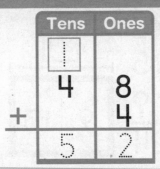

Tens	Ones
1	
4	8
+	4
5	2

Hi, I'm Daniel. This shows how to model a 2-digit addition problem.

TEKS 2.1A, 2.1B, 2.1C, 2.1D, 2.1E, 2.1F, 2.1G, 2.2F, 2.4B, 2.4C, 2.9C

Volume 1

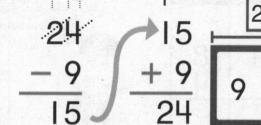

TOPIC 7 — Subtracting 2-Digit Numbers

Hi, it's Marta again. This shows how you can use addition to check subtraction.

⭐ TEKS 2.1A, 2.1B, 2.1C, 2.1D, 2.1E, 2.1F, 2.1G, 2.2F, 2.4, 2.4B, 2.4C, 2.4D, 2.9C

TOPIC 8 — 3-Digit Addition and Subtraction

Hi, I'm Alex. This shows how you can count on to find a missing part.

$100 \quad 100 \quad 10 \quad 10$

$440, 540, 640, 650, 660$

You counted on 220.

$440 + 220 = 660$

⭐ TEKS 2.1A, 2.1B, 2.1C, 2.1D, 2.1E, 2.1F, 2.1G, 2.4C, 2.4D

Volume 2

 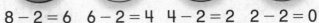

TOPIC 11 — Number Patterns and Algebra

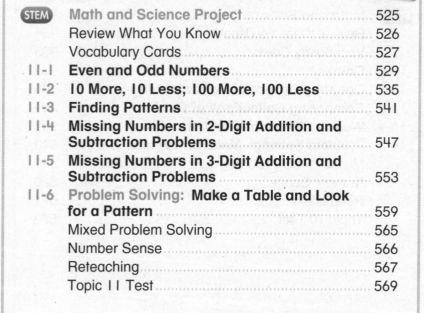

Hi, it's Emily again. This shows numbers that are 100 more as you read down each column.

TEKS 2.1A, 2.1B, 2.1C, 2.1D, 2.1E, 2.1F, 2.1G, 2.2C, 2.7, 2.7A, 2.7B, 2.7C

TOPIC 12 — Fractions

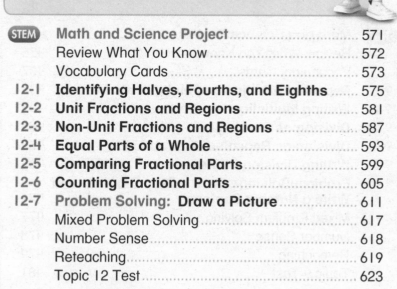

Hi, it's Jackson again. This shows that nine fourths is the same as two wholes and one fourth.

TEKS 2.1A, 2.1B, 2.1C, 2.1D, 2.1E, 2.1F, 2.1G, 2.3, 2.3A, 2.3B, 2.3C, 2.3D, 2.8E

Volume 2

TOPIC 13 — Geometry

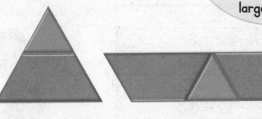

Hi, it's Marta again. This shows how you can use smaller shapes to make larger shapes.

TEKS 2.1A, 2.1B, 2.1C, 2.1D, 2.1E, 2.1F, 2.1G, 2.8, 2.8A, 2.8B, 2.8C, 2.8D, 2.8E

TOPIC 14 — Measurement

Hi, it's Daniel again. This shows 8:27 on two different clocks.

TEKS 2.1A, 2.1B, 2.1C, 2.1D, 2.1E, 2.1F, 2.1G, 2.9, 2.9A, 2.9B, 2.9D, 2.9E, 2.9F, 2.9G

TOPIC 15

Data

Hi, it's Emily again. This shows a pictograph that can be used to record and compare data.

Favorite Ball Games

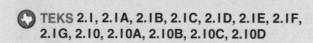

Baseball	🧍🧍
Soccer	🧍🧍🧍🧍🧍🧍🧍
Tennis	🧍🧍🧍🧍

Each 🧍 = 1 student

TEKS 2.1, 2.1A, 2.1B, 2.1C, 2.1D, 2.1E, 2.1F, 2.1G, 2.10, 2.10A, 2.10B, 2.10C, 2.10D

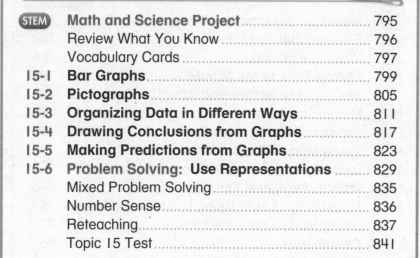

Volume 2

TOPIC 16

Personal Financial Literacy

Hi, it's Carlos again. This shows a chart that keeps track of how much money Joe pays back each week.

Week	Amount Joe Owes
1	$10 - $2 = $8
2	$8 - $2 = $6
3	$6 - $2 = $4
4	$4 - $2 = $2
5	$2 - $2 = $0

TEKS 2.1A, 2.1B, 2.1C, 2.1D, 2.1E, 2.1F, 2.1G, 2.10C, 2.11, 2.11A, 2.11B, 2.11C, 2.11D, 2.11E, 2.11F

Volume 2

Step Up to Grade 3

These lessons help prepare you for Grade 3.

TEKS 3.1A, 3.1B, 3.1C, 3.1D, 3.1E, 3.1F, 3.1G, 3.2, 3.2A, 3.2B, 3.2D, 3.3, 3.3A, 3.3C, 3.3D, 3.4, 3.4A, 3.5A

Addition Strategies

Essential Question: What are strategies for finding addition facts?

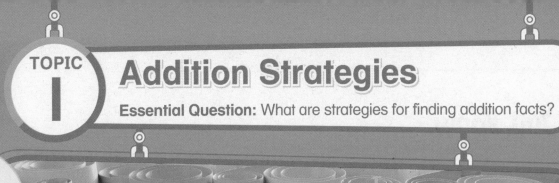

Look at the paper designs!

You can change an object like paper by cutting and folding it.

Wow! Let's do this project and learn more.

Math and Science Project: Arts, Crafts, and Addition

Find Out Gather sheets of paper, scissors, tape, or glue. Talk to your partner about ways to change the paper to make art.

Journal: Make a Book Show your paper art in a book. In your book, also:

- Compare the art to the sheets of paper you used.

- Make up and solve addition problems about the paper you changed to make art.

Name _____

Review What You Know

Vocabulary

1. Circle the sign for **plus**.

$3 + 2 = 5$

2. Circle the number of cubes **in all**.

$3 + 2 = 5$

3. Circle the fact that shows 8 as the **whole**.

$1 + 8 = 9$

$8 + 5 = 13$

$4 + 4 = 8$

Understanding Addition

4. Write an addition sentence to add the cubes.

____ + ____ = ____

5. Write an addition sentence to answer the question.

Bill has 4 baseballs.
Tess has 2 baseballs.
How many baseballs do they have in all?

____ + ____ = ____

Making 10

6. Write the numbers that show a way to make 10.

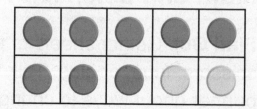

____ + ____ = ____

Study the words on the front of the card.
Complete the activity on the back.

A-Z

---

doubles

$$4 + 4 = 8$$

---

near doubles

$$4 + 5 = 9$$

---

addend

$$2 + 5 = 7$$

addends

---

sum

$$3 + 4 = 7$$

$$
\begin{array}{r}
4 \\
+3 \\
\hline
7
\end{array}
$$

sum ⟶ 7

My Word Cards

Use what you know to complete the sentences.
Extend learning by writing your own sentence using each word.

The numbers that are added are called

_____.

In a _____

_____

fact, the two numbers being added are one apart.

In a _____

fact, the two numbers being added are the same.

When adding, the total is called the

_____.

Solve & Share

You know that $2 + 2 = 4$.
Tell how knowing that fact can help you solve $2 + 3$.

⭐ **TEKS 2.4A** Recall basic facts to add and subtract within 20 with automaticity. **Mathematical Process Standards** 2.1D, 2.1F, 2.1G.

Digital Resources at SavvasTexas.com

Solve Learn Glossary Check Tools Games

$$2 + 2 = 4 \qquad\qquad 2 + 3 = \underline{}$$

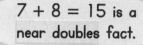

You can use a **doubles** fact to help you add.

Doubles

| 3 + 3 | 5 + 5 |

4 + 4

Find 7 + 8.

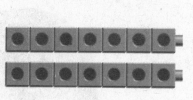

7 + 8 is 1 more than 7 + 7.

7 + 8 = 15 is a near doubles fact.

Do You Understand?

Show Me! Which doubles fact will help you add 8 + 9? How do you know which number to double?

☆ **Guided Practice** ☆

Complete the doubles facts.
Use the doubles facts to solve the near doubles.

1. 2 + 2 = __4__   2 + 3 = ____

2. ____ = 4 + 4   ____ = 4 + 5

3.
$$\begin{array}{r} 3 \\ + 3 \\ \hline \square \end{array}$$
$$\begin{array}{r} 3 \\ + 4 \\ \hline \square \end{array}$$

4.
$$\begin{array}{r} 7 \\ + 7 \\ \hline \square \end{array}$$
$$\begin{array}{r} 7 \\ + 8 \\ \hline \square \end{array}$$

6 six

Topic 1 | Lesson 1

Independent Practice

Complete the doubles facts. Use the doubles facts to solve the near doubles.

5. $6 + 6 =$ ___ $6 + 7 =$ ___   6. $5 + 5 =$ ___ $5 + 6 =$ ___

7. $7 + 7 =$ ___ $7 + 8 =$ ___   8. ___ $= 3 + 3$ ___ $= 3 + 4$

9.
$$2 \atop {+2}$$
☐

$$2 \atop {+3}$$
☐

10.
$$4 \atop {+4}$$
☐

$$4 \atop {+5}$$
☐

11.
$$8 \atop {+8}$$
☐

$$8 \atop {+9}$$
☐

12. **Extend Your Thinking** Complete the doubles and near doubles facts.

$9 +$ ☐ $= 18$ ☐ $+$ ☐ $= 19$

13. John drew 4 houses.
Then he drew 5 more houses.
How many houses did John draw in all?

Draw a picture and write a number sentence.

_____ + _____ = _____ houses

---

14. Kate's dog had 6 puppies.
Jim's dog had 1 more puppy than Kate's dog.

Which number sentence shows how many puppies in all?

○ 6 + 1 = 7

○ 6 + 7 = 13

○ 6 + 6 = 12

○ 7 + 7 = 14

15. Extend Your Thinking
Choose a doubles fact.
Use that doubles fact to draw a picture that shows a near doubles story.

Name _____

Another Look You can use a doubles fact to solve a near doubles fact.

To solve a near doubles fact, you can add 1 more to the doubles fact.

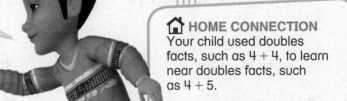

🏠 **HOME CONNECTION** Your child used doubles facts, such as $4 + 4$, to learn near doubles facts, such as $4 + 5$.

HOME ACTIVITY Have your child use common objects, such as pennies or buttons, to show doubles and near doubles. Then ask your child to write addition sentences to show the facts.

$6 + 6 =$ 12

Doubles Fact

$6 + 7 =$ 13

Near Doubles Fact

Write and solve the doubles facts and the near doubles facts.

1.

___ + ___ = ___   ___ + ___ = ___

2.

___ + ___ = ___   ___ + ___ = ___

Write an addition sentence to solve the problem. Use doubles facts to help you.

3. Algebra A number plus 6 equals 12.
What is the number?

___ + ___ = ___

The number is ___.

4. Algebra 7 plus a number equals 13.
What is the number?

___ + ___ = ___

The number is ___.

5. Algebra A number plus 9 equals 19.
What is the number?

___ + ___ = ___

The number is ___.

6. Terry's dollhouse has 7 windows on the first floor and 8 windows on the second floor.

Which shows how Terry found the number of windows in all?

○ 6 + 6 and 1 more is 13.

○ 7 + 7 and 1 more is 15.

○ 8 + 8 and 1 more is 17.

○ 9 + 9 and 1 more is 19.

7. Extend Your Thinking Draw a picture to show the story.
Then write an addition sentence for the story.

Jane has 5 books.
Fred has 1 more book than Jane.
How many books do Fred and Jane have in all?

___ + ___ = ___

_____ books

Name _____

 Solve & Share

Use cubes to show $4 + 5 = 9$.
What will happen to the total number of cubes if you change the order of the numbers being added? Explain.

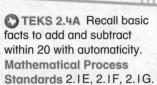

TEKS 2.4A Recall basic facts to add and subtract within 20 with automaticity. **Mathematical Process Standards 2.1E, 2.1F, 2.1G.**

Digital Resources at SavvasTexas.com

Solve Learn Glossary Check Tools Games

$4 + 5 = 9$ ___ + ___ = ___

You can write an addition sentence for this cube train.

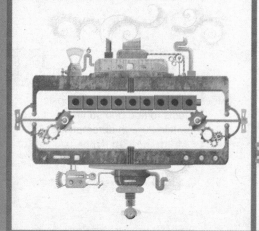

The machine changes the order of the **addends**, which are the numbers being added.

You can change the order of the addends.

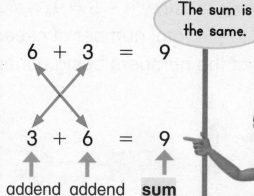

$$6 + 3 = 9$$

$$3 + 6 = 9$$

addend addend **sum**

You can write the facts this way, too.

The sum is the same.

$$\begin{array}{r} 6 \\ +3 \\ \hline 9 \end{array} \qquad \begin{array}{r} 3 \\ +6 \\ \hline 9 \end{array}$$

Do You Understand?

Show Me! How is $6 + 3$ similar to $3 + 6$?

Guided Practice Write the addition fact for the cubes. Then change the order of the addends.

1.

$$3 + 1 = 4$$

___ + ___ = ___

2.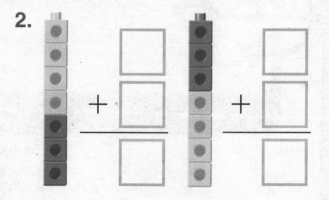

___ + ___

___ + ___

12 twelve

Topic 1 | Lesson 2

Independent Practice

Write the sum. Then change the order of the addends.

3. $8 + 2 = \underline{\quad}$

$\underline{\quad} + \underline{\quad} = \underline{\quad}$

4. $8 + 5 = \underline{\quad}$

$\underline{\quad} + \underline{\quad} = \underline{\quad}$

5. $9 + 3 = \underline{\quad}$

$\underline{\quad} + \underline{\quad} = \underline{\quad}$

6.
$$\begin{array}{r} 1 \\ + \ 5 \\ \hline \square \end{array} \qquad \begin{array}{r} \square \\ + \ \square \\ \hline \square \end{array}$$

7.
$$\begin{array}{r} 6 \\ + \ 2 \\ \hline \square \end{array} \qquad \begin{array}{r} \square \\ + \ \square \\ \hline \square \end{array}$$

8.
$$\begin{array}{r} 5 \\ + \ 6 \\ \hline \square \end{array} \qquad \begin{array}{r} \square \\ + \ \square \\ \hline \square \end{array}$$

9. **Extend Your Thinking** Write the missing numbers.
The same shapes are the same numbers.

$\blacksquare + 6 = 10$

$6 + \blacksquare = 10$

$\blacksquare + \blacktriangle = 9$

$\blacktriangle + \blacksquare = 9$

$\blacksquare = \underline{\quad}$

$\blacktriangle = \underline{\quad}$

10. Joy has 4 flowers in her garden.
Then she plants 3 more.
How many flowers does Joy have now?
Draw a picture. Then write facts for this
story with the addends in a different order.

___ + ___ = ___

___ + ___ = ___

11. Kate has 7 fish.
⭐ Nick has some fish.
Kate and Nick have 12 fish in all.

Choose the facts for this story.

7 + 5 = 12   7 + 12 = 19
5 + 7 = 12   5 + 12 = 17
  ○   ○

7 + 5 = 12   5 + 12 = 17
5 + 12 = 17   12 + 5 = 17
  ○   ○

12. **Extend Your Thinking** Find the group of
pictures in Box 1 and Box 2 that have the
same objects.
Write two addition sentences to show how
many there are in all.

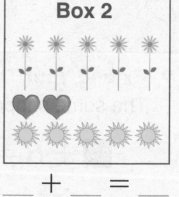

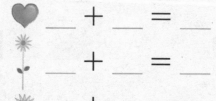

___ + ___ = ___   ___ + ___ = ___

___ + ___ = ___   ___ + ___ = ___

___ + ___ = ___   ___ + ___ = ___

Name _____

Another Look You can add two numbers in any order.
The sum is the same.

$5 + 2 = \underline{7}$

$2 + 5 = \underline{7}$

🏠 **HOME CONNECTION**
Your child added the same two numbers in a different order, such as 6 + 2 and 2 + 6, and found that the sum is always the same.

HOME ACTIVITY Have your child use small clothing items, such as socks or mittens, to model the addition facts 5 + 4 and 4 + 5. Then ask your child to use their models to explain why the sum is always 9.

Write addition facts for each picture.

1.

___ + ___ = ___

___ + ___ = ___

2.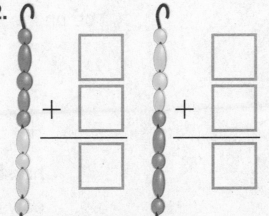

___ + ⬜ ⬜ ⬜

3.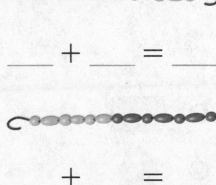

___ + ___ = ___

___ + ___ = ___

Write two addition facts for each story. Then solve.

4. Diego has 9 action figures.
He buys some more action figures.
Now he has 14 action figures.
How many action figures did Diego buy?

_____ + _____ = _____

_____ + _____ = _____

_____ action figures

5. Ana draws 3 circles.
Then she draws 8 more circles.
How many circles did Ana draw?

_____ + _____ = _____

_____ + _____ = _____

_____ circles

6. Which shape belongs in the sentence?

○

○

○

○

7. Extend Your Thinking Draw a picture to solve. Then write two addition facts for the story.

A farm has horses and cows. There are 15 animals in all. How many horses and cows could be on the farm?

_____ + _____ = 15

_____ + _____ = 15

_____ horses

_____ cows

Name _____

Solve & Share

You and two friends see some birds. You see 6 red birds, one friend sees 5 yellow birds, and the other friend sees 4 blue birds.

What are some different ways to find the sum of 6, 5, and 4? Select real objects, connecting cubes, technology tools, or paper and pencil to solve the problem. Show your work.

TEKS 2.4A Recall basic facts to add and subtract within 20 with automaticity. **Mathematical Process Standards** 2.1A, 2.1B, 2.1C, 2.1D, 2.1G.

Digital Resources at SavvasTexas.com

Solve   Learn   Glossary   Check   Tools   Games

How can you add these three numbers?

2
3
6

You can add $2 + 3 = 5$ and then add the **6**.
$5 + 6 = 11$

You can also add $6 + 3 = 9$ and then add **2** more.
$9 + 2 = 11$

You can add in any order and get the same sum.

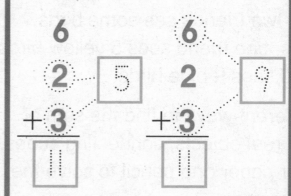

6
2
[5]
+3
[11]

6
2
[9]
+3
[11]

You can pick any two numbers to add first.

5
4
+1
[10]

$4 + 1$
$5 + 4$
$5 + 1$

Do You Understand?

Show Me! What are two different ways you could add $3 + 4 + 7$? Explain.

☆ **Guided Practice** ☆   Find each sum in two different ways. Circle the numbers you added first. Then write their sum in the box.

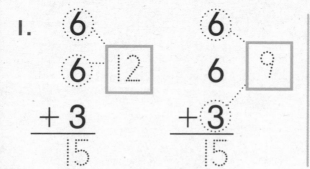

1.
6
6
[12]
+3
15

6
6
[9]
+3
15

2.
5
4
[ ]
+3

5
4
[ ]
+3

3.
[ ]
$4 + 6 + 4 =$ ___

[ ]
$4 + 6 + 4 =$ ___

Topic 1 | Lesson 3

Independent Practice

Write the sum. Circle the numbers you added first.

4. $3 + 8 + 2 =$ ___

5. $5 + 9 + 5 =$ ___

6. $3 + 4 + 6 =$ ___

7. ___ $= 9 + 4 + 1$

8. $6 + 5 + 7 =$ ___

9. ___ $= 2 + 8 + 1$

10.
$$\begin{array}{r} 9 \\ 9 \\ + 2 \\ \hline \end{array}$$

11.
$$\begin{array}{r} 8 \\ 3 \\ + 1 \\ \hline \end{array}$$

12.
$$\begin{array}{r} 3 \\ 5 \\ + 7 \\ \hline \end{array}$$

13.
$$\begin{array}{r} 2 \\ 6 \\ + 8 \\ \hline \end{array}$$

14.
$$\begin{array}{r} 8 \\ 2 \\ + 4 \\ \hline \end{array}$$

15.
$$\begin{array}{r} 7 \\ 1 \\ + 7 \\ \hline \end{array}$$

16. **Extend Your Thinking** Fill in the missing numbers. Then explain how the addition sentences are similar.

_____

_____

_____

$6 +$ ___ $+ 7 = 17$

___ $+ 6 + 4 = 17$

$4 + 7 +$ ___ $= 17$

17. Ron has 4 red crayons, 7 blue crayons, and 4 green crayons.

How many crayons does Ron have in all?

_____ crayons

18. Three teams scored 19 points in all.

The first team scored 6 points.

The second team scored 8 points.

How many points did the third team score?

_____ points

19. There are three kinds of balls.

List 3 different ways you can

add to find the total number of balls.

_____

_____

_____

20. Josie has 2 baseballs and her brother has 4 baseballs.

They then get 8 more baseballs and 2 basketballs.

How many baseballs do they now have in all?

6 ○   10 ○

14 ○   16 ○

21. Extend Your Thinking Shayla, Lucky, and Mia collected 15 cans in all on Clean-Up Day.

Complete the chart and the addition sentence to show how many cans each child could have collected.

Cans Collected		
Shayla	**Lucky**	**Mia**

____ + ____ + ____ = 15 cans

Name _____

Another Look There are different ways to add three numbers.
You can add any two numbers or try to make a 10.
You can also look for doubles or near doubles.
Then add the third number.

🏠 **HOME CONNECTION**
Your child added three numbers.

HOME ACTIVITY Have your child use pennies or other small objects to show different ways to add $9 + 1 + 4$. Continue by adding three other numbers less than 10.

Add any two numbers.

$$\begin{array}{r} 5 \\ 3 \\ + 8 \\ \hline 16 \end{array} \qquad \boxed{8}$$

$$\begin{array}{r} + 8 \\ \hline 16 \end{array}$$

Try to make a 10.

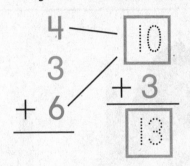

$$\begin{array}{r} 4 \\ 3 \\ + 6 \end{array} \qquad \boxed{10}$$

$$\begin{array}{r} + 3 \\ \hline 13 \end{array}$$

Look for doubles.

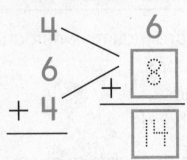

$$\begin{array}{r} 4 \\ 6 \\ + 4 \end{array} \qquad \begin{array}{r} 6 \\ + \boxed{8} \\ \hline 14 \end{array}$$

 Find the sums.
Draw lines from the first two numbers you add.

1.
$$\begin{array}{r} 7 \\ 4 \\ + 3 \\ \hline \end{array} \qquad \begin{array}{r} 4 \\ + \square \\ \hline \square \end{array}$$

2.
$$\begin{array}{r} 8 \\ 4 \\ + 8 \\ \hline \end{array} \qquad \begin{array}{r} 4 \\ + \square \\ \hline \square \end{array}$$

3.
$$\begin{array}{r} 2 \\ 6 \\ + 7 \\ \hline \end{array} \qquad \begin{array}{r} 2 \\ + \square \\ \hline \square \end{array}$$

4. Algebra Which number is missing?

$$3 + 7 + \underline{} = 15$$

    3   5   6   7
    ○   ○   ○   ○

5. Algebra Which number is missing?

$$\underline{} + 8 + 2 = 13$$

    8   6   3   2
    ○   ○   ○   ○

6. Algebra Which number is missing?

$$2 + \underline{} + 6 = 14$$

    2   4   5   6
    ○   ○   ○   ○

---

7. Adam and his friends are making wristbands.
Adam makes 7 wristbands.
Teri makes 6 wristbands.
Connor makes 5 wristbands.

Use pictures, numbers, or words to show three different ways to find the total number of wristbands.

---

8. Lila cut out 14 shapes in all.
Lila cut out 3 rainbows.
She cut out some moons.
She cut out 7 stars.
How many moons did Lila cut out?

   ○   7

   ○   6

   ○   5

   ○   4

9. Extend Your Thinking Add across and down. Write the missing numbers.

9	3	2	14
	6		14
1		8	14
14	14	14	

Name _____

Solve & Share

How can thinking about 10 help you solve 9 + 3?
Use the ten-frames and counters to help show how.

⭐ TEKS 2.4A Recall basic facts to add and subtract within 20 with automaticity. Also, 2.4. Mathematical Process Standards 2.1C, 2.1D, 2.1G.

Digital Resources at SavvasTexas.com

Solve   Learn   Glossary   Check   Tools   Games

$$\begin{array}{r} 9 \\ +\ 3 \\ \hline \end{array}$$

You can make a 10 to help you add 8.

$\begin{array}{r} 8 \\ +5 \\ \hline \boxed{?} \end{array}$

Move 2 counters to make a 10.

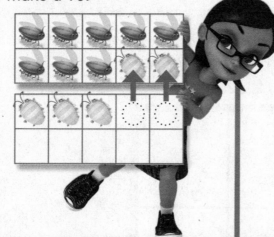

Add with 10.

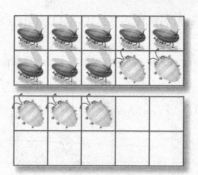

$\begin{array}{r} 10 \\ +3 \\ \hline 13 \end{array}$ so, $\begin{array}{r} 8 \\ +5 \\ \hline 13 \end{array}$

Do You Understand?

Show Me! Why do you move 2 counters to add 8 + 5?

☆ **Guided Practice** ☆ Make a 10 to add. Use counters and ten-frames.

1. $\begin{array}{r} 7 \\ +4 \\ \hline \boxed{?} \end{array}$

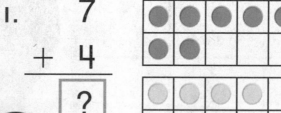

$\begin{array}{r} 10 \\ +\boxed{\vdots} \\ \hline \boxed{\vdots\vdots} \end{array}$ so, $\begin{array}{r} 7 \\ +\boxed{} \\ \hline \boxed{} \end{array}$

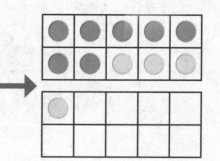

✰ Independent ✰ Practice

Make a 10 to add. Use counters and ten-frames.

2. 8
   + 4
   ☐

3. 3
   + 9
   ☐

4. 6
   + 7
   ☐

5. 5
   + 8
   ☐

6. 7
   + 5
   ☐

7. $5 + 9 =$ ___

8. $3 + 8 =$ ___

9. $4 + 9 =$ ___

10. $7 + 9 =$ ___

Algebra Which number is missing?

11. $8 + 5 = \boxed{} + 3$

12. $6 + 9 = 10 + \boxed{}$

13. $8 + 9 = 10 + \boxed{}$

14. **Extend Your Thinking** Can you make a 10 to help you add $7 + 2 + 5$? Explain.

15. Tan's team has 9 points.
They score 7 more points.
How many points do they have in all?

_____ points

16. The school has a coat drive for charity.
Ana's class donates 8 coats. Nico's class donates 8 coats.
How many coats were donated in all?

_____ coats

17. Mary wrote an addition sentence.
Which number makes her addition sentence true?

Find the missing number!

$$7 + \underline{} = 9 + 5$$

5 ○   6 ○

7 ○   8 ○

18. **Extend Your Thinking** Draw a picture to show how you can make a 10 to help you add $3 + 5 + 9$.

Name _____

Another Look You can make a 10 to help you add.

This shows 8 + 4.

Show 10 + 2.
Move 2 counters to make a 10.

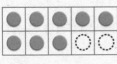
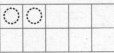

The sums are the same!

🏠 **HOME CONNECTION**
Your child explored strategies for adding by making 10.

HOME ACTIVITY Have your child use buttons to make a group of 9 and a group of 5. Ask your child to show you how to make a group of 10 buttons to help find the sum.

8 + 4 is the same as 10 + 2.

$8 + 4 = \underline{12}$ $10 + 2 = \underline{12}$

Make a 10 to help you add.

1. Find 9 + 7.   Move 1 counter to make a 10.

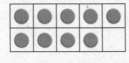

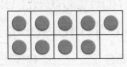
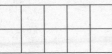

9 + 7 is the same as 10 + ___.

$9 + 7 = \underline{}$ $\underline{} + \underline{} = \underline{}$

2. Find 7 + 5.

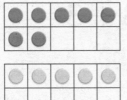

Move ___ counters to make a 10.

7 + 5 is the same as 10 + ___.

$7 + 5 = \underline{}$ $\underline{} + \underline{} = \underline{}$

3. Beth has 8 fish and 7 snails. ★
How can Beth make a 10 to find how many fish and snails she has in all?

$10 + 9$ $10 + 8$ $10 + 7$ $10 + 5$
  ○   ○   ○   ○

4. Ari has 7 new pens and 4 old pens. ★
How can he make a 10 to find how many pens he has in all?

$10 + 1$ $10 + 3$ $10 + 5$ $10 + 7$
  ○   ○   ○   ○

Add. Then draw lines to match addition problems with the same sum.

5. $9 + 6 =$ _____

6. $7 + 5 =$ _____

7. $9 + 5 =$ _____

8. $5 + 8 =$ _____

$10 + 2 =$ _____

$10 + 3 =$ _____

$10 + 4 =$ _____

$10 + 5 =$ _____

9. Extend Your Thinking Blanca wants to add $5 + 8 + 3$. Describe how she can make a 10 to solve.

$5 + 8 + 3 =$ _____

_____

_____

_____

10. Extend Your Thinking Jay has 14 blocks in all.
He has 6 yellow blocks.
The rest of the blocks are green.
How many green blocks does Jay have?
Make a 10 to solve.
Jay has _____ green blocks.

Explain how you solved the problem!

_____

_____

_____

Name _____

Solve & Share

Explain how to use the make a 10 strategy to add 7 + 9.

⭐ **TEKS 2.1G** Display, explain, and justify mathematical ideas and arguments using precise mathematical language in written or oral communication. Also, 2.4A. **Mathematical Process Standards** 2.1B, 2.1D, 2.1E.

Digital Resources at SavvasTexas.com

Solve Learn Glossary Check Tools Games

Analyze and Plan

$$6 + 7 = ?$$

Andi wants to write an explanation for Ben about how to use a doubles fact to add $6 + 7$.

How can Andi write a good math explanation?

Good written explanations tell others how you are thinking about a problem.

Solve and Justify

Here is what Andi wrote:

We already know that $6 + 6 = 12$.

$6 + 7$ is just one more.

$6 + 7$ is one more than 12.
$6 + 7 = 13$

Evaluate

Andi used words, pictures, and number sentences in her explanation.

Guided Practice

Explain how to make a 10 to add $9 + 5$.

Do You Understand?

Show Me! How did the pictures help Andi write an explanation?

1.

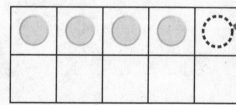

To make a 10, add ____ to ____.

Then add $10 +$ ____.

$10 +$ ____ $=$ ____

So, ____ $+$ ____ $=$ ____.

Topic 1 | Lesson 5

Name _____

Explain how to find each sum.

2. $7 + 8$

3. $8 + 3$

4. $4 + 9 + 5$

5. $7 + 5 + 1$

6. **Extend Your Thinking** Jen wrote an explanation about how to find $8 + 9$.
   Is Jen's explanation correct? Explain how you know.

> We already know that $9 + 9 = 18$.
> $8 + 9$ is just one more.
> So, $8 + 9$ is one more than 18.
> $8 + 9 = 19$

Solve the problems below.

7. Rob picked 7 daisies and 5 tulips from his garden. Explain how you can find the number of flowers Rob picked in all.

8. Donna wrote the addition sentence below.

$$4 + \underline{?} = 9$$

Explain how to find the missing number.

9. Ali wrote the explanation below about how to add $6 + 5$.

> We already know that ___?___.
> $6 + 5$ is just one more.
> So, $6 + 5$ is one more than 10.
> $6 + 5 = 11$

Which is the missing addition fact?

○ $5 + 4 = 9$

○ $5 + 5 = 10$

○ $5 + 6 = 11$

○ $6 + 6 = 12$

10. **Extend Your Thinking** Brin has 19 apples. He has 9 red apples, 8 green apples, and some yellow apples. Explain how to find the number of yellow apples Brin has.

Another Look You can use words, pictures, and number sentences in a math explanation.

What strategy can you use to add 8 + 4?

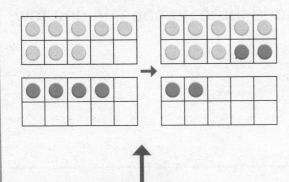

You can make a 10 to help you add 8.

Move _2_ counters to make a 10.

Then add with 10 to get 10 + _2_ = _12_.

The sums are the same, so 8 + 4 = _12_.

Pictures   **Words**   **Number Sentences**

🏠 **HOME CONNECTION**
Your child used pictures, words, and number sentences to write explanations about how to add.

HOME ACTIVITY With your child, write a word problem that can be solved by adding 7 + 6. Then ask your child to write an explanation telling you how to use a strategy to solve the problem.

Explain how you would solve each problem.

1. Alan has 8 animal stickers. Lucy has 9 animal stickers. How many animal stickers do Alan and Lucy have in all?

2. Tasha jumped rope for 8 minutes. Then she jumped rope for 6 more minutes. How many minutes did Tasha jump rope in all?

Use the magic square below. The numbers in each row, column, and diagonal all have the same sum.

8	1	6
3	5	7
4	9	2

3. Explain how you can use a near doubles fact to add the numbers in one row, column, or diagonal.

_____

4. Explain how you can make a 10 to add three numbers in one row, column, or diagonal.

5. Karen wrote the explanation below about how to add three numbers.

Look for a near double to get 13. Then add 4 to get 17.

Which could be the three numbers Karen added?

- ○ $4 + 7 + 6$
- ○ $6 + 4 + 6$
- ○ $6 + 7 + 6$
- ○ $7 + 4 + 7$

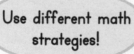
Use different math strategies!

6. Extend Your Thinking Paola solves $7 + 3 + 8$ two different ways. The numbers she added first are circled. Explain how to find the sum each way.

⑦ + ③ + 8

⑦ + 3 + ⑧

Name _____

You can **select tools** like real objects, manipulatives, technology, and paper and pencil to solve problems.

I chose a digital Math Tool to show how to make a 10 to add 7 + 5. The tool makes it easy to show and move counters in ten-frames. 10 + 2 = 12, so 7 + 5 = 12.

Tell whether you would select real objects, manipulatives, technology, or paper and pencil to solve each problem.

1. A bowl has 4 walnuts, 6 peanuts, and 4 pecans. How many nuts are there in all?

_____

_____

_____

2. How is 8 + 5 like 5 + 8?

_____

_____

_____

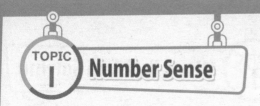

Complete It!

1. Petra likes to explore patterns.
She sees an addition pattern.
Figure out the pattern.
Then fill in the rest of the table.

Addends	Sum
$0 + 1 + 2 =$	3
$1 + 2 + 3 =$	
$2 + 3 + 4 =$	9
$\_\_ + 4 + 5 =$	12
$4 + \_\_ \_\_ =$	
$\_\_ \_\_ =$	

What's Wrong?

2. Kai says, "Doubles are 11, 22, 33, 44, 55, and so on."
Draw a picture of a doubles fact with a sum of 18 to show Kai his mistake.

Code Math

3. Use the code to write the missing numbers.

▲ = 3	● = 6
■ = 4	★ = 7
➡ = 5	✳ = 8

$$\text{✳} + \_\_\_ = 16$$

$$\_\_\_ = \text{➡} + \text{★} + \text{➡}$$

$$\_\_\_ + \text{●} = 13$$

$$\text{➡} + \text{●} = \text{■} + \_\_\_$$

Name _____

Set A

You can use doubles to help you add a near double.

$4 + 4 =$ _8_

So, $3 + 4 =$ _7_ .

$4 + 4 = 8$
$3 + 4$ is one
less than $4 + 4$.
So, $3 + 4 = 7$.

Use digital tools to solve these and other Reteaching problems.

Complete the doubles facts.
Use the doubles facts to solve
the near doubles.

1.　$8 + 8 =$ _____

So, $7 + 8 =$ _____ .

2.　$5 + 5 =$ _____

So, $6 + 5 =$ _____ .

Set B

You can change the order of the addends.
The sum will stay the same.

$4 + 2 =$ _6_

_2_ $+$ _4_ $=$ _6_

Write the sum. Then change the
order of the addends and complete
the problem.

3.　$9 + 3 =$ _____

_____ $+$ _____ $=$ _____

4.　$6 + 4 =$ _____

_____ $+$ _____ $=$ _____

Topic 1

thirty-seven　**37**

You can add any two numbers first.

6 + 4 = 10

Then add the 3.

10 + 3 = 13

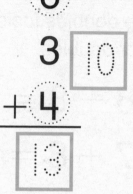

6
3 $\boxed{10}$
+ 4
$\boxed{13}$

Circle the numbers you add first.
Write their sum in the box at the right.
Then complete the problem.

5.
2
7 $\boxed{}$
+ 3
$\boxed{}$

6.
8
8 $\boxed{}$
+ 2
$\boxed{}$

You can make a 10 to help you add 8.

8 + 6 = ?

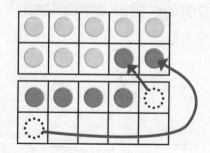

10 + 4 = 14

So, 8 + 6 = 14.

Make a 10 to add 8.

7.
8 + 4 = ?

10
+ $\boxed{}$
$\boxed{}$

8
so, + 4
$\boxed{}$

Name _____

1. Tia has 6 stickers.
   Kay has 1 more sticker than Tia.
   Which shows the number of stickers
   Tia and Kay have in all?

   ○ 13

   ○ 14

   ○ 15

   ○ 16

2. Which is the missing number?

   $$9 + \boxed{} + 2 = 18$$

   ○ 5

   ○ 6

   ○ 7

   ○ 8

3. Tom drew 5 ladybugs.
   Gina drew 6 ladybugs.
   Which number sentence shows how
   many ladybugs there are in all?

   ○ $5 + 5 = 10$

   ○ $5 + 6 = 11$

   ○ $6 + 6 = 12$

   ○ $6 + 7 = 13$

4. Which number sentence shows
   the addends in a different order?

   $$4 + 3 = \underline{}$$

   ○ $7 + 3 = 10$

   ○ $3 + 7 = 10$

   ○ $3 + 4 = 7$

   ○ $4 + 3 = 7$

5. Which number completes the number sentence?

$$7 + 5 = 10 + \underline{\quad}$$

- ○ 2
- ○ 3
- ○ 4
- ○ 5

6. Explain how to find the sum.

$$6 + 7 = ?$$

$$6 + 7 = \underline{\quad}$$

---

7. Three friends made a table to show how many posters they made.

Posters Made			
	Horses	Cats	Dogs
Brian	9	1	3
Fernando	7	6	2
Laurel	4	0	8

Choose one of the friends.
How many posters did that friend make?
Write a number sentence to solve.

I chose _____.

_____ + _____ + _____ = _____

_____ posters

Subtraction Strategies

Essential Question: What are strategies for finding subtraction facts?

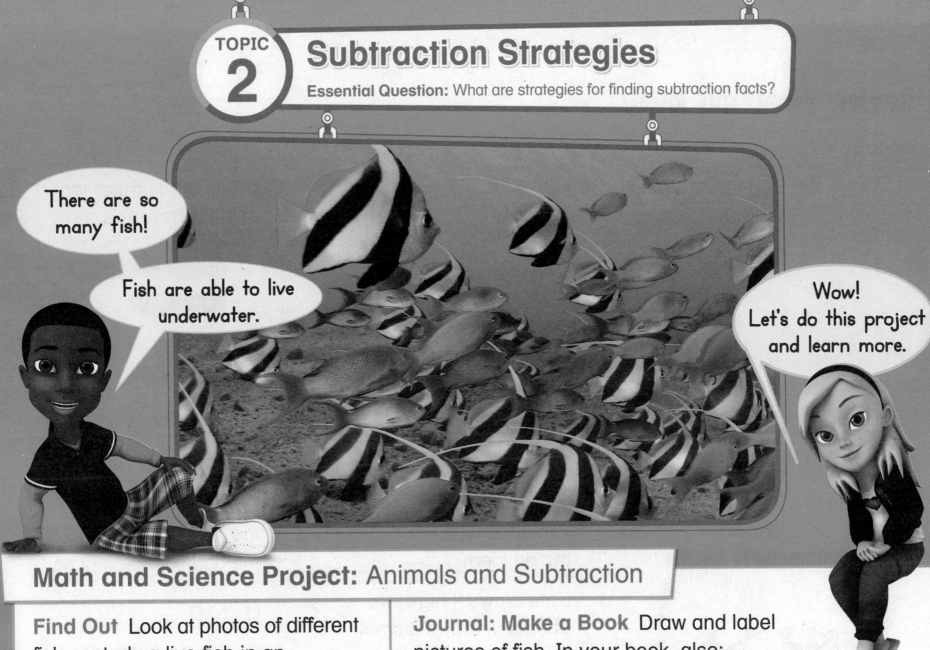

Math and Science Project: Animals and Subtraction

Find Out Look at photos of different fish or study a live fish in an aquarium. Talk to your partner about the body parts that help a fish live in the water.

Journal: Make a Book Draw and label pictures of fish. In your book, also:

- Compare fish to animals that live on land.
- Make up and solve subtraction problems about fish or other animals.

Name _____

Review What You Know

Vocabulary

1. Circle the sign for **equals.**

$$- \quad + \quad =$$

2. Circle the sign for **minus.**

$$- \quad + \quad =$$

3. Circle the number that is the **difference.**

$$6 - 4 = 2$$

Subtraction Stories

4. There are 7 birds on a fence. 2 fly away. How many birds are left?

_____ birds

Doubles Facts

5. Write an addition sentence to solve the problem.

Kate draws 4 big stars. Then she draws 4 small stars. How many stars does Kate draw?

_____ + _____ = _____

Adding in Any Order

6. Change the order of the addends to complete the addition sentences.

$$4 + 3 = \underline{}$$

$$\underline{} + \underline{} = \underline{}$$

My Word Cards

Study the words on the front of the card.
Complete the activity on the back.

related

$2 + 3 = 5$

$5 - 2 = 3$

fact family

$2 + 4 = 6$

$4 + 2 = 6$

$6 - 2 = 4$

$6 - 4 = 2$

My Word Cards

Use what you know to complete the sentences.
Extend learning by writing your own sentence using each word.

A group of related addition and subtraction facts is called a

_____

_____.

Addition facts and subtraction facts are

_____

if they have the same numbers.

Name _____

Solve & Share

14 ladybugs are on a leaf. 6 ladybugs fly away. How can thinking about 10 help you find how many ladybugs are left? Explain.

⭐ TEKS 2.4A Recall basic facts to add and subtract within 20 with automaticity. Also, 2.4. Mathematical Process Standards 2.1C, 2.1E, 2.1G.

Digital Resources at SavvasTexas.com

Solve	Learn	Glossary	Check	Tools	Games

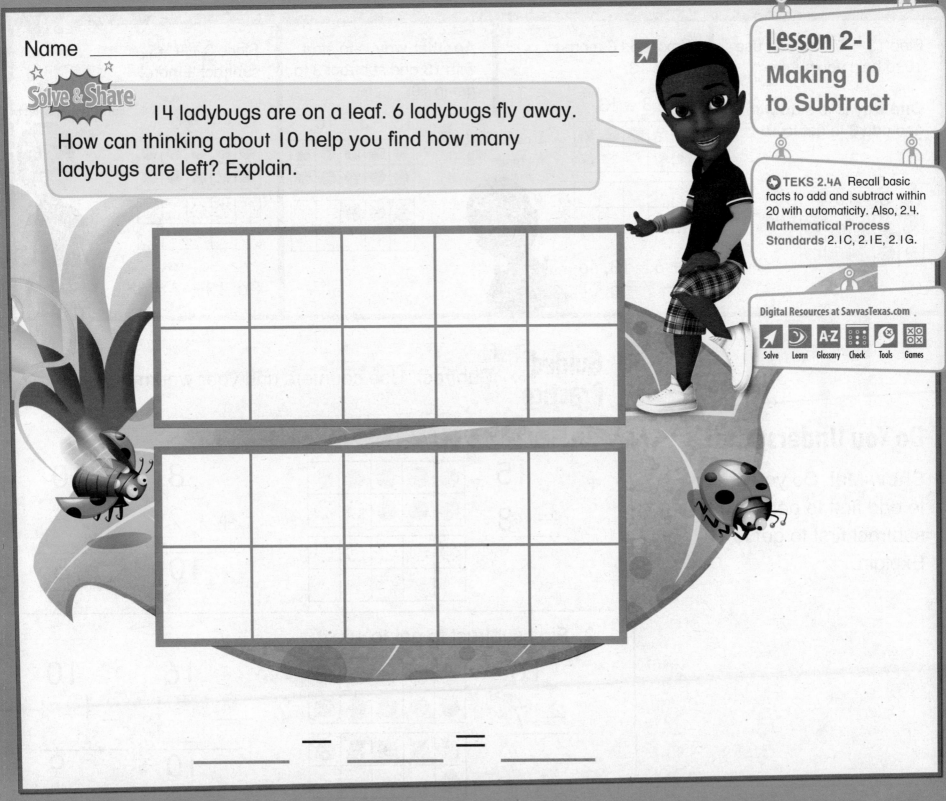

_____ − _____ = _____

Find 13 − 7. You can use 10 to help you subtract.

One way is to start with 7 and add 3 to get to 10.

7 + 3 = 10

Next, add 3 more to make 13.

10 + 3 = 13

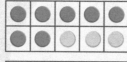

7 + 6 = 13, so
13 − 7 = 6.

I added 6 to 7 to make 13.

Another way is to start with 13 and subtract 3 to get to 10.

13 − 3 = 10

Since 3 + 4 = 7, subtract 4 more.

10 − 4 = 6

I subtracted 7 and have 6 left.

So, 13 − 7 = 6.

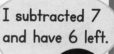
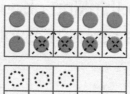

Do You Understand?

Show Me! Do you prefer to add first to get to 10 or subtract first to get to 10? Explain.

☆ **Guided Practice** ☆ Subtract. Use counters and your workmat.

1. First add to get to 10.

$$\begin{array}{r} 15 \\ -\ 8 \\ \hline 7 \end{array}$$

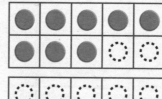

$$\begin{array}{r} 8 \\ +\ 2 \\ \hline 10 \end{array} \qquad \begin{array}{r} 10 \\ +\ 5 \\ \hline 15 \end{array}$$

2. First subtract to get to 10.

$$\begin{array}{r} 16 \\ -\ 7 \\ \hline \end{array}$$

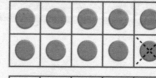
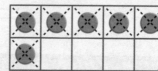

$$\begin{array}{r} 16 \\ -\ \square \\ \hline 10 \end{array} \qquad \begin{array}{r} 10 \\ -\ \square \\ \hline 9 \end{array}$$

Topic 2 | Lesson 1

Name _____

Use 10 to subtract. Use counters and your workmat.

Think of the ways you know to make 10.

3. 11
    − 4

4. 14
    − 8

5. 12
    − 7

6. 12
    − 4

7. 18
    − 9

8. 17
    − 8

9. 16
    − 8

10. 13
    − 4

11. **Extend Your Thinking** Carol wants to subtract
    6 from 15. She first added to get to 10
    and then added again to find her answer.
    Her answer was 10.
    Is Carol correct? Explain.

_____

_____

_____

_____

12. Chen has 12 animal stickers. Mosi has 5 animal stickers. How many more animal stickers does Chen have than Mosi?

_____ animal stickers

13. Angie bought 13 strawberries. She ate 8 of the strawberries. How many strawberries does Angie have now?

_____ strawberries

14. 17 birds are in a pond. Some birds fly away. 9 birds are still in the pond. How many birds flew away?

| 6 | 7 | 8 | 9 |
| ○ | ○ | ○ | ○ |

15. Extend Your Thinking Show how you can use 10 to find 15 − 9.

Name _____

Another Look You can use 10 to help you subtract. Find $13 - 5$.

One way

Subtract $13 - 3 = 10$.
Subtract 2 more to subtract 5 in all. $10 - 2 = 8$

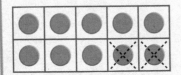

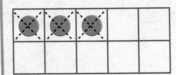

You have 8 left. So, $13 - 5 = 8$.

Another way

Add $5 + 5 = 10$.
Add 3 more to make 13.
$10 + 3 = 13$

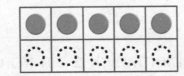

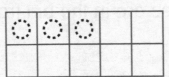

You added $5 + 8 = 13$. So, $13 - 5 = 8$.

Use the ten-frames to subtract. Think about the parts and the whole.

1. $11 - 7 =$ ____

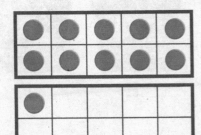

2. $14 - 6 =$ ____

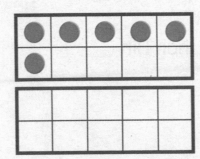

3. $12 - 5 =$ ____

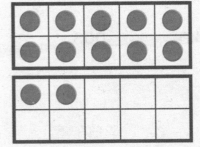

4. Which addition sentences show you how to find $16 - 9$?

- ○ $9 + 1 = 10, 10 + 5 = 15$
- ○ $9 + 1 = 10, 10 + 6 = 16$
- ○ $9 + 2 = 11, 11 + 6 = 17$
- ○ $9 + 1 = 10, 10 + 9 = 19$

5. Which subtraction sentences show you how to find $15 - 7$?

- ○ $15 - 6 = 9, 9 - 8 = 1$
- ○ $15 - 5 = 10, 10 - 5 = 5$
- ○ $15 - 5 = 10, 10 - 2 = 8$
- ○ $15 - 2 = 13, 13 - 2 = 11$

Extend Your Thinking For each problem, pick a bin from each row. Subtract to find how many more bottles are in the bin from the top row than the bin from the bottom row.

6. Bin _____ has _____ more bottles than Bin _____.

7. Bin _____ has _____ more bottles than Bin _____.

8. Bin _____ has _____ more bottles than Bin _____.

9. Bin _____ has _____ more bottles than Bin _____.

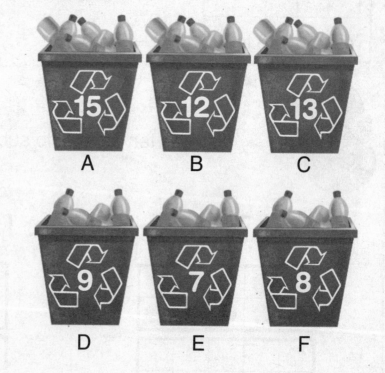

A   15   B   12   C   13

D   9   E   7   F   8

Name ____________________

Solve & Share

How can you use counters to show parts of 12? What addition and subtraction sentences can you write for the counters you show?

12

___ + ___ = ___

___ + ___ = ___

___ − ___ = ___

___ − ___ = ___

Lesson 2-2

Connecting Addition and Subtraction

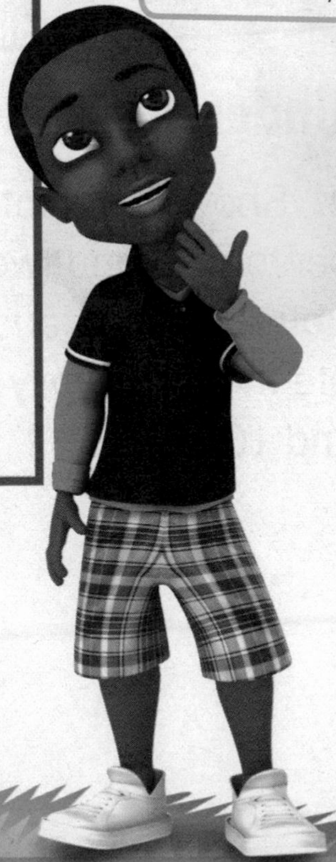

TEKS 2.4A Recall basic facts to add and subtract within 20 with automaticity. **Mathematical Process Standards** 2.1C, 2.1D, 2.1F.

Digital Resources at SavvasTexas.com

Solve | Learn | Glossary | Check | Tools | Games

You can write addition and subtraction sentences to show the whole and the parts.

6 is one part. 5 is the other part. So, 11 is the whole.

These two related addition sentences show the same parts and the same whole.

$$6 + 5 = 11$$
$$5 + 6 = 11$$

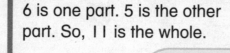

11 is the whole. 6 is one part. So, 5 is the hidden part.

Let's write a related subtraction sentence.

$$11 - 6 = 5$$

11 is the whole. 5 is one part. So, 6 is the hidden part.

That completes the fact family for 5, 6, and 11.

$$11 - 5 = 6$$

Do You Understand?

Show Me! Show two related addition sentences and two related subtraction sentences to complete the fact family for 7, 3, and 10.

☆ **Guided Practice** ☆ Write two related addition sentences for the model. Then write two related subtraction sentences for the model.

1. ☐9☐

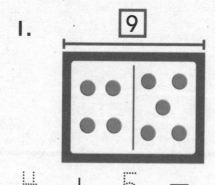

$$4 + 5 = 9$$
$$5 + 4 = 9$$
$$9 - 4 = 5$$
$$9 - 5 = 4$$

2. ☐14☐

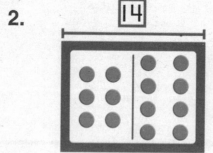

$$\_\_ + \_\_ = \_\_$$
$$\_\_ + \_\_ = \_\_$$
$$\_\_ - \_\_ = \_\_$$
$$\_\_ - \_\_ = \_\_$$

Independent Practice

Write two related addition sentences for the model.
Then write two related subtraction sentences for the model.

3. 13

____ + ____ = ____

____ + ____ = ____

____ − ____ = ____

____ − ____ = ____

4. 16

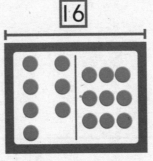

____ + ____ = ____

____ + ____ = ____

____ − ____ = ____

____ − ____ = ____

5. 15

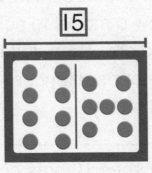

____ = ____ + ____

____ = ____ + ____

____ = ____ − ____

____ = ____ − ____

---

6. Extend Your Thinking Find the related addition facts.

$12 - 5 = 7$ ☐ + ☐ = ☐ $17 - 8 = 9$ ☐ + ☐ = ☐

$12 - 7 = 5$ ☐ + ☐ = ☐ $17 - 9 = 8$ ☐ + ☐ = ☐

7. Yoshi has 6 red toys.
He has 3 yellow toys. How many
toys does Yoshi have in all?
Draw a model to solve the
problem. Then write the related
number sentences for that
fact family.

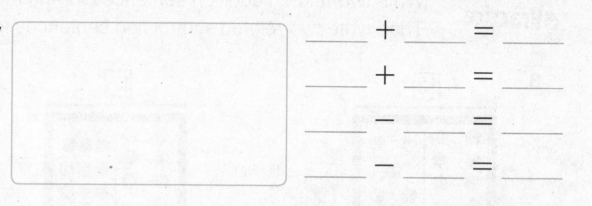

_____ + _____ = _____

_____ + _____ = _____

_____ − _____ = _____

_____ − _____ = _____

8. Jan sees 10 ants on a rock.
⭐ Some ants walk off.
There are 6 ants left.

Which number sentence shows the story?

10 + 6 = 16   4 + 6 = 10
    ○   ○

10 − 4 = 6   6 − 4 = 2
    ○   ○

9. **Extend Your Thinking** Complete the
model. Write a whole and two parts.
Then use the model to write a fact family.

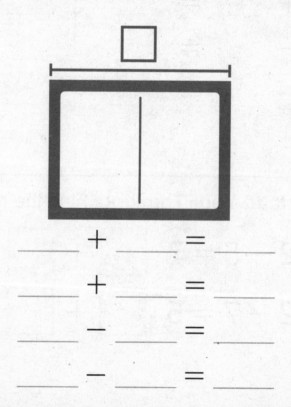

_____ + _____ = _____

_____ + _____ = _____

_____ − _____ = _____

_____ − _____ = _____

Name _____

Another Look You can write an addition sentence to add the parts.
The subtraction sentences use the same numbers.

9 | Whole

Part   Part

$$6 + 3 = 9$$
Part   Part   Whole

$$3 + 6 = 9$$
Part   Part   Whole

$$9 - 3 = 6$$
Whole   Part   Part

$$9 - 6 = 3$$
Whole   Part   Part

🏠 **HOME CONNECTION**
Your child wrote two addition sentences and two subtraction sentences using the same set of three numbers.

HOME ACTIVITY Put seven small objects, such as marbles or buttons, in two groups. Have your child tell you two related subtraction facts and two related addition facts for the numbers; for example:
$7 - 2 = 5$, $7 - 5 = 2$,
$2 + 5 = 7$, $5 + 2 = 7$.

Solve each problem.

1. Draw two parts to complete the model.

12

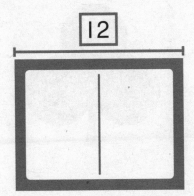

2. Write related number sentences for the model.

_____ + _____ = _____

_____ + _____ = _____

_____ − _____ = _____

_____ − _____ = _____

Which number sentence is a part of the fact family?

3. ⭐ 11

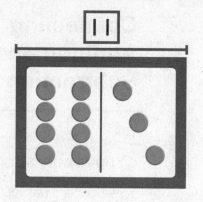

$? + 8 = 11$

$8 + ? = 11$

$11 - ? = 8$

$19 - 8 = 11$ ○

$8 + 11 = 19$ ○

$8 - 3 = 5$ ○

$11 - 8 = 3$ ○

4. ⭐ 13

$7 + ? = 13$

$13 - 7 = ?$

$13 - ? = 7$

$13 - 5 = 8$ ○

$6 + 7 = 13$ ○

$6 + 13 = 19$ ○

$13 + 7 = 20$ ○

Extend Your Thinking Draw the missing counters. Then write two addition sentences and two subtraction sentences.

5.

____ + ____ = ____

____ + ____ = ____

____ − ____ = ____

____ − ____ = ____

6.

____ = ____ + ____

____ = ____ + ____

____ = ____ − ____

____ = ____ − ____

Name _____

Solve & Share

How can knowing $3 + 4 = 7$ help you solve $7 - 4$? Use counters to help show how.

TEKS 2.4A Recall basic facts to add and subtract within 20 with automaticity. Also, 2.7C. **Mathematical Process Standards** 2.1C, 2.1D, 2.1F.

Digital Resources at SavvasTexas.com

 Solve Learn Glossary Check Tools Games

$$3 + 4 = 7$$

$$\text{So, } 7 - 4 = \underline{\quad}.$$

Find $10 - 8$.

Think 8 plus how many more is 10?

$10 - 8 = \underline{}$

$8 + \underline{} = 10$

You know this shows $8 + 2 = 10$.

So, you also know $10 - 8 = 2$.

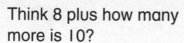

$10 - 8 = \underline{2}$

$8 + \underline{2} = 10$

Both number sentences use the same numbers!

Do You Understand?

Show Me! What addition fact can help you solve $8 - 5$? Explain why.

1. $5 - 2 = ?$

$2 + \underline{3} = 5$

So, $5 - 2 = \underline{3}$.

2. $6 - 4 = ?$

$4 + \underline{} = 6$

So, $6 - 4 = \underline{}$.

3. $7 - 2 = ?$

$2 + \underline{} = 7$

So, $7 - 2 = \underline{}$.

4. $8 - 7 = ?$

$7 + \underline{} = 8$

So, $8 - 7 = \underline{}$.

Independent Practice

Subtract. Write the addition fact that helped you.

5. $7 - 4 =$ _____

$4 + $ _____ $= 7$

6. $8 - 6 =$ _____

$6 + $ _____ $= 8$

7. $9 - 3 =$ _____

$3 + $ _____ $= 9$

8. $\begin{array}{r} 9 \\ - 4 \\ \hline \square \end{array}$ $\begin{array}{r} 4 \\ + \square \\ \hline 9 \end{array}$

9. $\begin{array}{r} 6 \\ - 2 \\ \hline \square \end{array}$ $\begin{array}{r} 2 \\ + \square \\ \hline 6 \end{array}$

10. $\begin{array}{r} 5 \\ - 3 \\ \hline \square \end{array}$ $\begin{array}{r} 3 \\ + \square \\ \hline 5 \end{array}$

11. **Extend Your Thinking** Write the missing numbers.
Then write and solve your own problem with missing numbers.

If $2 + $ _____ $= 9$, then $9 - 2 =$ _____ .

If _____ $+$ _____ $=$ _____ , then _____ $-$ _____ $=$ _____ .

Addition facts can help you subtract!

Problem Solving
Use counters to help you solve.
Then write an addition fact that can help you subtract.

12. Ping has 8 seeds.
His friend has 2 fewer seeds.
How many seeds does Ping's friend have?

Ping's friend has _____ seeds.

_____ + _____ = _____

So, _____ − _____ = _____ .

13. Jack is playing with 5 dogs. He only has 3 dog toys. He wants to give each dog a toy.

Which sentence can help you find how many more toys Jack needs?

3 + 2 = 5
○

3 − 2 = 1
○

5 + 2 = 7
○

5 + 3 = 8
○

14. **Extend Your Thinking** Choose 2 numbers. Use the numbers to write or draw a subtraction story.
Then write an addition fact to solve it.

_____ + _____ = _____

Name _____

Another Look Addition facts can help you subtract.
Use the pictures to find the missing numbers.

Addition Fact

Subtraction Fact

Think $2 + \underline{8} = 10$.

So, $10 - 2 = \underline{8}$.

Use addition facts to help you subtract.

1.

Think $3 + \underline{\hphantom{0}} = 7$.

So, $7 - 3 = \underline{\hphantom{0}}$.

2.

Think $7 + \underline{\hphantom{0}} = 8$.

So, $8 - 7 = \underline{\hphantom{0}}$.

3. Chris has 7 whistles. He needs 10 whistles for his party.
⭐ Which number sentence can help you find how many more whistles Chris needs?

$7 + 10 = 17$ $7 - 3 = 4$ $7 + 3 = 10$ $4 + 3 = 7$

    ○   ○   ○   ○

---

4. Draw a picture to solve the subtraction story. Write an addition fact that can help you solve it. Then write a subtraction sentence.

Becky has 5 crayons.
Joy has 3 fewer crayons than Becky.
How many crayons does Joy have?

_____ + _____ = _____

_____ − _____ = _____ crayons

Extend Your Thinking Solve each problem.

5. If △ + ○ = □, then □ − △ = _____.

6. If ↑ − ◇ = ∩, then ◇ + _____ = ↑.

Name ____________________

Solve & Share

How can you use an addition fact to solve $14 - 6$?
Use counters to help show how.

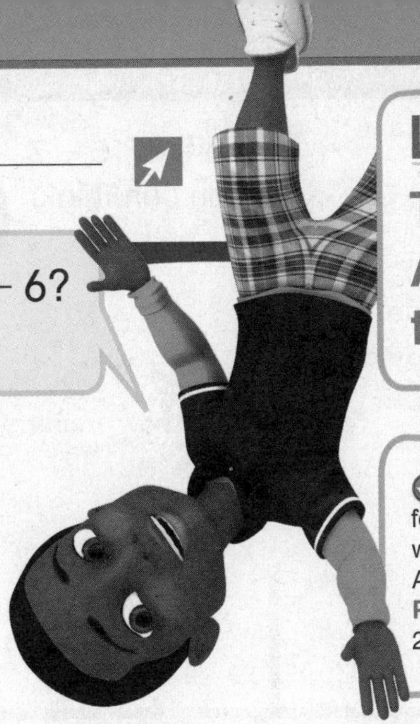

Lesson 2-4

Thinking Addition to 20 to Subtract

TEKS 2.4A Recall basic facts to add and subtract within 20 with automaticity. Also, 2.7C, 2.4. **Mathematical Process Standards** 2.1B, 2.1C, 2.1F, 2.1G.

Digital Resources at SavvasTexas.com

Solve Learn Glossary Check Tools Games

___ + ___ = ___

So, $14 - 6 =$ ___.

Find 15 − 7.

One way to subtract is to think about addition.

To find 15 − 7, you can think:

7 plus how many more is 15?
or
7 + ___ = 15

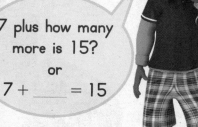

The missing number is the same in both number sentences.

7 + ___ = 15

15 − 7 = ___

You know the addition fact.

7 + __8__ = 15

You also know the subtraction fact.

15 − 7 = __8__

Guided Practice

Think addition to help you subtract.

Do You Understand?

Show Me! How do you know which addition fact to use to complete the subtraction fact?

1. 6 − 4 = ?

4 + _2_ = 6

So, 6 − 4 = _2_.

2. 9 − 3 = ?

3 + ___ = 9

So, 9 − 3 = ___.

3. 14 − 5 = ?

5 + ___ = 14

So, 14 − 5 = ___.

4. 13 − 6 = ?

6 + ___ = 13

So, 13 − 6 = ___.

Independent ☆ ☆ Practice
Subtract. Write the addition fact that helped you.

5. $8 - 5 =$ ____

$5 + $ ____ $= 8$

6. $10 - 2 =$ ____

$2 + $ ____ $= 10$

7. $15 - 6 =$ ____

$6 + $ ____ $= 15$

8.
$$\begin{array}{r} 18 \\ -\ 8 \\ \hline \square \end{array}$$

$$\begin{array}{r} 8 \\ +\ \square \\ \hline 18 \end{array}$$

9.
$$\begin{array}{r} 16 \\ -\ 9 \\ \hline \square \end{array}$$

$$\begin{array}{r} 9 \\ +\ \square \\ \hline 16 \end{array}$$

10.
$$\begin{array}{r} 19 \\ -\ 9 \\ \hline \square \end{array}$$

$$\begin{array}{r} 9 \\ +\ \square \\ \hline 19 \end{array}$$

Extend Your Thinking Use a related addition fact to complete the subtraction fact.

11. $11 - $ ____ $= 5$

____ $+$ ____ $=$ ____

12. $15 - $ ____ $= 8$

____ $+$ ____ $=$ ____

13. $12 - $ ____ $= 8$

____ $+$ ____ $=$ ____

14. Kate had 6 pens.
She got 5 more pens from John.
How many pens does
Kate have in all?

_____ + _____ = _____

_____ pens

15. John had 11 pens.
He gave 5 pens to Kate.
How many pens does
John have now?

_____ − _____ = _____

_____ pens

16. Pam has 16 cherries.
She eats 7 cherries.
Which addition fact can help you
find how many cherries Pam has left?

7 + 4 = 11   7 + 6 = 13
○   ○

7 + 9 = 16   9 + 9 = 18
○   ○

17. Extend Your Thinking Write a subtraction
story using the numbers 18, 10, and 8.
Then write an addition fact that can
help you solve your story.

_____

_____

_____

_____

_____ + _____ = _____

Another Look Addition facts can help you subtract.
Use the pictures to find the missing numbers.

Addition Fact   Subtraction Fact

   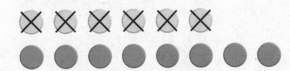

Think $6 + \underline{8} = 14$.   So, $14 - 6 = \underline{8}$.

 HOME CONNECTION
Your child used addition facts
to help complete subtraction
facts.

HOME ACTIVITY Make
up problems during daily
activities such as, "If I have
12 eggs and I use 3 of them,
how many eggs do I have
left?" Have your child write
and solve the subtraction
sentence using addition facts.

 Addition facts can help you subtract.
Use the pictures to find the missing numbers.

1. Think $9 + \underline{} = 13$.   So, $13 - 9 = \underline{}$.

2. Think $8 + \underline{} = 17$.   So, $17 - 8 = \underline{}$.

3. Maria has 11 rings. She loses 3 rings. Which addition fact can help you find how many rings Maria has left?

$3 + 1 = 4$ ○ $6 + 5 = 11$ ○

$3 + 8 = 11$ ○ $11 + 3 = 14$ ○

4. Subtract. Write the addition fact that helped you.

$19 - 9 =$ _____

$9 +$ _____ $= 19$

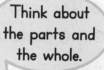

Think about the parts and the whole.

Extend Your Thinking Circle the addition fact that will help you subtract. Write a subtraction sentence to solve each problem.

5. Lucy has 12 books. Michael has 3 books. How many more books does Lucy have than Michael?

$3 + 12$

$3 + 9$

$6 + 6$

_____ $-$ _____ $=$ _____

_____ more books

6. Pam has 20 marbles. She puts 10 marbles in a jar. How many marbles are not in the jar?

$20 + 10$

$9 + 9$

$10 + 10$

_____ $-$ _____ $=$ _____

_____ marbles

Name ______________________________

Solve & Share

Write four related facts that use both the numbers 7 and 9 as quickly as you can. Hold up your hand when you are done. Then, tell how you found each fact.

Lesson 2-5

Addition and Subtraction Facts

TEKS 2.4A Recall basic facts to add and subtract within 20 with automaticity. Also, 2.7C. **Mathematical Process Standards** 2.1C, 2.1F, 2.1G.

Digital Resources at SavvasTexas.com

Solve | Learn | Glossary | Check | Tools | Games

____ + ____ = ____ | ____ − ____ = ____

____ + ____ = ____ | ____ − ____ = ____

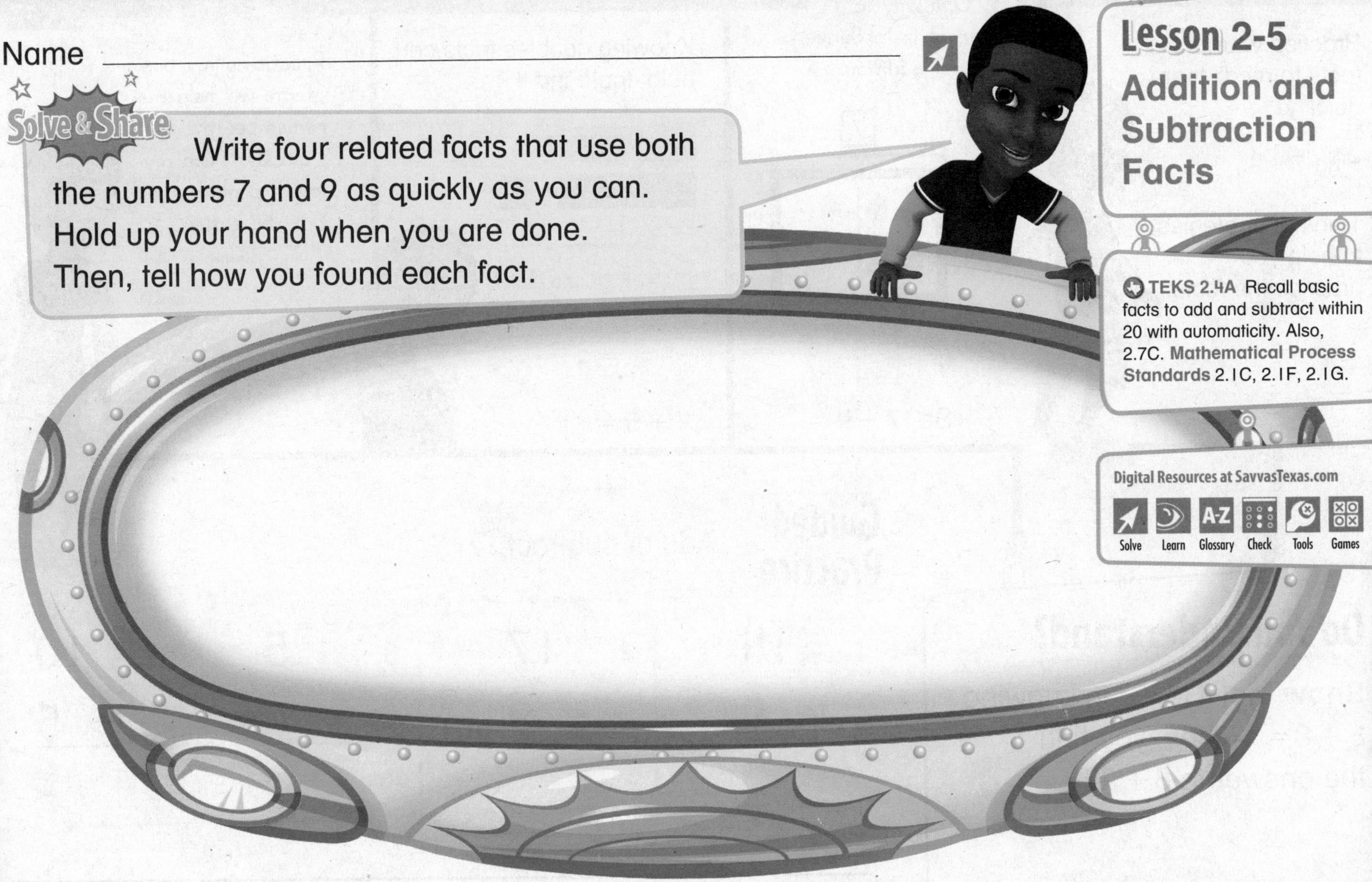

Practice your basic facts to recall them quickly.

Find 7 − 4.

Think of strategies to help you practice the facts.

One way to subtract is to think about addition.

7

$4 + \boxed{3} = 7$

So, $7 - 4 = \boxed{3}$.

Knowing doubles facts can help, too! Find 4 + 5.

4 + 4 and 1.

$4 + 5 = \boxed{9}$

Practicing my basic facts will help me remember the facts quickly. Then my math problems will be easier.

Do You Understand?

Show Me! How can knowing $8 + 8 = 16$ help you find the answer to $8 + 9$?

☆ Guided Practice ☆   Add or subtract.

1.
$$\begin{array}{r} 14 \\ -\ 9 \\ \hline 5 \end{array}$$

2.
$$\begin{array}{r} 17 \\ -\ 9 \\ \hline \end{array}$$

3.
$$\begin{array}{r} 5 \\ +\ 7 \\ \hline \end{array}$$

4.
$$\begin{array}{r} 10 \\ -\ 5 \\ \hline \end{array}$$

5.
$$\begin{array}{r} 6 \\ -\ 4 \\ \hline \end{array}$$

6.
$$\begin{array}{r} 9 \\ +\ 9 \\ \hline \end{array}$$

7.
$$\begin{array}{r} 12 \\ -\ 4 \\ \hline \end{array}$$

8.
$$\begin{array}{r} 10 \\ +\ 10 \\ \hline \end{array}$$

Name _____

Add or subtract.

9. $14 - 7 =$ _____

10. $3 + 4 =$ _____

11. $8 + 7 =$ _____

12. $13 - 6 =$ _____

13. $10 + 9 =$ _____

14. $17 - 8 =$ _____

15. $18 - 9 =$ _____

16. $9 - 6 =$ _____

17. $7 + 4 =$ _____

18. $6 + 6 =$ _____

19. $16 - 9 =$ _____

20. $20 - 10 =$ _____

Extend Your Thinking Write the missing number.

21. $6 + \boxed{} = 14 - 5$

22. $12 - 4 = \boxed{} + 2$

23. $14 - \boxed{} = 5 + 6$

Problem Solving Solve the problems below.

24. Danielle made 17 bracelets.
Talisa made 8 bracelets.
How many more bracelets
did Danielle make than Talisa?
Write a number sentence to solve.

_____ ◯ _____ = _____

_____ more bracelets

25. Diego saw 5 frogs on a rock.
He also saw 7 frogs swimming.
How many frogs did Diego see in all?
Write a number sentence to solve.

_____ ◯ _____ = _____

_____ frogs

26. ⭐ Deshawn had some shells.
He gave 3 shells to his brother.
Now, Deshawn has 8 shells.
How many shells did Deshawn have at first?

5   8
◯   ◯

11   14
◯   ◯

Use different
strategies to solve
the problems!

27. **Extend Your Thinking** Glen counts on
to solve 8 + 9. How could he solve
this problem more quickly?

_____

_____

_____

_____

_____

_____

Name _____

Another Look You can use models or strategies to help you practice addition and subtraction facts.

Find 12 − 7.

12

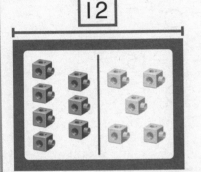

12 − 7 = 5

You can use a model. You can also think addition and use related facts.

7 plus how many more is 12?

or

7 + 5 = 12

So, 12 − 7 = 5.

🏠 **HOME CONNECTION**
Your child practiced recalling addition and subtraction facts.

HOME ACTIVITY Give your child the following numbers: 5, 6, and 11. Tell your child to write the fact family for these numbers as quickly as he or she can.

Use models or strategies to solve.

1. 11 − 5 6	2. 12 − 6	3. 7 + 6	4. 2 + 3	5. 12 − 3	6. 8 + 8

7. $9 - 3 =$ _____ | **8.** $10 + 9 =$ _____ | **9.** $10 - 5 =$ _____

10. What addition doubles fact can help you solve $4 + 5$? Explain how you know.

_____

_____

_____

11. Which addition sentence can help you find $9 - 6$?

$6 + 3 = 9$ ○ $8 + 8 = 16$ ○

$6 + 6 = 12$ ○ $6 + 9 = 15$ ○

Extend Your Thinking Complete the squares so that the sums on the right side and the sums on the bottom are correct.

12.

	3	11
7		10
15	6	

13.

6		10
	9	18
15		

14.

	7	12
8		17
13	16	

15.

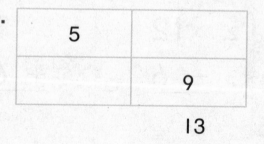

5		9
	9	
	13	

☆ ☆
Solve & Share

Diego and Gail pick 13 apples in all. Gail picks 7 apples.
How many apples does Diego pick?
Do you add or subtract to solve this problem?
How do you know?

Problem Solving

Lesson 2-6
Use Tools

⭐ **TEKS 2.1C** Select tools ... and techniques ... to solve problems. Also, 2.4A, 2.7C. **Mathematical Process Standards** 2.1A, 2.1B, 2.1D.

Digital Resources at SavvasTexas.com

Solve   Learn   Glossary   Check   Tools   Games

add   subtract   _____ ◯ _____ ◯ _____

Analyze

Maria has 8 crayons.
She gives 3 crayons to Seth.
How many crayons does
Maria have left?

Maria gives
away crayons.
So, I subtract.

Plan

8

I can use
counters to
solve.

Solve and Justify

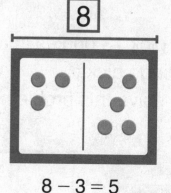

8

$8 - 3 = 5$

Evaluate

Check your work.

I know $5 + 3 = 8$.
So, $8 - 3 = 5$.

Do You Understand?

Show Me! How did Jackson
solve the problem above?

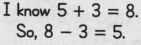
☆ **Guided** ☆
Practice

Use counters and your workmat. Circle **add** or
subtract. Then write a number sentence and solve.

1. Sam has 5 green tomatoes
   and 3 red tomatoes.
   How many tomatoes
   does he have in all?

   (add)   subtract

        tomatoes

---

2. There are 9 party hats.
   The children wear some of them.   add   subtract
   There are 7 hats left.
   How many hats did the children wear?

   ____ ◯ ____ ◯ ____   ____ hats

Topic 2 | Lesson 6

Name _____

Use counters and your workmat. Circle **add** or **subtract**.
Then write a number sentence and solve.

3. Cho has 9 toy horses.
Cho has 3 more toy horses than Hakeem.
How many toy horses does Hakeem have?

add   subtract

____ ◯ ____ ◯ ____

____ horses

4. There are 10 peaches.
The children eat 3 of them.
How many peaches are left?

add   subtract

____ ◯ ____ ◯ ____

____ peaches

5. Juan reads 5 books.
Betty reads some books.
They read 7 books in all.
How many books did Betty read?

add   subtract

____ ◯ ____ ◯ ____

____ books

6. Some grapes are in a bowl.
Sarah eats 6 grapes.
There are 5 grapes left.
How many grapes were in the bowl before?

add   subtract

____ ◯ ____ ◯ ____

____ grapes

7. **Extend Your Thinking** Explain how you could add or subtract to solve Exercise 3.

_____

8. Maria has some rings.
She buys 3 more rings.
Now she has 11 rings.
Which number sentence could help find how many rings Maria had to start with?

$8 + 11 = 19$
○

$3 + 8 = 11$
○

$3 + 11 = 14$
○

$12 - 8 = 4$
○

9. Annika saves 10 dimes.
Leroy saves 7 dimes.
How many more dimes does Annika save than Leroy?

Write a number sentence and solve.

_____ ◯ _____ ◯ _____

_____ more dimes

10. Extend Your Thinking Write a story problem about the numbers 4 and 6.
Draw a picture to show how you would solve your problem.
Then write a number sentence to match your story problem.

_____

_____

_____

_____ ◯ _____ = _____

Name _____

Another Look You can use counters to solve this problem.
You need to add to find how many in all.

5 frogs are on a rock.
3 frogs join them.
How many frogs in all?

5 (+) 3 = 8 frogs
Part — Part — Whole

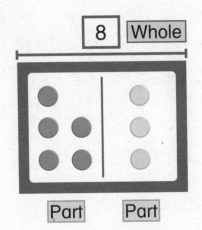

8 | Whole

Part   Part

🏠 **HOME CONNECTION**
Your child used objects and decided whether to add or subtract to solve a math story problem.

HOME ACTIVITY Make up word problems. Ask your child to use small objects such as paper clips or pennies to add or subtract to solve the problems.

Use objects to solve.
Circle **add** or **subtract.** Then write the number sentence.

1. 2 bugs are on a leaf.
   4 bugs join them.
   How many bugs are there in all?

   add or subtract?

   ____ ◯ ____ = ____ bugs

2. 10 toads are in a pond.
   5 toads jump out.
   How many toads are left?

   add or subtract?

   ____ ◯ ____ = ____ toads

Use objects.
Choose the number sentence that helps solve the problem.

3. Jan has some dolls. Kat has 4 dolls.
⭐ They have 11 dolls in all.
How many dolls does Jan have?

$7 - 4 = 3$ ○

$11 + 4 = 15$ ○

$4 + 3 = 7$ ○

$4 + 7 = 11$ ○

4. Pat has 9 cards. Mia has 7 cards.
⭐ Al has 2 cards.
How many more cards does
Pat have than Al?

$9 + 7 = 16$ ○

$9 + 2 = 11$ ○

$9 - 2 = 7$ ○

$7 - 5 = 2$ ○

Extend Your Thinking Jack made this design with pattern blocks.

Jack used four different types of pattern blocks.

5. How many △ and ⬡ did Jack use in all? _____

6. How many ◊ and ⬭ did Jack use in all? _____

7. How many more ◊ than ⬭ did Jack use? _____

8. How many fewer ⬡ than ⬭ did Jack use? _____

Name _____

Connect addition and subtraction to cheer the champions!

1. How many more medals did Marta win than Carlos?
Write a number sentence to show your answer.

_____

2. Which two athletes won a total of 20 medals? Explain.

_____

_____

Emily

Marta

Carlos

---

3. Use the numbers of medals Carlos and Emily won to write a fact family. Show two addition and two subtraction sentences.

_____

_____

4. Who won more medals: Marta alone or Carlos and Emily together?
How many more? Explain your thinking.

_____

_____

_____

_____

Go Figure!

1. Jake made a table with ten
   part + part = whole facts. Each column has
   a pattern from top to bottom. Figure out the
   patterns. Then fill in the missing numbers.
   Make sure that each row makes sense.

Part	Part	Whole
10	10	20
	10	19
	9	18
8		
	8	
7		
		14
	7	13
	6	

What's Wrong?

2. One model cannot be finished. Cross it out.
   Finish the other model so it makes sense.

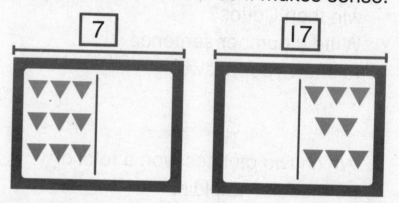

Code Math

3. Use the code to solve the number sentences.

$$5 + \square = + $$

$$\blacklozenge - \square = 7$$

$$\square - 10 = \square$$

$$\square + \square = 16$$

▼ = 7	✓ = 9
□ = 10	+ = 15
♦ = 16	○ = 20

Name _____

Set A

You can make a 10 to subtract.
Find 17 − 8.

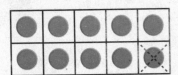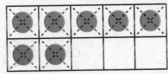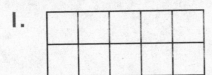

$$17 − 7 = 10$$
$$10 − 1 = 9$$
$$17 − 8 = \boxed{9}$$

Reteaching

Make a 10 to find 13 − 8.
Draw counters to show your work.

1.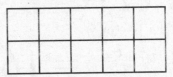

$$13 − \rule{1cm}{0.4pt} = 10$$
$$10 − \rule{1cm}{0.4pt} = \rule{1cm}{0.4pt}$$
$$13 − 8 = \rule{1cm}{0.4pt}$$

Set B

You can write four related facts to
show the whole and the parts.

13

$$5 + 8 = 13$$
$$8 + 5 = 13$$
$$13 − 5 = 8$$
$$13 − 8 = 5$$

Write two addition sentences for the model.
Then write two subtraction sentences for the model.

2.

13

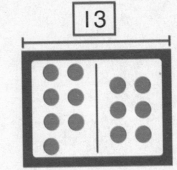

$$\rule{1cm}{0.4pt} + \rule{1cm}{0.4pt} = \rule{1cm}{0.4pt}$$
$$\rule{1cm}{0.4pt} + \rule{1cm}{0.4pt} = \rule{1cm}{0.4pt}$$
$$\rule{1cm}{0.4pt} − \rule{1cm}{0.4pt} = \rule{1cm}{0.4pt}$$
$$\rule{1cm}{0.4pt} − \rule{1cm}{0.4pt} = \rule{1cm}{0.4pt}$$

You can think addition to help you subtract.

$$16 - 9 = \underline{7}$$

$$9 + \underline{7} = 16$$

Subtract. Write the addition fact that helped you.

3. $13 - 7 = \underline{}$

$7 + \underline{} = 13$

4. $17 - 9 = \underline{}$

$9 + \underline{} = 17$

You can use doubles facts to help you subtract.

$$12 - 6 = \underline{6}$$

$$\underline{6} + \underline{6} = \underline{12}$$

Subtract. Write the doubles fact that helped you. Use cubes if you need to.

5. $14 - 7 = \underline{}$

$\underline{} + \underline{} = \underline{}$

6. $16 - 8 = \underline{}$

$\underline{} + \underline{} = \underline{}$

Name _____

1. Which number sentence completes the fact family?

○ 9 − 6 = 3

○ 9 − 3 = 6

○ 15 − 5 = 10

○ 15 − 6 = 9

15

9 + 6 = 15

6 + 9 = 15

15 − 9 = 6

____ − ____ = ____

Choose the addition fact that can help you subtract.

2. 7 friends go to the movies.
   They have 4 tickets.
   How many more tickets do they need?

   ○ 2 + 4 = 6

   ○ 4 + 3 = 7

   ○ 7 + 3 = 10

   ○ 7 + 4 = 11

3. Dave has 12 grapes.
   He gives 6 to his sister.
   How many grapes does
   Dave have left?

   ○ 3 + 3 = 6

   ○ 4 + 4 = 8

   ○ 6 + 6 = 12

   ○ 10 + 10 = 20

4. Marty made 12 puppets.
Tomás made 5 puppets.
How many more puppets
did Marty make than Tomás?

○ 6

○ 7

○ 17

○ 19

5. Make a 10 to subtract.

$$17 - 8 = \underline{}$$

○ 8

○ 10

○ 7

○ 9

6. Which addition
fact can you use to
solve $7 - \underline{} = 5$?

○ $7 + 5 = 12$

○ $2 + 9 = 11$

○ $5 + 2 = 7$

○ $5 + 1 = 6$

---

7. Ray has 6 coins. Clinton has 8 coins.
How many more coins does
Clinton have than Ray?
Write a number sentence to solve.

$\underline{} \bigcirc \underline{} = \underline{}$

$\underline{}$ coins

---

8. Use counters and your workmat.
Circle **add** or **subtract**.
Then write the number sentence.

There are 14 birds on a rock.
Some birds fly away.
There are 5 birds left.
How many birds flew away?

add   subtract

$\underline{} \bigcirc \underline{} \bigcirc \underline{}$

$\underline{}$ birds

Numbers to 1,200

Essential Question: How can you count, read, and show numbers up to the thousands?

The market sells many different fruits and vegetables.

Different fruits and vegetables are grown on farms near us.

Wow! Let's do this project and learn more.

Math and Science Project: Counting with Fruits and Vegetables

Find Out Visit the library to learn about local farms or visit a farm stand or farmer's market with your family. Find out which crops grow well in your region.

Journal: Make a Book Draw pictures and write sentences to show what you learned about local farms. In your book, also:

- Choose a number up to 1,200. Write sentences about that many pieces of fruit.

- Show the number in different ways.

Name _____

Review What You Know

Vocabulary

1. Circle the number that is 1 **less** than 48.

38   49

47

2. Circle the number that is 10 **more** than 26.

16   36

27

3. Circle the **ten**.

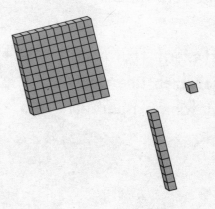

Tens and Ones

4. Show 38.

_____ tens _____ ones

5. Show 75.

_____ tens _____ ones

Counting

6. Write the missing numbers.

11			15				20
	22	23		26	28		
		33		36		39	40

My Word Cards

Study the words on the front of the card. Complete the activity on the back.

A-Z

hundred

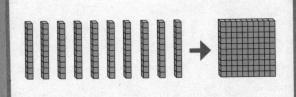

digit

43 has 2 digits.

43

standard form

436 is the standard form for $400 + 30 + 6$.

expanded form

$400 + 60 + 3 = 463$

number word

The number word for 23 is twenty-three.

thousand

My Word Cards

Use what you know to complete the sentences.
Extend learning by writing your own sentence using each word.

Using the

_____

_____

is a way to write a number
showing only its digits.

Numbers have 1 or more

_____.

---

10 tens make 1

_____.

---

10 hundreds make 1

_____.

A _____

_____

shows a number using
words.

Using the

_____

_____

is a way to write a number
showing the place value of
each digit.

Name _____

Solve & Share

How can you use place-value blocks to show 125? Explain.

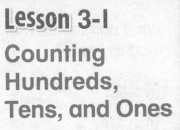

⭐ TEKS 2.2 Understand how to represent and compare whole numbers ... and relationships within the numeration system related to place value. Also, 2.2B. Mathematical Process Standards 2.1C, 2.1D, 2.1E.

Digital Resources at SavvasTexas.com

Solve   Learn   Glossary   Check   Tools   Games

What number do the models show?

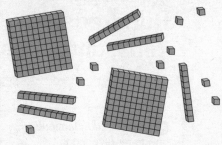

Remember, 10 ones make I ten.
10 tens make I **hundred**.

First, count the hundreds.

Hundreds	Tens	Ones
2		

Then count the tens.

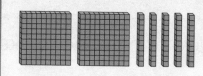

Hundreds	Tens	Ones
2	5	

Then count the ones.

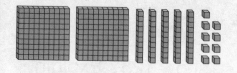

Hundreds	Tens	Ones
2	5	9

The models show 259.
259 has 3 digits.

Do You Understand?

Show Me! How many hundreds are in 395? How many tens? How many ones?

Guided Practice Write the numbers shown.
Use models and your workmat if needed.

I.

Hundreds	Tens	Ones
	7	0

70

2.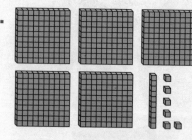

Hundreds	Tens	Ones

Independent Practice

Write the numbers shown. Use models and your workmat if needed.

3.

Hundreds	Tens	Ones

_____

4.

Hundreds	Tens	Ones

_____

5.

Hundreds	Tens	Ones

_____

6.

Hundreds	Tens	Ones

_____

7.

Hundreds	Tens	Ones

_____

8.

Hundreds	Tens	Ones

_____

9. Extend Your Thinking Find the number. It has 5 hundreds. The digit in the tens place is between 5 and 7. The number of ones is 2 less than 4. _____

10. Complete the chart.
A number has an 8 in the hundreds place.
It does not have any tens.
It has a 3 in the ones place.

Hundreds	Tens	Ones

What is the number? _____

11. Katie used these models to show a number.
⭐ Which number would be shown if Katie
used 1 more hundreds flat?

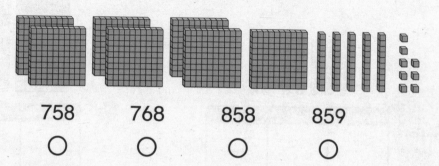

758   768   858   859

  ◯   ◯   ◯   ◯

_____

12. **Extend Your Thinking** Choose
a three-digit number.
Draw models to show the hundreds,
tens, and ones for your number.
Write the number below.

_____

Name _____

Another Look Use models and your workmat to sort and count.

First, put the hundreds flats on your mat. Next, put the tens rods on your mat. Last, put the ones cubes on your mat.

Write the number of hundreds, tens, and ones.

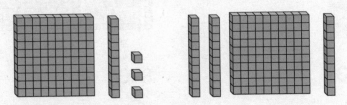

Hundreds	Tens	Ones
2	4	3

Write the numbers.
Use models and your workmat if needed.

1.

Hundreds	Tens	Ones

2.

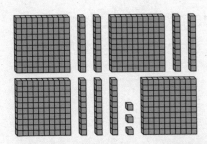

Hundreds	Tens	Ones

What number is shown? Use models and your workmat if needed.

3. ⭐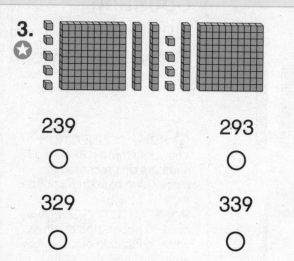

239 ⭕   293 ⭕

329 ⭕   339 ⭕

4. ⭐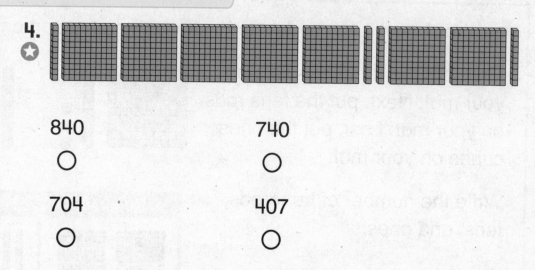

840 ⭕   740 ⭕

704 ⭕   407 ⭕

---

5. Extend Your Thinking Use the clues to solve the number puzzle.

I have a 5 in my ones place. The digit in my tens place is 3 plus the digit in my ones place. The digit in my hundreds place is 2 less than the digit in my ones place. What number am I?

_____

6. Extend Your Thinking Write your own place-value number puzzle. Give it to a friend to solve.

_____

_____

_____

_____

Name _____

Solve & Share

What is another way to write the number 231? Explain.

 TEKS 2.2B Use standard, word, and expanded forms to represent numbers up to 1,200. Also, 2.2A. Mathematical Process Standards 2.1A, 2.1C, 2.1D, 2.1F.

Digital Resources at SavvasTexas.com

Solve Learn Glossary Check Tools Games

Way 1

231

Way 2

What number is shown by the models?

You can write the number in different ways.

One way to show the number is by using the **expanded form**.

$300 + 20 + 8$

Another way is to use the **standard form**.

328

Write the hundreds first, then the tens, then the ones.

The third way is to use the **number word** form.

three hundred twenty-eight

All three ways show the same number!

☆ **Guided Practice** ☆ Solve each problem.

Do You Understand?

Show Me! How many hundreds, tens, and ones does the number six hundred forty have?

1. Read the number. Write the number in expanded form. Then write it in standard form.

   three hundred twenty-five

   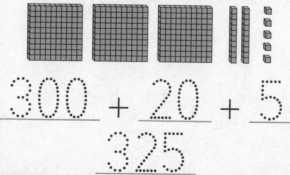

   $\underline{300} + \underline{20} + \underline{5}$

   $\underline{325}$

2. Use the models to write the number in expanded form. Then write it in number word form.

   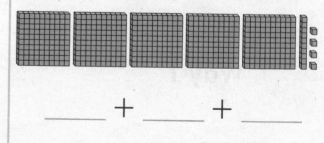

   ___ + ___ + ___

   _____

Topic 3 | Lesson 2

Name _____

Write the number in both number word form and standard form.

3. $300 + 80 + 2$

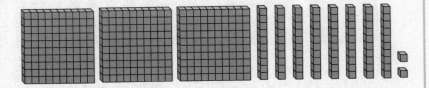

_____

_____

4. $200 + 0 + 6$

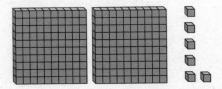

_____

_____

5. $600 + 90 + 5$

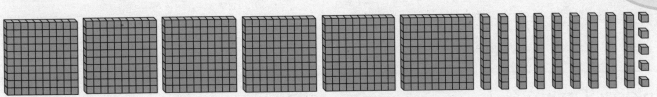

_____

_____

You can count the models!

6. **Extend Your Thinking** Write the number in two different ways.
It has 5 hundreds. The tens digit is 1 less than the hundreds digit.
The ones digit is 2 more than the hundreds digit.

Standard form: _____   Expanded form: _____

7. There are 493 pages in a book.
Write the number in expanded form.
Then write it in number word form.

_____ + _____ + _____

_____

8. The model shows a three-digit number.
⭐ What is the standard form of the number?

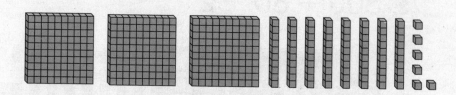

$300 + 80 + 6$ $300 + 90 + 7$
○   ○

386   397
○   ○

9. Extend Your Thinking Draw
hundreds, tens, and ones models
to show a three-digit number.
Then write the expanded form of
the number and use the number
word in a sentence.

_____ + _____ + _____

Name _____

Another Look You can write and show numbers in different ways.

Expanded form uses addition signs to show hundreds, tens, and ones.

$$200 + 60 + 4$$

You can draw models to show expanded form.

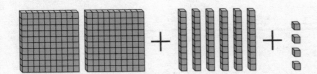

The **number word** is two hundred sixty-four.

The **standard form** is

_264_ .

🏠 **HOME CONNECTION**
Your child identified and wrote the expanded form, the number word, and the standard form for three-digit numbers.

HOME ACTIVITY Say a three-digit number, such as eight hundred fifty-one. Write it down in number word form. Ask your child to write the number in both standard form and expanded form.

 Solve each problem.

1. Draw models to show the expanded form. Write the number in standard form.

$$400 + 30 + 8$$

four hundred thirty-eight

_____

2. Write the number in both expanded form and standard form.

five hundred fourteen

_____ + _____ + _____

3. Write the number in standard form.
Then write it in number word form.

$$400 + 70 + 8$$

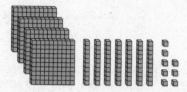

_____

4. 329 cars and 293 trucks are parked in a parking lot.

What is the expanded form of the number of cars parked?

$200 + 90 + 3$ ○ $600 + 20 + 2$ ○

$300 + 20 + 9$ ○ $300 + 90 + 2$ ○

Extend Your Thinking Use the clues to fill in the number puzzle.

Across

5. $500 + 20 + 3$

7.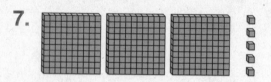

9. $400 + 20 + 9$

10.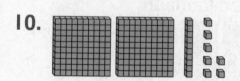

13. Two hundred sixty-nine

Down

6. $300 + 40 + 7$

7. Three hundred ninety-seven

8. $500 + 60 + 9$

11.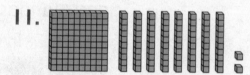

12. Four hundred thirty-eight

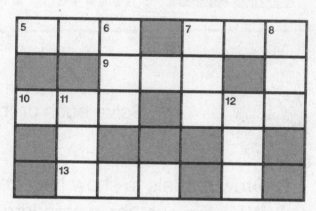

Solve & Share

Students from Alex's school have collected 1,127 coupons. How can you use place-value blocks to show the number of coupons? Explain.

1, 1 2 7

Lesson 3-3
Counting Thousands, Hundreds, Tens, and Ones

TEKS 2.2 Understand how to represent and compare whole numbers ... and relationships within the numeration system related to place value. Also, 2.2B. **Mathematical Process Standards 2.1C, 2.1D, 2.1E, 2.1G.**

Digital Resources at SavvasTexas.com

Solve   Learn   Glossary   Check   Tools   Games

Remember that 10 hundreds make 1 **thousand**.

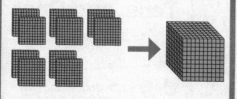

Use models to show 1,132.

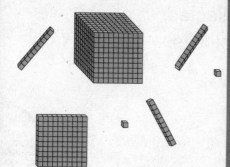

First, count the thousands.
Next, count the hundreds.
Then, count the tens and ones.

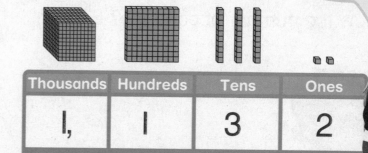

A comma goes between the hundreds and thousands places: 1,132.

Thousands	Hundreds	Tens	Ones
1,	1	3	2

Do You Understand?

Show Me! How many thousands are in 1,108? How many hundreds? How many tens? How many ones?

Guided Practice

Write the numbers. Use models and your workmat to help you.

1.
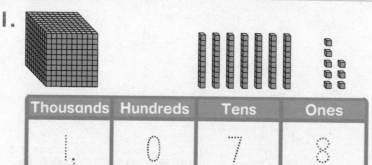

Thousands	Hundreds	Tens	Ones
1,	0	7	8

1,078

2.
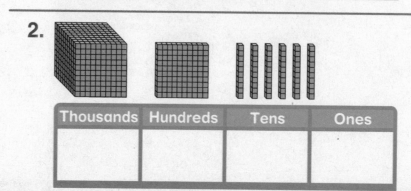

Thousands	Hundreds	Tens	Ones

Name _____

Write the numbers. Use models and your workmat to help you.

3.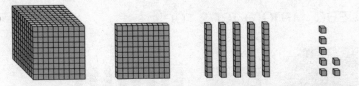

Thousands	Hundreds	Tens	Ones

_____

4.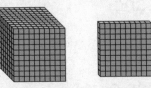

Thousands	Hundreds	Tens	Ones

_____

5. **Extend Your Thinking** Find the number.

It has 1 thousand.

There are no hundreds.

The number of tens is between 6 and 9, and is less than 8.

The number of ones is greater than 2 and less than 4.

_____

Think about where each digit goes!

6. Complete the chart.

A number has 1 thousand.

It has 2 hundreds.

It has no tens.

The digit 0 is in the ones place.

Thousands	Hundreds	Tens	Ones

What is the number? _____

7. Gwen used these models to show a number. Which number would be shown if Gwen used 1 more tens rod?

1,185   1,186
○   ○

1,195   1,196
○   ○

---

8. Extend Your Thinking Write a four-digit number that is less than 1,200. The sum of its digits should equal 12. Draw place-value models and write the number.

_____

Thousands	Hundreds	Tens	Ones

Name _____

Another Look You can use models and your workmat to help you write numbers.

First, place the thousands.
Next, place the hundreds.
Finally, place the tens and ones.

Thousands	Hundreds	Tens	Ones
1,	1	5	3

🏠 **HOME CONNECTION**
Your child learned four-digit numbers and recorded the place value of each digit.

HOME ACTIVITY Write a four-digit number that is 1,200 or less. Have your child tell how many thousands, how many hundreds, how many tens, and how many ones are in the number. Repeat for several other four-digit numbers that are less than 1,200.

Write the numbers. Use models and your workmat to help you.

1.

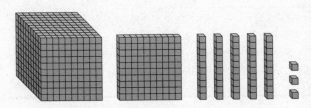

Thousands	Hundreds	Tens	Ones
1,	0		

2.

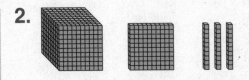

Thousands	Hundreds	Tens	Ones

3. Which number is shown?

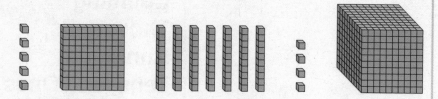

1,079 ○   1,097 ○

1,179 ○   1,197 ○

4. Extend Your Thinking Greg wrote 112 to match the model. What mistake did he make? What number should he have written?

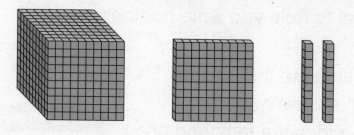

_____

_____

5. Extend Your Thinking Use some of these models to make a number that is less than 1,200. The sum of its digits should be 8. Draw the models you used to make your number. Then write your number.

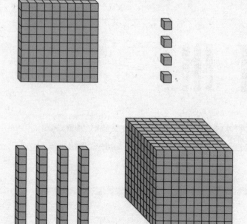

My number is _____.

Solve & Share

Toss a number cube two times to make the missing digits. Write the digits in the empty boxes.
What are the standard, expanded, and number word forms for the number you made?

⭐ **TEKS 2.2B** Use standard, word, and expanded forms to represent numbers up to 1,200. Also, 2.2A. **Mathematical Process Standards** 2.1C, 2.1D, 2.1E.

Digital Resources at SavvasTexas.com

Solve   Learn   Glossary   Check   Tools   Games

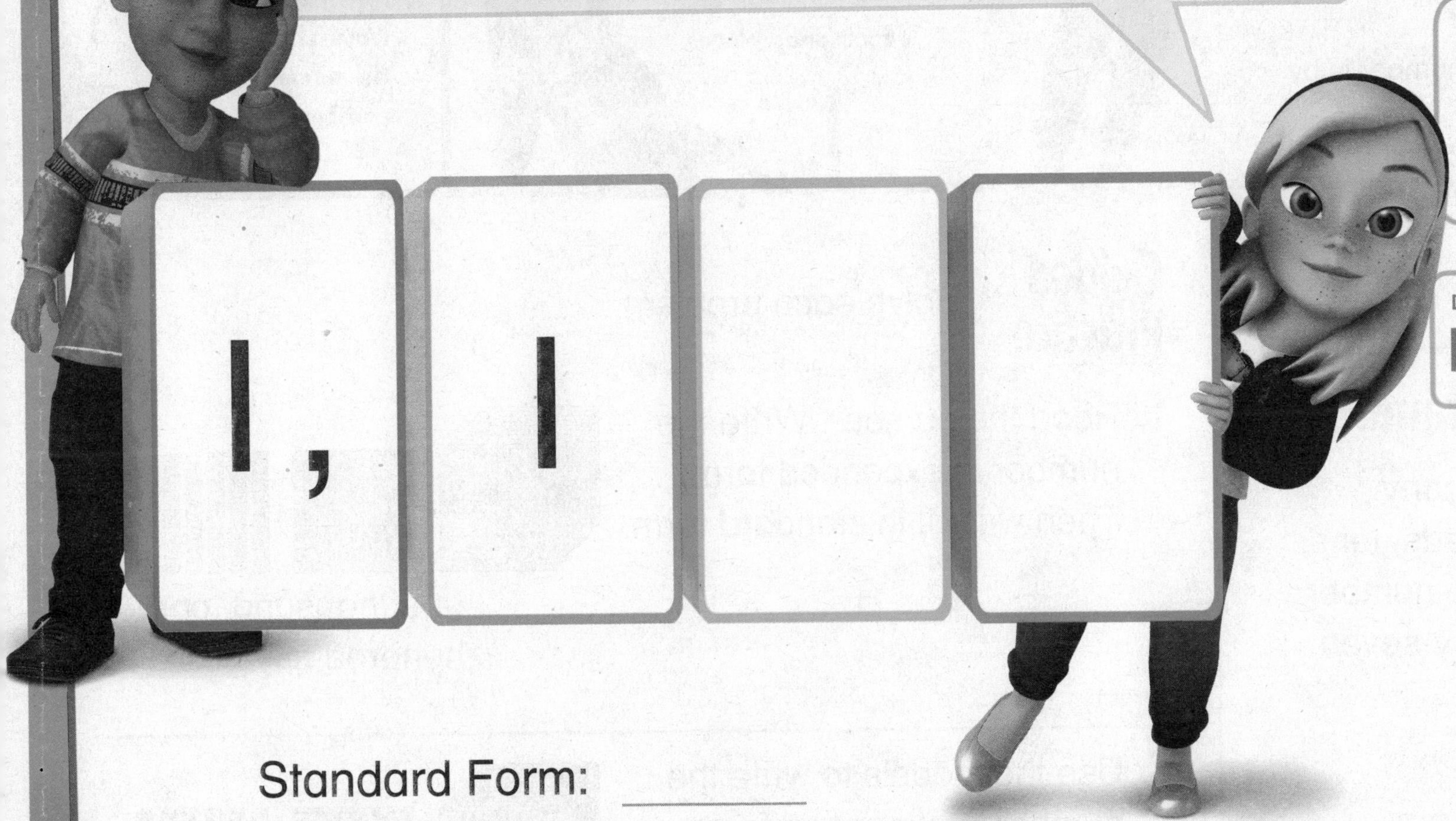

1, 1

Standard Form: _____

Expanded Form: _____ + _____ + _____ + _____

Number Word: _____

What number is shown by the models?

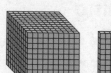

$$1,000 + 100 + 50 + 3$$

One way to write the number is by using expanded form.

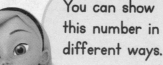
You can show this number in different ways.

Another way is the standard form.

1,153

Remember the comma between the hundreds and thousands places.

A third way is the number word.

One thousand, one hundred fifty-three

All three ways show the same number.

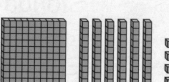

Do You Understand?

Show Me! How many thousands, hundreds, tens, and ones does the number one thousand, forty-seven have?

☆ Guided Practice ☆ Solve each problem.

1. Read the number. Write the number in expanded form. Then write it in standard form.

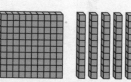

_____ + _____ + _____ + _____

_____

one thousand, one hundred fifty-six

2. Use the models to write the number in expanded form. Then write the number in word form.

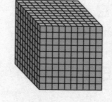

_____ + _____ + _____ + _____

Topic 3 | Lesson 4

Name _____

Write the number in word form. Then write it in standard form.

3. $1,000 + 100 + 30 + 2$

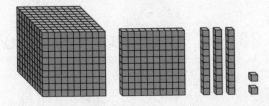

_____

_____

4. $1,000 + 0 + 40 + 8$

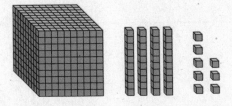

_____

_____

5. $1,000 + 100 + 9$

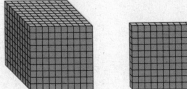

_____

_____

6. **Extend Your Thinking** Write the number in two different ways.

It has a 1 in the thousands place, 2 in the tens place, 0 in the hundreds place, and 0 in the ones place.

Standard form: _____   Expanded form: _____

7. There are 1,193 entries in an art contest.
Write the number in expanded form.

_____ + _____ + _____ + _____

---

8. The model shows a four-digit number.
⭐ What is the standard form of the number?

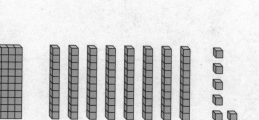

$1,000 + 100 + 80 + 6$ ◯

$1,000 + 100 + 80 + 7$ ◯

1,186 ◯

1,187 ◯

---

9. **Extend Your Thinking** Choose a four-digit number up to 1,200.
Write the standard form and the expanded form of the number.
Then use the number word in a sentence.

Standard Form: _____

Expanded Form: _____ + _____ + _____ + _____

_____

_____

Name _____

Another Look You can write and show numbers in different ways.

Expanded form uses addition signs to show thousands, hundreds, tens, and ones.

$$1,000 + 100 + 50 + 4$$

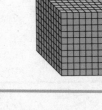

You can use models to show expanded form.

The **number word** is one thousand, one hundred fifty-four.

The **standard form** is

_1,154_.

🏠 **HOME CONNECTION**
Your child identified and wrote the standard form, the expanded form, and the number word form for numbers up to 1,200.

HOME ACTIVITY Write and say a number that is less than 1,200, such as one thousand, one hundred sixty-two. Ask your child to write the number in standard form and expanded form.

 Write the number in word form.
Then write the number in standard form.

1. $1,000 + 200$

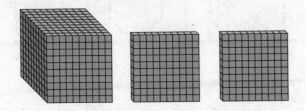

_____

_____

2. $1,000 + 100 + 80 + 2$

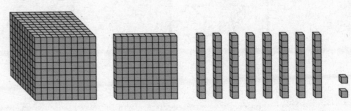

_____

_____

3. There are 1,129 students at school on Monday and 1,143 students at school on Tuesday.

What is the expanded form of the number of students at school on each day?

Monday: _____

Tuesday: _____

4. Which of these is NOT a way to write the number shown by the models?

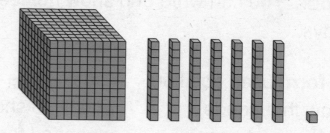

○ 1,071

○ one thousand, seventy-one

○ 1,000 + 70 + 1

○ 1,017

Extend Your Thinking Each shape stands for a digit.

Look at each chart. Write the number in expanded form and standard form.

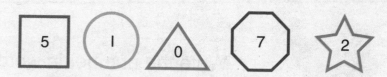

5.

Thousands	Hundreds	Tens	Ones
○	☆	△	△

_____

_____

6.

Thousands	Hundreds	Tens	Ones
○	○	⬡	□

_____

_____

Name _____

Solve & Share

Show two ways to make 213 with place-value blocks. Tell how your ways are alike and different.

Make your models here.

⭐ **TEKS 2.2A** Use concrete and pictorial models to compose and decompose numbers up to 1,200 in more than one way as a sum of so many thousands, hundreds, tens, and ones. **Mathematical Process Standards** 2.1C, 2.1D, 2.1G.

Digital Resources at SavvasTexas.com

 Solve Learn Glossary Check Tools Games

Draw your models here.

Way 1	Way 2

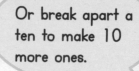

You can show 1,123 in lots of different ways. Here is one way.

Thousands	Hundreds	Tens	Ones

$$1,123 = 1,000 + 100 + 20 + 3$$

Break apart the thousand to make 10 more hundreds.

Thousands	Hundreds	Tens	Ones

$$1,123 = 1,100 + 20 + 3$$

Or break apart the hundred to make 10 more tens.

Thousands	Hundreds	Tens	Ones

$$1,123 = 1,000 + 120 + 3$$

Or break apart a ten to make 10 more ones.

Thousands	Hundreds	Tens	Ones

$$1,123 = 1,000 + 100 + 10 + 13$$

Do You Understand?

Show Me! How are 5 hundreds and 4 tens the same as 4 hundreds and 14 tens?

Guided Practice

Use place-value blocks to count the thousands, hundreds, tens, and ones. Show two other ways to make the number.

1.

Thousands	Hundreds	Tens	Ones

$$1,132 = \underline{1,000 + 100 + 30 + 2}$$

$$1,132 = \underline{\hspace{4cm}}$$

$$1,132 = \underline{\hspace{4cm}}$$

Name _____

Use place-value blocks to count the thousands, hundreds, tens, and ones.
Then show two other ways to make the number.

2.
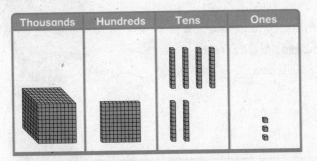

Hundreds	Tens	Ones

$418 =$ _____

$418 =$ _____

$418 =$ _____

3.

Thousands	Hundreds	Tens	Ones

$1,163 =$ _____

$1,163 =$ _____

$1,163 =$ _____

4.

Thousands	Hundreds	Tens	Ones

$1,025 =$ _____

$1,025 =$ _____

$1,025 =$ _____

Extend Your Thinking Write the missing number.

5. $698 = 500 + \underline{\quad} + 8$

6. $1,139 = 1,100 + 20 + \underline{\quad}$

7. Carl made this model to show a number.

Thousands	Hundreds	Tens	Ones

What number is shown? _____

Draw models to show another way
Carl could make this number.

8. Which of these is NOT a way
to show 1,187?

○ 1,000 + 100 + 80 + 7

○ 1,100 + 100 + 80 + 7

○ 1,100 + 80 + 7

○ 1,000 + 100 + 70 + 17

Remember, you can show numbers in different ways.

9. **Extend Your Thinking** Make 572 as hundreds, tens, and ones.

Write as many ways as you can.

_____   _____

_____   _____

Name _____

Another Look You can show a number in different ways.

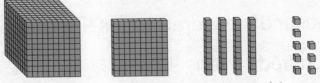

__1__ thousand __1__ hundred __4__ tens __8__ ones

$1,148 = \underline{1,000} + \underline{100} + \underline{40} + \underline{8}$

is the same as

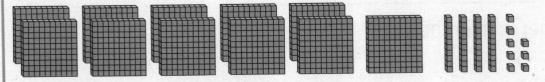

11 hundreds 4 tens 8 ones

$1,148 = \underline{1,100} + \underline{40} + \underline{8}$

Show a different way to make the number. You can use place-value blocks to help.

1. 734 is ____ hundreds ____ tens ____ ones.

   $734 = \underline{\hspace{1cm}} + \underline{\hspace{1cm}} + \underline{\hspace{1cm}}$

   734 is ____ hundreds ____ tens ____ ones.

   $734 = \underline{\hspace{1cm}} + \underline{\hspace{1cm}} + \underline{\hspace{1cm}}$

2. What number does the model show?

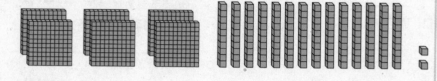

_____

3. Which of these is NOT a way to show 1,164?

○   11 hundreds 5 tens 14 ones

○   1 thousand 1 hundred 6 tens 4 ones

○   11 hundreds 6 tens 4 ones

○   1 thousand 1 hundred 5 tens 24 ones

Extend Your Thinking Write each number 3 different ways.

4. 936

Hundreds	Tens	Ones

Hundreds	Tens	Ones

Hundreds	Tens	Ones

---

5. 1,152

Thousands	Hundreds	Tens	Ones

Thousands	Hundreds	Tens	Ones

Thousands	Hundreds	Tens	Ones

Name _____

I am thinking of a 4-digit number.

It has 1 thousand.

It has 15 tens.

It has less than 5 ones.

Which number am I thinking of?

Explain how you found the number.

⭐ TEKS 2.1G Display, explain, and justify mathematical ideas and arguments using precise mathematical language in written or oral communication. Also, 2.2, 2.2B. Mathematical Process Standards 2.1B, 2.1E.

Digital Resources at SavvasTexas.com

Solve   Learn   Glossary   Check   Tools   Games

1,190

694

1,153

1,035

986

1,158

1,107

Mystery number: _____

Analyze

Which number am I?

I have 1 thousand.
I have 0 hundreds.
My ones are the sum of 3 + 5.

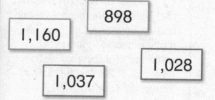

898

1,160

1,037

1,028

Plan

I will cross out the numbers that do not match the clues.

~~1,160~~

~~898~~

~~1,037~~

1,028

Solve and Justify

1,028 is the mystery number.

~~1,160~~

~~898~~

~~1,037~~

1,028

Evaluate

1,028 has 1 thousand.
It also has 0 hundreds.
3 + 5 = 8 and 1,028 has 8 ones.
All the clues describe 1,028.

Do You Understand?

Show Me! How does crossing out numbers that do not match the clues help you find the answer?

☆ Guided Practice ☆

Cross out the numbers that do not match the clues. Circle the number that answers the question.

1. Which number am I?
I have 1 thousand.
I have 1 hundred.

~~1,066~~

~~572~~

(1,132)

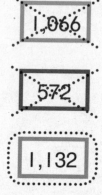

2. Which number am I?
I have more than 2 tens.
I do not have 6 ones.

1,116

1,078

1,056

☆ Independent ☆ Practice

Cross out the numbers that do not match the clues.
Circle the number that answers the question.

3. Which number am I?
I have 1 thousand.
I have 19 ones.

| 1,111 | 1,019 | 819 | 1,020 |

4. Which number am I?
I have no hundreds.
I have the same number of tens and ones.

| 1,199 | 1,027 | 1,055 | 1,200 |

5. Which number am I?
I have 7 ones.
I have 11 hundreds.
I have more than 4 tens.

 1,187   1,163   1,147   1,037

6. Which number am I?
I have 15 tens.
I have less than 6 ones.
I have 1 thousand.

1,065   1,153   152   167

7. Extend Your Thinking This riddle is missing a clue.
Write the last clue to find the mystery number.

I have the same number of tens and ones.
I do not have 7 hundreds.

| 633 | 1,045 | 766 | 1,200 |

_____

Which number am I? _____

8. Kim's house number is a
four-digit number.
It has more ones than tens.
It does not have 0 hundreds.
Circle Kim's house.

 1,012   1,046   1,159   1,095

9. Juanita pulled a number out of
the bag. It has 18 tens. It has
more ones than hundreds.
Circle Juanita's number.

582	1,080
1,180	1,182

10. Ari won a new top score in a game.
It has more ones than tens.
It has more hundreds than ones.
Which number could NOT be
Ari's top score?

310 ○   726 ○

857 ○   908 ○

11. Extend Your Thinking Use the numbers on the
cards to make 3 different three-digit numbers.
Then write a riddle about the numbers.

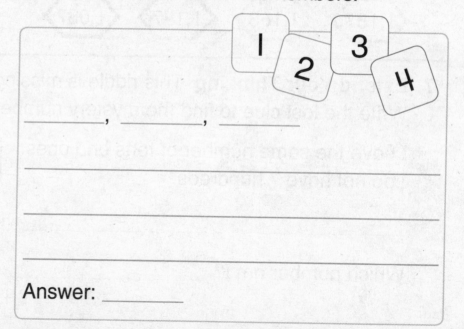

_____, _____, _____

_____

_____

_____

Answer: _____

Another Look Read the clues. Cross out the number that does not fit each clue.

Which number am I?
I have 1 hundred.
I have more ones than tens.

| 1,093 | 1,193 | 1,139 |

To find the number, think:
- It has 1 hundred.
  Cross out 1,093.
- It has more ones than tens.
  Cross out 1,193.
- Circle the number that is
  not crossed out.

🏠 **HOME CONNECTION**
Your child used clues to solve problems about four-digit numbers up to 1,200.

HOME ACTIVITY Show your child some four-digit numbers up to 1,200. Tell clues about one of them. Ask your child to explain how to use the clues to eliminate numbers and identify the "mystery number" you chose.

Cross out the numbers that do not match the clues.
Circle the number that answers the questions.

1. I have more than 5 tens.
I have 9 hundreds.
Which number am I?

| 1,995 | 1,935 | 1,865 |

2. I have 4 ones.
I have the same number of
tens and hundreds.
Which number am I?

| 424 | 441 | 664 |

3. I have 6 tens.
I have less than 8 ones.
Which number am I?

| 1,168 | 1,167 | 1,143 |

4. I have 6 ones.
I have 11 hundreds.
Which number could I NOT be?

1,106	1,036
○	○

1,186	1,136
○	○

5. 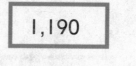 Solve 15 − 7 to find my tens digit.
Solve 8 − 6 to find my ones digit.
Which number am I?

1,190	1,082
○	○

1,186	1,199
○	○

6. Extend Your Thinking Three friends are playing a game. Each friend
has a secret number. Use the numbers and clues to find each friend's number.
Cross out the numbers that do not match the clues.

CLUES
- No number has 2 hundreds.
- All the numbers have more than 1 one.
- Jess has 1 hundred.
- Nina has less than 3 tens.
- Ben has more ones than tens.

1,187	1,125
1,101	1,095
1,200	1,068

Jess: _____

Nina: _____

Ben: _____

Name _____

Use the *Digit Gadget* to **think about numbers** and **represent** them in different ways.

Digit Gadget

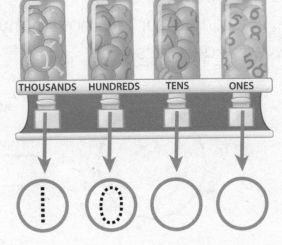

THOUSANDS HUNDREDS TENS ONES

1. Every digit keeps the value the *Digit Gadget* gives it.
   The thousands and hundreds digits are shown.
   Pick digits for tens and ones. Write all the digits below.

   Thousands   Hundreds   Tens   Ones

   (I)   (0)   (   )   (   )

2. Write your 4-digit number in expanded form.

   _____

3. Show your number in three other ways.
   Use place-value blocks to help.

   _____ = _____

   _____ = _____

   _____ = _____

4. The *Digit Gadget* costs $15.
   If you have $9, how much more money do
   you need to save to buy it? Explain.

   _____

   _____

   _____

Code Math

1. Nina plays a dart game.
   She tosses 5 darts.
   The ring color tells how many points each dart gets.

key	
———	1,000
———	100
———	10
———	1

Nina scores 320 points.
Where do her darts hit?

_____

_____

_____

Nina tosses 5 darts. She scores BELOW 100.
Where do her darts hit?

_____

What's Wrong?

2.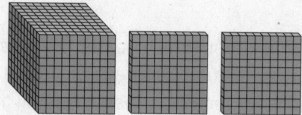

Javon says, "My models show one hundred twenty."
What is Javon's mistake? Fix it!

_____

_____

_____

Number Riddles

3. Solve the riddle.

   I have four different digits.
   I have no hundreds. I have 1 thousand.
   My greatest digit is 3.
   What number am I? _____

Name _____

Set A

You can use place value to help you write numbers.

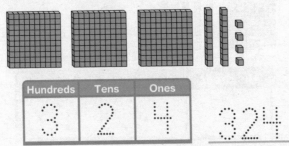

Hundreds	Tens	Ones
3	2	4

324

There are 3 hundreds, 2 tens, and 4 ones in 324.

Reteaching

Write the numbers. Use the models and your workmat if needed.

1.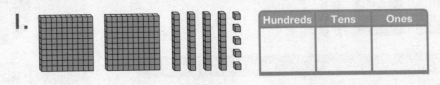

Hundreds	Tens	Ones

_____

2.

Hundreds	Tens	Ones

_____

Set B

You can write a number using the expanded form, number word form, or standard form.

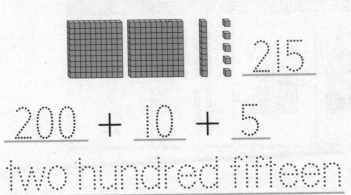

215

200 + 10 + 5

two hundred fifteen

Write the number in standard form, expanded form, and number word form.

3.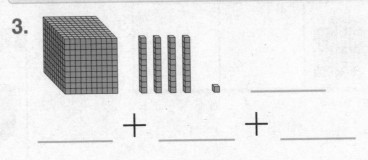

_____

___ + ___ + ___

_____

You can use place value to help you write numbers.

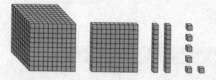

Thousands	Hundreds	Tens	Ones
1	1	2	6

There is 1 thousand, 1 hundred, 2 tens, and 6 ones in 1,126.

Write the numbers. Use models and your workmat to help you.

4.

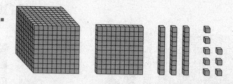

Thousands	Hundreds	Tens	Ones

You can write numbers in different ways.

Thousands	Hundreds	Tens	Ones

$1,200 = \underline{1,000} + \underline{100} + \underline{90} + \underline{10}$

$1,200 = \underline{1,000} + \underline{190} + \underline{10}$

Show two different ways to write the number. Use blocks and draw pictures to help.

5.

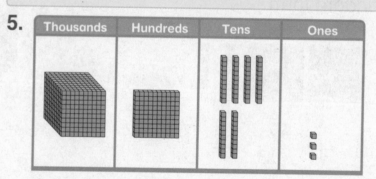

$1,163 = \underline{\hphantom{000}} + \underline{\hphantom{000}} + \underline{\hphantom{000}} + \underline{\hphantom{000}}$

$1,163 = \underline{\hphantom{000}} + \underline{\hphantom{000}} + \underline{\hphantom{000}}$

Name _____

1. Which number does the model show?

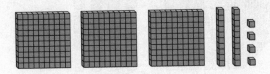

- ○ 423
- ○ 342
- ○ 324
- ○ 234

2. Which is the number word for the number shown by the blocks?

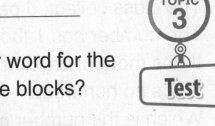

- ○ four hundred fifty-six
- ○ four hundred forty-six
- ○ 400 + 40 + 6
- ○ 446

3. Which is the standard form of the number shown by the models?

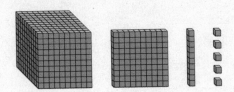

- ○ 1,115
- ○ one thousand, one hundred fifteen
- ○ 1,000 + 100 + 10 + 5
- ○ 1,151

4. Which is the expanded form of the number shown by the models?

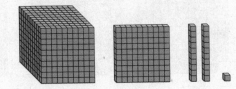

- ○ 1,121
- ○ one thousand, one hundred twenty-one
- ○ 1,000 + 100 + 20 + 1
- ○ 1,000 + 100 + 10 + 2

5. The class collected pennies in a bowl.
The number has 1 thousand.
It has more ones than tens.
It has no hundreds.
Which is the number of pennies?

1,154   1,016   1,108   1,020
  ○   ○   ○   ○

6. Which number is shown by the model?

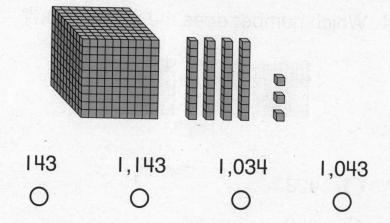

143   1,143   1,034   1,043
  ○   ○   ○   ○

7. Danny made this model.
What number does it show?

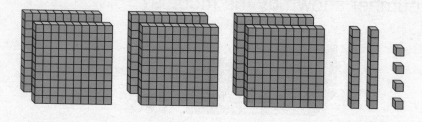

___ = ___ + ___ + ___

8. Show three different ways to write 563.

563 = _____

563 = _____

563 = _____

132   one hundred thirty-two

Topic 3

Comparing and Ordering to 1,200

Essential Question: How can number lines be used to locate numbers?

Jets carry passengers all over the world.

A jet could take me to many different places!

Wow! Let's do this project and learn more.

Math and Science Project: Travel and Numbers

Find Out Ask friends or family to describe trips they have taken to faraway places. Find out where they visited and how they traveled there.

Journal: Make a Book Draw pictures to show what you learned about your friends' and family's travels. In your book, also:

- Choose a city in the United States that you would like to visit. Tell why you would like to visit there.

- Find the distance in miles from your town to the city you chose. Show the distance on a number line.

Name _____

Review What You Know

Vocabulary

1. Circle the **thousands** digit.

1,073

2. Circle the number that is **less than** 20.

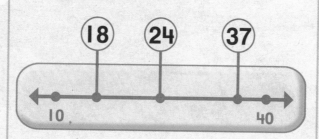

3. Circle the sign for **greater than**.

>   <   =

Understanding Place Value

4. Write the number to match the model.

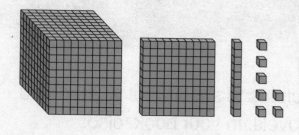

_____

5. A number has 9 in the hundreds place. It does not have any tens. It has 5 in the ones place.

What is the number?

Comparing Numbers

6. Write the number of cubes.

Circle >, <, or =.

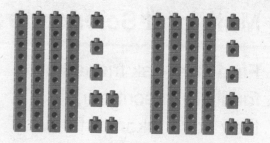

_____ > < = _____

number line

```
1  2  3  4  5  6  7  8  9  10
```

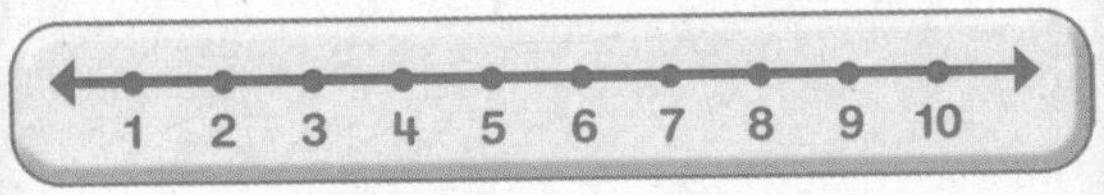

compare

147 $>$ 143

147 is greater than 143.

equal to (=)

36 = 36

36 is equal to 36.

less than (<)

2 < 6

greater than (>)

5 > 1

least

35 47 58 61

least

My Word Cards

Use what you know to complete the sentences.
Extend learning by writing your own sentence using each word.

36 is _____ 36.

When you _____

numbers, you find out if a number is greater than, less than, or equal to another number.

A line that shows numbers in order from left to right is

called a _____

_____.

The _____

is the number or group with the smallest value.

5 is _____

_____ 1.

2 is _____

_____ 6.

A-Z

My Word Cards Study the words on the front of the card. Complete the activity on the back.

greatest

35 47 58 (61)

greatest

order

(27) 72 107 117 (171)

least   greatest

increase

224, 324, 424, 524

The pattern rule is increase by 100.

My Word Cards

Use what you know to complete the sentences.
Extend learning by writing your own sentence using each word.

When you _____ a number you add to its value.

Numbers can be put in counting _____ from least to greatest or from greatest to least.

The _____ is the number or group with the largest value.

Name _____

Solve & Share

Are there different ways to find the missing number? Explain.

⊕ TEKS 2.2F Name the whole number that corresponds to a specific point on a number line. Also, 2.2, 2.2D. Mathematical Process Standards 2.1C, 2.1F.

Digital Resources at SavvasTexas.com

Solve   Learn   Glossary   Check   Tools   Games

630 631 632 633 634 **?** 636 637 638 639 640

_____ is the missing number.

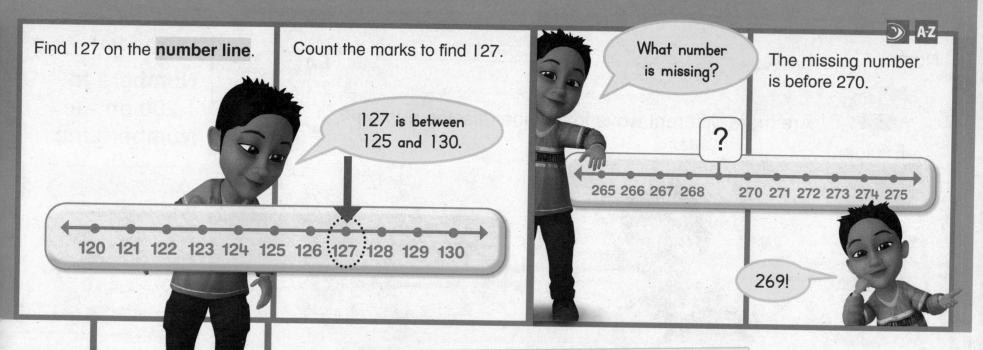

Find 127 on the **number line**.

Count the marks to find 127.

127 is between 125 and 130.

120 121 122 123 124 125 126 127 128 129 130

What number is missing?

The missing number is before 270.

?

265 266 267 268 270 271 272 273 274 275

269!

Do You Understand?

Show Me! Explain how to find a missing number on a number line.

Write the missing numbers.

1.

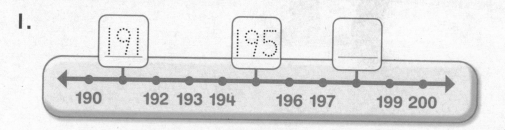

191 195 ___

190 192 193 194 196 197 199 200

2.

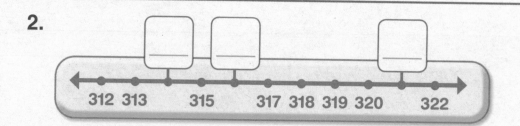

312 313 315 317 318 319 320 322

Topic 4 | Lesson 1

Independent Practice

Write the missing numbers.

3.

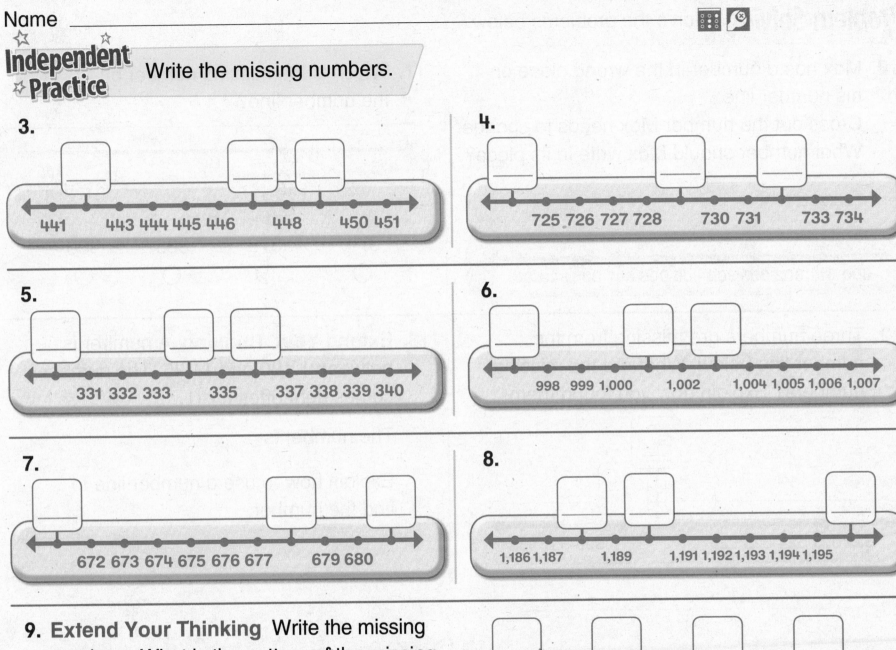

441 ___ 443 444 445 446 ___ 448 ___ 450 451

4.

___ 725 726 727 728 ___ 730 731 ___ 733 734

5.

___ 331 332 333 ___ 335 ___ 337 338 339 340

6.

___ 998 999 1,000 ___ 1,002 ___ 1,004 1,005 1,006 1,007

7.

___ 672 673 674 675 676 677 ___ 679 680

8.

1,186 1,187 ___ 1,189 ___ 1,191 1,192 1,193 1,194 1,195 ___

9. Extend Your Thinking Write the missing numbers. What is the pattern of the missing numbers?

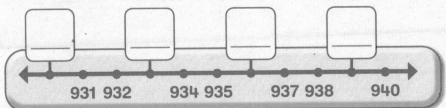

931 932 ___ 934 935 ___ 937 938 ___ 940

10. Max has a number in the wrong place on his number line.

Cross out the number Max needs to change. What number should Max write in its place?

_____

800 810 802 803 804 805 806 807 808 809 810

11. Which is the missing number on the number line?

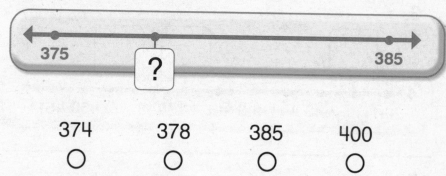
375   ?   385

374   378   385   400
○   ○   ○   ○

12. Three numbers are missing from the number line below. What are the missing numbers? Explain how you found them.

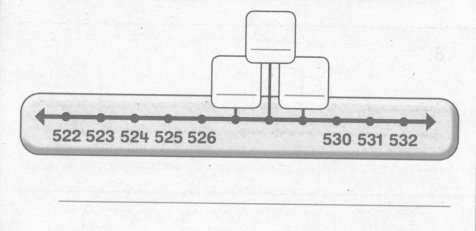
522 523 524 525 526   530 531 532

13. Extend Your Thinking A number is between 1,140 and 1,145. The number comes right after 1,141.

The number is _____.

Explain how to use a number line to find the number.

Topic 4 | Lesson 1

Name _____

Another Look

What numbers are missing on the number line?
You can count to find out. Start at 355.
Count up to the missing number.
Then count back to the other missing number.

🏠 **HOME CONNECTION**
Your child learned how to find missing numbers on a number line.

HOME ACTIVITY Draw a number line from 1,000 to 1,010. Leave three numbers unlabeled. Ask your child to find the missing numbers and explain how to find them.

Count back.   Count up.
355, 354, 353, 352   355, 356, 357

350 351   353 354 355 356   358 359 360

352   357

Solve the problems.

1. Circle 286 on the number line.
   Use 286 to find the missing numbers.

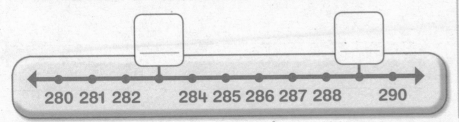

280 281 282   284 285 286 287 288   290

2. Explain how you found the missing numbers.

_____

_____

Write the missing numbers.

3.

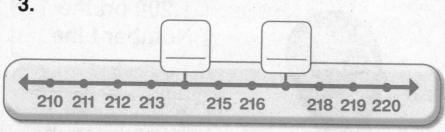

210 211 212 213 ___ 215 216 ___ 218 219 220

4.

980 981 ___ 983 984 985 986 987 988 ___ 990

Use the number lines to solve.

5. I am between 857 and 861.
I have a 6 in my tens place.

What number am I? _____

855   865

6. Which is the missing number on the number line?

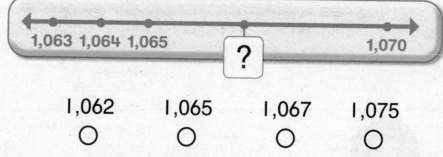

1,063 1,064 1,065   **?**   1,070

◯ 1,062   ◯ 1,065   ◯ 1,067   ◯ 1,075

7. Extend Your Thinking A number is missing on a number line. The number is between 1,155 and 1,165. One of the digits is a 7.

What is the number? _____

Explain your thinking.

_____

_____

_____

_____

_____

Name _____

Solve & Share

Use number cards to make a number between 70 and 90. Draw a point to show where your number should be on the number line. Explain how you know.

My number

⭐ TEKS 2.2E Locate the position of a given whole number on an open number line. Also, 2.2. **Mathematical Process Standards** 2.1B, 2.1C, 2.1F.

Digital Resources at SavvasTexas.com

Solve   Learn   Glossary   Check   Tools   Games

70   90

Do You Understand?

Show Me! Explain how you can use an open number line to show where to place 48 and 84.

☆ **Guided Practice** ☆ Draw lines to show where each number should go on the number line.

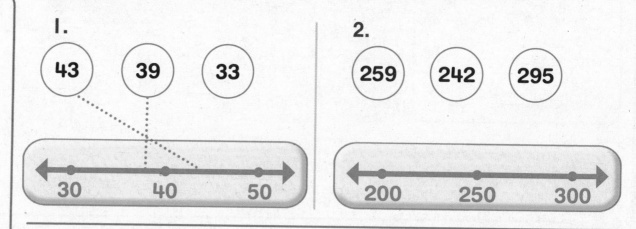

1.

43 39 33

30   40   50

2.

259 242 295

200 250 300

3. What number is halfway between 500 and 600?

_____

500   600

Name _____

Draw lines to show where each number should go on the number line.

4.

(92)   (82)   (89)

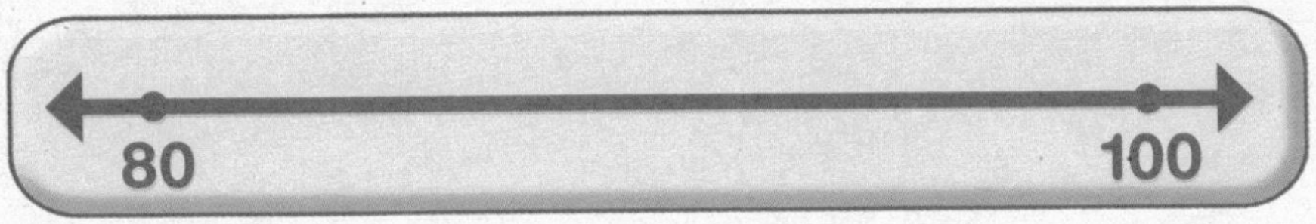

←———————————•—→
80   100

5.

(451)   (495)   (447)

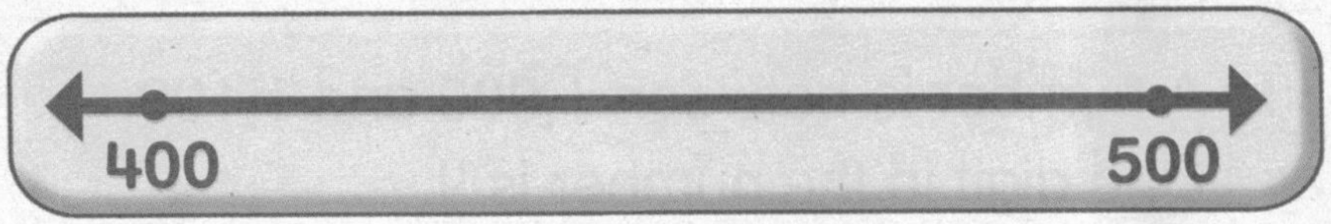

←•————————————•→
400   500

6.

(859)   (905)   (895)

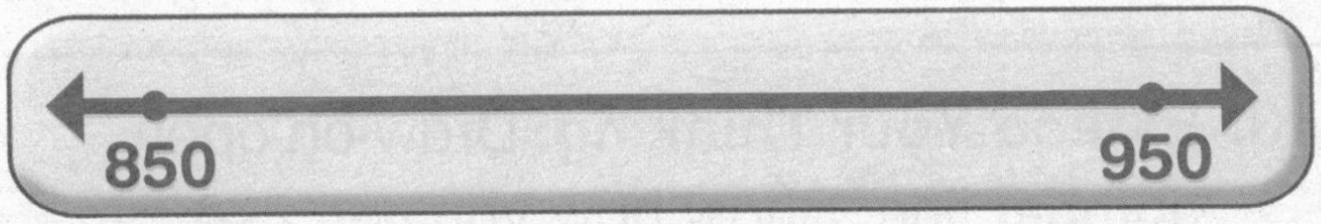

←•————————————•→
850   950

7.

(1,147)   (1,115)   (1,185)

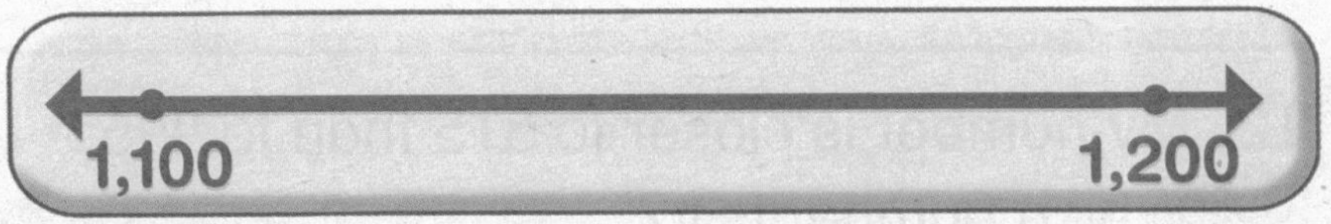

←•————————————•→
1,100   1,200

8. Extend Your Thinking Draw lines to show the order of these numbers on the number line.

(845)   (770)   (800)   (820)

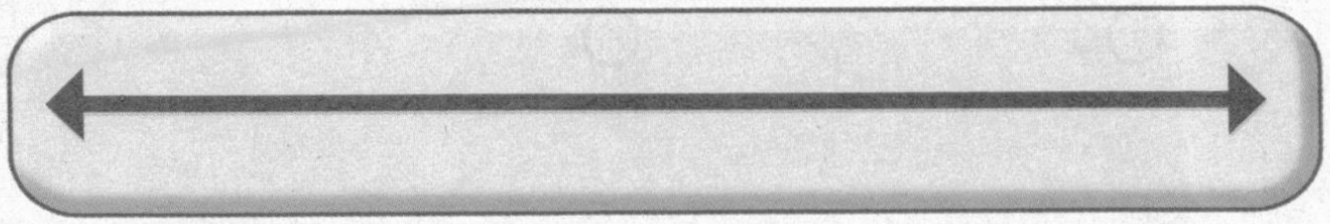

←——————————————————→

9. Sara's number is between 540 and 550.
One of the digits in Sara's number is 6.
Is Sara's number closer to 540 or 550?

closer to _____

10. A number is between 880 and 890.
It is closer to 890 than to 880.
The ones digit is greater than 8.
What is the number?

_____

11. A number is between 1,000 and 1,100.
One digit in the number is 4.
Another digit in the number is 2.
Write the number.
Draw a line to place it on the number line.

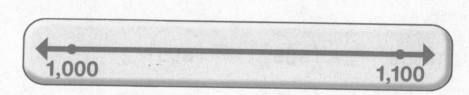

1,000   1,100

12. My number is closer to 515 than to 495.
Which number is it?

475   500
○   ○

485   525
○   ○

13. **Extend Your Thinking** Draw an open
number line. Show how you can use
this to place 830 and 790.

Topic 4 | Lesson 2

Another Look You can place 460, 410, and 490 on an open number line.

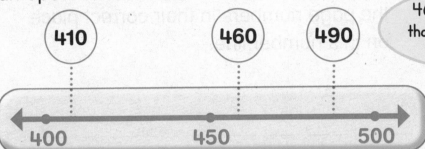

410   460   490

400   450   500

460 is a little more than halfway between 400 and 500.

460 is **after** 450. It is **closer to** 450 than to 500.

410 is **before** 450. It is **closer to** 400 than to 450.

490 is **after** 450. It is **closer to** 500 than to 450.

The numbers are in order: 410, 460, 490.

🏠 **HOME CONNECTION**
Your child has learned how to place numbers on an open number line.

HOME ACTIVITY With your child, draw an open number line from 700 to 900. Ask your child to place the numbers 870, 790, and 810 on the number line. Have your child explain how to place the numbers.

Write the numbers to show their place on the number line.

1. 681   627   659

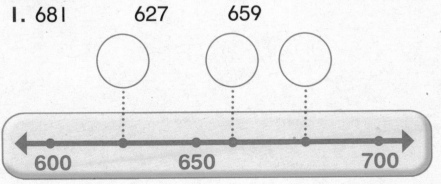

600   650   700

2. 1,090   989   1,011

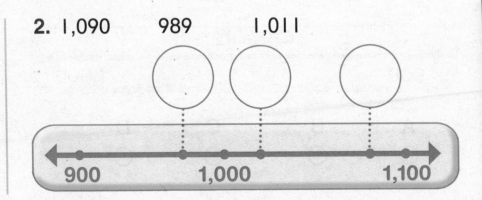

900   1,000   1,100

3. A number is between 625 and 675. Two of the digits in the number are 5. Is the number closer to 625 or 675?

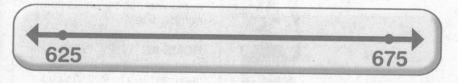

625   675

closer to _____

4. Some pages are out of order. The page numbers are 420, 590, and 510. Show the page numbers in their correct place on this number line.

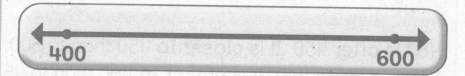

400   600

5. Which letter shows the number 958 on the number line?

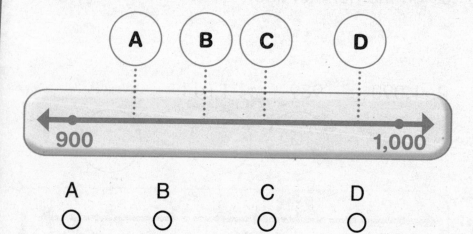

A   B   C   D

900   1,000

A   B   C   D
○   ○   ○   ○

6. Extend Your Thinking Draw an open number line. Place the numbers 480, 590, 430, and 560 on the number line.

Topic 4 | Lesson 2

Name _____

Solve & Share

Which number is greater? How can you tell? Explain.

1,065   1,120

★ TEKS 2.2D Use place value to compare and order whole numbers up to 1,200 using comparative language, numbers, and symbols (>, <, or =). Also, 2.2. **Mathematical Process Standards** 2.1A, 2.1C, 2.1E, 2.1F.

Digital Resources at SavvasTexas.com

Solve   Learn   Glossary   Check   Tools   Games

_____ is greater than _____.

Compare 1,115 and 225.

To compare numbers, start with the digit that has the greatest place value.

1,115 ◯ 225	1,135 ◯ 1,200	1,163 ◯ 1,163
Compare the thousands first.	If the thousands are equal, compare the hundreds.	The thousands, hundreds, tens, and ones are equal.
1,000 is **greater than** 0 thousands.	100 is **less than** 200	1,163 is **equal to** 1,163.
So, 1,115 _⟨>⟩_ 225.	So, 1,135 _⟨<⟩_ 1,200.	So, 1,163 _⟨=⟩_ 1,163.

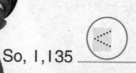

Do You Understand?

Show Me! How would you compare 1,126 and 890?

☆ **Guided Practice** ☆ Compare. Write greater than, less than, or equal to. Then write >, <, or =.

1.
1,064 is _greater than_ 178.

1,064 ⊙> 178

2.
540 is _____ 560.

540 ◯ 560

3.
846 is _____ 819.

846 ◯ 819

4.
1,143 is _____ 1,143.

1,143 ◯ 1,143

Name _____

Independent Practice

Compare. Write greater than, less than, or equal to. Then write >, <, or =.

5.

572 is _____ 1,177.

572 ◯ 1,177

6.

256 is _____ 243.

256 ◯ 243

7.

837 is _____ 837.

837 ◯ 837

8.

1,076 is _____ 1,074.

1,076 ◯ 1,074

9.

208 is _____ 208.

208 ◯ 208

10.

936 is _____ 836.

936 ◯ 836

11.

821 is _____ 1,028.

821 ◯ 1,028

12.

1,117 is _____ 1,171.

1,117 ◯ 1,171

13.

286 is _____ 189.

286 ◯ 189

14. Extend Your Thinking What number makes both comparisons true?

_____ < 1,011   _____ > 1,009

15. Ming sells 319 tickets.
Josie sells 315 tickets.
Who sells more tickets?

319 ◯ 315

_____ sells more tickets.

16. Jared earned 1,189 pennies doing chores.
Tara earned 1,200 pennies doing chores.
Who earned more?

1,189 ◯ 1,200

_____ earned more.

17. Solve the riddle to find the number of coins in the second chest.
Then compare the numbers.

The two numbers have the same digits. The tens and ones digits are in a different order.

1,056 coins   ? coins

1,056 < 1,106   1,056 = 1,056
    ◯   ◯

1,056 > 1,065   1,056 < 1,065
    ◯   ◯

18. Extend Your Thinking Compare the numbers 1,098 and 1,089. Write the comparison two ways. Explain your thinking.

_____ ◯ _____

_____ ◯ _____

_____

_____

_____

_____

Name _____

Another Look First compare the digits with the greatest place value.

If the thousands are equal, compare the hundreds.
If the hundreds are equal, compare the tens.
If the tens are equal, compare the ones.

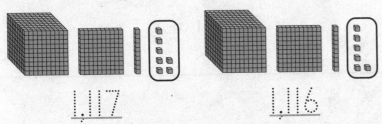

1,117   1,116

7 is __greater than__ 6. So 1,117 ⊃ 1,116.

Use models to help!

⌂ **HOME CONNECTION**
Your child compared numbers using words (greater than, less than, equal to) and symbols (>, <, =).

HOME ACTIVITY Ask your child if 1,142 is greater than or less than 1,124. Then have your child explain his or her answer.

Compare. Write >, <, or =.

1. 341 ◯ 432

2. 1,190 ◯ 1,090

3. 621 ◯ 639

4. 890 ◯ 880

5. 546 ◯ 546

6. 1,005 ◯ 995

Use the numbers in the triangles. Write a number that will make each sentence true.

7.

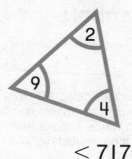

_____ < 717

8.

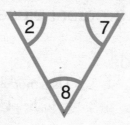

792 > _____

9.

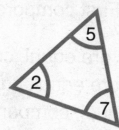

591 > _____

---

10. Nyla compared 1,090 and 1,009.
Her work is shown at the right.

Is Nyla's comparison correct? If not, correct her mistake.

_____

_____

_____

> 1,090 < 1,009
>
> I compared the ones. 0 is less than 9.
>
> So, 1,090 < 1,009.

---

11. This week, 1,161 fans watched a soccer game. Last week, 1,116 fans watched a soccer game.
Which comparison is correct?

1,116 = 1,161   1,116 > 1,161
    ○   ○

1,161 < 1,116   1,116 < 1,161
    ○   ○

12. Extend Your Thinking Circle hundreds, tens, and ones to show your answer.

This number is less than 200 and greater than 100. The ones digit is 5 less than 10. The tens digit is 2 more than the ones digit. What is the number?

_____

Name _____

Solve & Share

How can you order these three numbers in two different ways? Explain.

⭐ TEKS 2.2D Use place value to compare and order whole numbers up to 1,200 using comparative language, numbers, and symbols (>, <, or =). Also, 2.2. Mathematical Process Standards 2.1C, 2.1E, 2.1F.

| 1,066 | 1,135 | 798 |

Digital Resources at SavvasTexas.com

Solve Learn Glossary Check Tools Games

Way 1

Way 2

_____ , _____ , _____   _____ , _____ , _____

Write the numbers in order from **least** to **greatest**.

387 407 389

_____ , _____ , _____
least   greatest

First compare the hundreds digits.

4 hundreds is greater than 3 hundreds.

387

407 389

_____ , _____ , 407
least   greatest

Then compare the tens digits.

387

389

They are the same!

_____ , _____ , 407
least   greatest

Now compare the ones digits.

387

7 is less than 9.

389

So 387 is less than 389.

387 , 389 , 407
least   greatest

Guided Practice

Write the numbers in order from least to greatest.

Do You Understand?

Show Me! Is a number with 3 digits always greater than a number with 2 digits? How do you know?

1.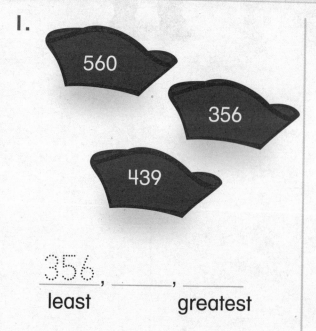

560

356

439

356 , _____ , _____
least   greatest

2.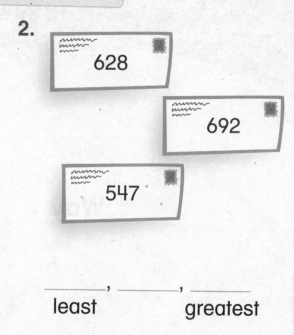

628

692

547

_____ , _____ , _____
least   greatest

Topic 4 | Lesson 4

Name _____

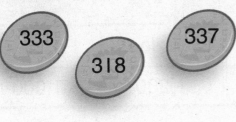

Independent Practice

Write the numbers in order from least to greatest.

3.

333   318   337

_____ , _____ , _____
least   greatest

4.

1,101   1,130   1,103

_____ , _____ , _____
least   greatest

5.

109   91   190

_____ , _____ , _____
least   greatest

Write the numbers in order from greatest to least.

6.

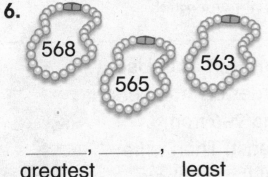

568   565   563

_____ , _____ , _____
greatest   least

7.

127   7   123

_____ , _____ , _____
greatest   least

8.

429   412   434

_____ , _____ , _____
greatest   least

9. Extend Your Thinking Three students play a game. Read the clues.
Use symbols to compare the scores. Then write names to match their scores.

• Tia has fewer points than Raj.
• Allie has the least number of points.

_____ ◯ _____ ◯ _____

_____ 603

_____ 568

_____ 564

10. Three students read books. Order the number of pages they read from least to greatest.

_____, _____, _____

11. Each puzzle has a different number of pieces.

Puzzle A	Puzzle B	Puzzle C
750	1,200	1,000

Order the number of puzzle pieces from greatest to least.

_____, _____, _____

I can write a story about the number of fans at a game!

12. The numbers of stamps that Ray, Josie, and Ming have form a pattern.
Ray has 111 stamps.
Josie has 121 stamps.
Ming has the greatest number of stamps.

| 111 | 121 | ? |

Choose the number of stamps that Ming has.

101   131   121   112
○   ○   ○   ○

13. **Extend Your Thinking** Use > or < to order the numbers 964, 694, and 946 from greatest to least. Then write a story about the numbers.

_____ ○ _____ ○ _____

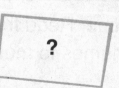

Topic 4 | Lesson 4

Name _____

Another Look Put the numbers in order from least to greatest.

273	250	499

Step 1. Compare the hundreds digits to find the greatest number.

273   250   499

> 4 hundreds is greater than 2 hundreds. 499 is the greatest number.

Step 2. Then compare the tens digits.

273   250

250, 273, 499
least   greatest

> 7 tens is greater than 5 tens. So, 250 is the least number.

🏠 **HOME CONNECTION**
Your child ordered three numbers up to 1,200 from least to greatest.

HOME ACTIVITY Have your child choose three numbers up to 1,200. Then ask your child to explain how to order the three numbers from least to greatest.

Write the numbers in order from least to greatest.

1.

187	126	219

_____, _____, _____
least   greatest

2.

489	352	327

_____, _____, _____
least   greatest

3.

734	632	638

_____, _____, _____
least   greatest

4. Which set of numbers is NOT ordered from least to greatest?

529 531 560 568 ○

513 652 661 701 ○

199 208 398 409 ○

956 865 849 798 ○

Fill in the missing numbers. Use each number in the box once.

| 362 | 240 | 429 | 719 | 885 | 226 |

These numbers are in order from greatest to least.

5. 562, 467, 431, _____, 387, _____, 341

6. 973, 960, _____, 841, 769, _____, 700

7. 437, 411, 365, 271, _____, _____, 199

| 321 | 478 | 625 | 415 | 701 | 589 |

These numbers are in order from least to greatest.

8. 215, 297, _____, 341, 402, _____, 437

9. 482, 521, 618, _____, _____, 750

10. 389, 413, 459, _____, 532, _____, 599

11. Extend Your Thinking Circle the greatest number. Then tell how to find the greatest number.

1,122   1,120   1,126

Which digits do I compare first?

Topic 4 | Lesson 4

Name ______________________________

Solve & Share

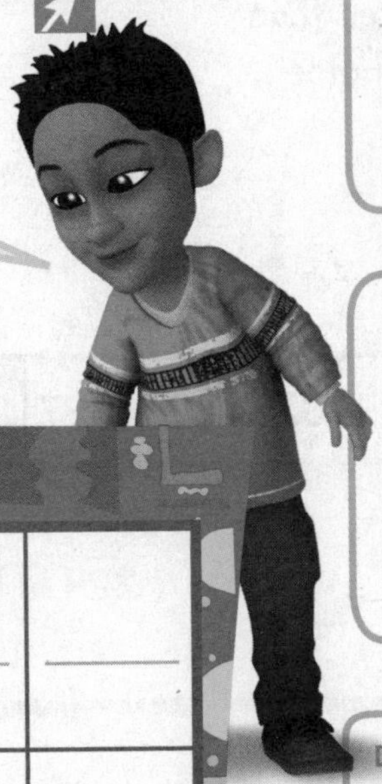

This chart shows only one number.
How can you find a number that is greater than 256?
How can you find a number that is less than 256?

Lesson 4-5
Greater Than and Less Than

TEKS 2.2C Generate a number that is greater than or less than a given whole number up to 1,200. Also, 2.2. **Mathematical Process Standards** 2.1C, 2.1D, 2.1F, 2.1G.

Digital Resources at SavvasTexas.com

Solve | Learn | Glossary | Check | Tools | Games

____	____	____	____	____	____	____	____	____	____
____	____	____	____	____	256	____	____	____	____
____	____	____	____	____	____	____	____	____	____

______ is greater than 256.

______ is less than 256.

You can write numbers that are greater than or less than another number.

$\underline{324} < 325$

| 321 | 322 | 323 | 324 | 325 | 326 | 327 | 328 | 329 | 330 |

324 is less than 325.

$\underline{329} > 325$

| 323 | 324 | 325 | 326 | 327 | 328 | 329 | 330 |

329 is greater than 325.

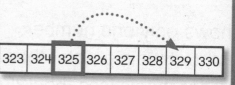

$\underline{325} > 321$

$\underline{325} < 330$

| 321 | 322 | 323 | 324 | 325 | 326 | 327 | 328 | 329 | 330 |

325 is greater than 321 and less than 330.

Do You Understand?

Show Me! How could you write a number that is less than 330 and greater than 328?

☆ Guided Practice ☆ Write a number to make each correct.

1. $\underline{461} < 467$

2. $\underline{} < 188$

3. $1,019 < \underline{}$

4. $432 < \underline{}$

5. $1,200 > \underline{}$

6. $901 > \underline{}$

Name _____

Independent Practice

Write a number to make each correct.

7. 421 > _____

8. _____ < 884

9. 959 < _____

10. _____ < 619

11. 1,103 < _____

12. 566 > _____

13. 394 < _____

14. _____ < 417

15. _____ > 789

Write < or > to make each correct.

16. 107 ◯ 106

17. 630 ◯ 629

18. 1,032 ◯ 1,033

19. **Extend Your Thinking** Write a number to make each correct.
Place the numbers on the number lines.

_____ < 780 < _____

_____ > 457 > _____

Solve the problems below.

20. Kim is thinking of a number.
It is greater than 447.
It is less than 635.
What could the number be?

_____

21. Ken is thinking of a number.
It is less than 1,082.
It is greater than 1,050.
What could the number be?

_____

22. Which number is neither greater than nor less than the number shown?

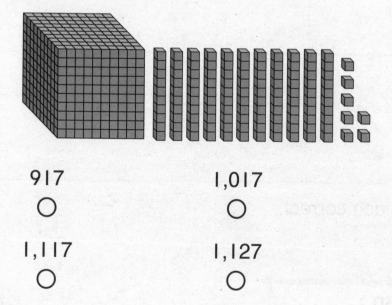

917
○

1,017
○

1,117
○

1,127
○

23. Extend Your Thinking Monty picked a number card. The number is greater than 282. It is less than 284. What is the number? Explain.

_____

_____

_____

_____

_____

Name _____

Another Look Think about the order of numbers.

150	151	152	153	154	155	156	157	158	159
160	161	162	163	164	165	166	167	168	169

Use the words **less than** and **greater than** to describe numbers.

<u>150</u> is **less than** 153.   <u>168</u> is **greater than** 167.

<u>161</u> is **greater than** 160 and **less than** 162.

 HOME CONNECTION
Your child wrote numbers that are greater than or less than another number up to 1,200.

HOME ACTIVITY Have your child choose a number up to 1,200. Then ask your child to explain how to write a number that is greater than that number and less than that number.

Write a number to make each correct.
Use the number chart to help you.

300	301	302	303	304	305	306	307	308	309
310	311	312	313	314	315	316	317	318	319

1. _____ is **less than** 304.

2. _____ is **greater than** 307.

3. _____ is **greater than** 314 and **less than** 316.

Write three different numbers to make each correct.

4. 805 > _____ > 795

805 > _____ > 795

805 > _____ > 795

5. 457 < _____ < 462

457 < _____ < 462

457 < _____ < 462

6. 1,200 > _____ > 1,190

1,200 > _____ > 1,190

1,200 > _____ > 1,190

7. Which two numbers are greater than 297?

213 and 298 ○   751 and 157 ○

307 and 299 ○   200 and 300 ○

8. Which two numbers are less than 1,079 and greater than 1,068?

1,076 and 1,082 ○   1,078 and 1,070 ○

1,070 and 1,120 ○   1,100 and 1,097 ○

9. Extend Your Thinking Match each soccer player with a team number. Write the number in the box.

Team Numbers			
192	319	198	420

Carlos: My number is greater than 197 and less than 199.

Jada: My number is less than Carlos's number.

Marta: My number is less than 421 and greater than 419.

Jackson: My number is greater than Carlos's number and less than Marta's number.

Carlos

Jada

Marta

Jackson

Topic 4 | Lesson 5

Name _____

☆ Solve & Share ☆

Order the numbers 825, 925, 1,025, 725, and 1,125 from least to greatest.

Explain one number pattern that you see.

⊕ **TEKS 2.1F** Analyze mathematical relationships to connect and communicate mathematical ideas. Also, 2.2D, 2.7, 2.7B. **Mathematical Process Standards** 2.1B, 2.1G.

[ ] [ ] [ ] [ ] [ ]

Digital Resources at SavvasTexas.com

  A-Z
Solve   Learn   Glossary   Check   Tools   Games

Number pattern

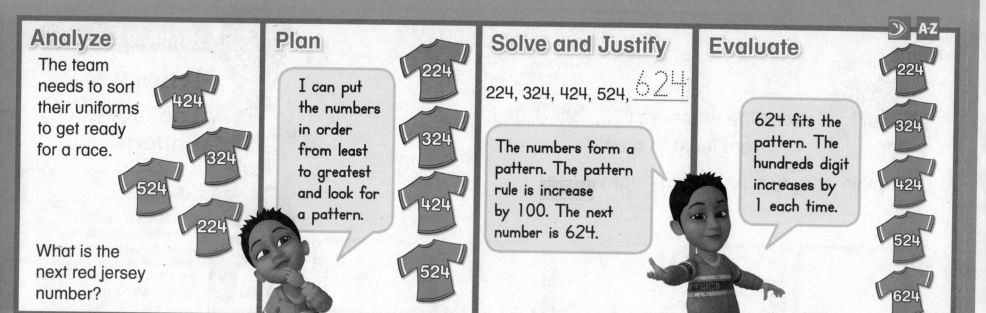

Analyze

The team needs to sort their uniforms to get ready for a race.

What is the next red jersey number?

Plan

I can put the numbers in order from least to greatest and look for a pattern.

Solve and Justify

224, 324, 424, 524, 624

The numbers form a pattern. The pattern rule is increase by 100. The next number is 624.

Evaluate

624 fits the pattern. The hundreds digit increases by 1 each time.

Do You Understand?

Show Me! How can you find the next three red jersey numbers after 624?

☆ Guided Practice ☆ Look for a number pattern to solve.

1. Put the yellow jersey numbers in order from least to greatest.

409, 419, 429, 439

What is the pattern rule?

+10

What is the next yellow jersey number? 449

2. Put the blue jersey numbers in order from least to greatest.

_____, _____, _____, _____

What is the pattern rule?

_____

What is the next blue jersey number? _____

Name _____

Independent Practice

Look for a number pattern to solve.

850   810   870   830

375   775   175   575

1,090   1,060   1,120   1,030

3. Put the library book numbers in order from least to greatest.

_____ , _____ , _____ , _____

What is the pattern rule?

_____

What is the next library book number? _____

4. Put the library book numbers in order from least to greatest.

_____ , _____ , _____ , _____

What is the pattern rule?

_____

What is the next library book number? _____

5. Put the library book numbers in order from least to greatest.

_____ , _____ , _____ , _____

What is the pattern rule?

_____

What is the next library book number? _____

6. Extend Your Thinking
Show a number pattern. Write a story about your pattern.

_____

_____

_____

Sam delivered mail to houses numbered 154, 194, 114, and 234. Look for a number pattern to solve.

7. Sam started at the house with the smallest number and continued in order to the house with the greatest number.

Write the numbers on the houses.
If the number pattern continues, what is the next house number Sam will deliver

mail to? _____

8. If Sam's last delivery was to house number 354, which shows the next 3 houses in the pattern?

364, 374, 384
○

374, 394, 414
○

394, 404, 414
○

394, 434, 474
○

9. Extend Your Thinking Look at the pattern. What is the first number in the pattern?

_____, 950, 975, 1,000

10. Extend Your Thinking Look at the pattern. What is the missing number?

400, 425, _____, 475

Name _____

Another Look Put these numbers in order from least to greatest.

How do the numbers change each time? Look for a pattern.

240   210   230   250   220

210 , 220 , 230 , 240 , 250

The pattern rule is +10

🏠 **HOME CONNECTION**
Your child learned that finding number patterns is a way to solve problems.

HOME ACTIVITY Write the numbers 285, 265, 255, 275, and 245 on small pieces of paper. Ask your child to order the numbers from least to greatest. Then ask your child to tell you the pattern rule and to find the next number in the pattern.

Look for a number pattern to solve.

1. Put the room number signs in order from least to greatest.

_____, _____, _____, _____

The pattern rule is _____

What room number would come next? _____

315   310   300   305

2. Put the taxis in order by number from least to greatest.

_____, _____, _____, _____

The pattern rule is _____

What taxi number would come next? _____

405   105   305   205

3. Look for a number pattern to solve.

Put the numbers on the bears in order from least to greatest.

_____, _____, _____, _____

What is the pattern rule? _____

What is the next number? _____

4. The numbers on the mailboxes follow the same pattern rule. What is the missing number?

922   932   942   962
○   ○   ○   ○

5. Extend Your Thinking Two teams need to sort their helmets for a bike race. Each team uses a different number pattern. There are five members on each team.

Write the missing numbers for Team A's helmets.

116, 126, 136, _____, _____

The pattern rule for Team A is _____.

Write the missing numbers for Team B's helmets.

112, 132, 152, _____, _____

The pattern rule for Team B is _____.

Name _____

The circus is in town! **Explain** what the math tells you about attendance.

Circus Attendance

Show Day	Tickets Sold
Thursday	726
Friday	781
Saturday	1,195
Sunday	1,032

1. How many people saw the circus on Friday? _____

2. Write the numbers of tickets sold from greatest to least.

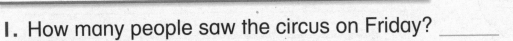
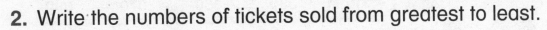

_____ _____ _____ _____

3. On which day was the greatest number of tickets sold? Explain how you know.

_____

_____

4. The circus sells fewer tickets on Monday than on Sunday. Write 3 different numbers of tickets the circus could have sold on Monday.

_____ _____ _____

TOPIC 4 Number Sense

What's the Number?

1. Look for a number pattern to solve. Write the number that comes next.

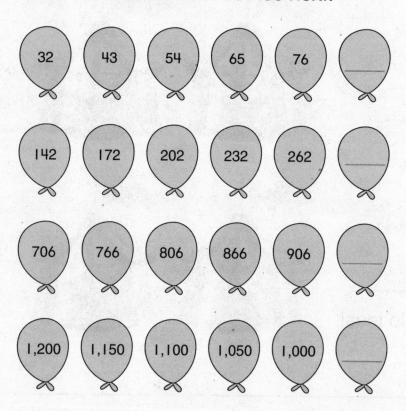

32   43   54   65   76   ___

142   172   202   232   262   ___

706   766   806   866   906   ___

1,200   1,150   1,100   1,050   1,000   ___

What's Wrong?

2. Rewrite this comparison so that it is correct.
   518 > 433 < 376

Complete It!

3. Oops! Four numbers fell off the number line. Write the numbers from least to greatest. Draw a line from each number to the number line to show where it belongs.

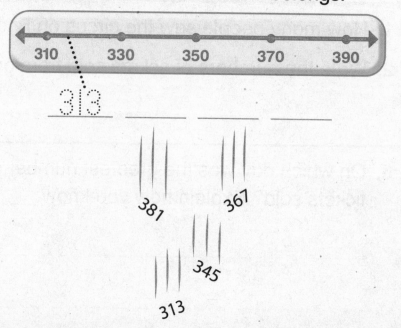

310   330   350   370   390

313   ___   ___   ___

381   367

313   345

Name _____

Set A

You can find a missing number
on a number line.

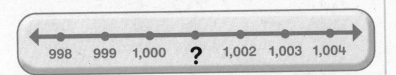

998   999   1,000   **?**   1,002   1,003   1,004

1,000 is the number before _1,001_.

1,002 is the number after _1,001_.

The missing number is _1,001_.

Find the missing number.

1.

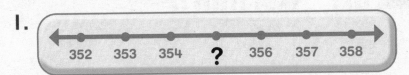

352   353   354   **?**   356   357   358

The missing number is _____.

2.

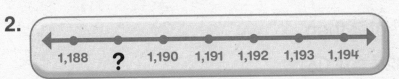

1,188   **?**   1,190   1,191   1,192   1,193   1,194

The missing number is _____.

Set B

You can place numbers on
a number line.

436   481

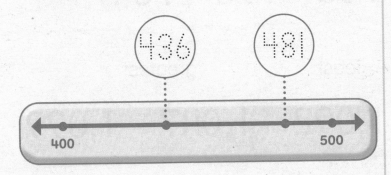

436 is closer to _450_ than 400.

481 is closer to _500_ than 450.

Show the numbers in their correct place
on the number line.

3. 1,177   1,193   1,137

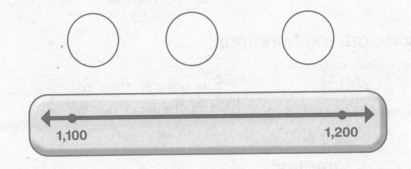

You can use place value to compare numbers.

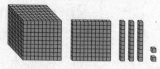 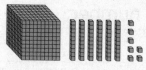

1,132   1,067

The thousands are equal, so compare the hundreds.

1 is greater than 0.

So, 1,132 > 1,067.

Compare each pair of numbers. Write <, >, or =.

4. 785 ◯ 793

5. 1,168 ◯ 1,162

You can compare and order numbers. Compare the thousands.

| 884 | 1,020 | 965 |

1 thousand is greater than 0 thousand. 1,020 is the greatest number.

Then compare the hundreds.

| 884 | 965 |

9 is greater than 8. 884 is the least number.

884, 965, 1,020
least   greatest

Write the numbers in order from least to greatest.

6. 763   776   764

_____, _____, _____
least   greatest

7. 1,092   1,047   1,099

_____, _____, _____
least   greatest

Name _____

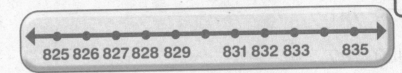

1. Jim has 1,019 songs. Pilar has 1,104 songs. Megan has the least number of songs. Which is the number of songs that Megan has?

○ 1,140

○ 1,041

○ 1,040

○ 1,014

2. Which numbers are missing?

825 826 827 828 829   831 832 833   835

○ 830, 833

○ 830, 834

○ 831, 832

○ 831, 834

3. This year, 1,050 students attended Lake School. Last year, 1,035 students attended Lake School.

Which comparison is correct?

○ 1,050 < 1,035

○ 1,050 = 1,035

○ 1,035 > 1,050

○ 1,050 > 1,035

4. Erica's number is closer to 925 than 1,025. Which number is it?

○ 950

○ 990

○ 1,010

○ 1,125

5. Which two numbers are less than 742?

- ○ 732, 743
- ○ 739, 741
- ○ 400, 789
- ○ 700, 800

6. Which numbers are in order from greatest to least?

- ○ 683, 679, 687
- ○ 679, 683, 687
- ○ 679, 687, 683
- ○ 687, 683, 679

7. Show the numbers in their correct places on the number line.

945   720   834

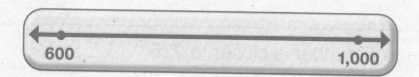

8. Put the cards in order from least to greatest.
Then write the number that comes next in the pattern.

Exploring Addition and Subtraction

Essential Question: How can sums and differences be found mentally?

This beach is covered in rocks.

Some rocks are jagged and some rocks are smooth!

Wow! Let's do this project and learn more.

Math and Science Project: Rocks

Find Out Look for different kinds of rocks in your neighborhood. Find 5 rocks of different shapes, sizes, or textures. Discuss how the rocks are alike and different.

Journal: Make a Book Draw pictures to show the different rocks you found. In your book, also:

• Describe ways that people use rocks.

• Make up and solve addition and subtraction problems about rocks.

Review What You Know

Vocabulary

1. Circle the **sum** in the addition sentence.

$$10 + 5 = 15$$

2. Circle the **difference** in the subtraction sentence.

$$17 - 9 = 8$$

3. Circle the sign that shows **subtraction**.

$$- \quad + \quad =$$

Addition and Subtraction

4. A year ago, Rosa's puppy weighed 6 pounds.
Now her puppy weighs 5 pounds more.
How much does Rosa's puppy weigh now?

_____ pounds

5. James wrote a number to make the number sentence true.
What number did he write?

$$16 - \rule{1cm}{0.4pt} = 9$$

Mental Math

6. Use mental math to solve.

Al has 8 trucks. Logan has 7 trucks. Al and Logan put their trucks together. How many trucks are there in all?

_____ trucks

My Word Cards

Study the words on the front of the card.
Complete the activity on the back.

A-Z

mental math

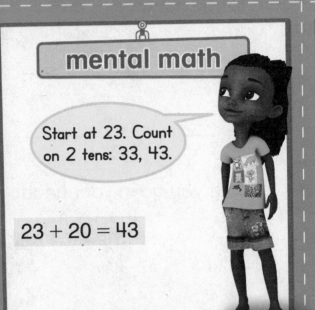

Start at 23. Count on 2 tens: 33, 43.

$23 + 20 = 43$

tens digit

38

↑

tens digit

next ten

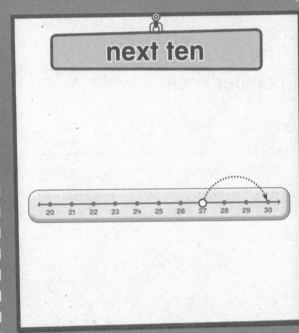

difference

$14 - 6 = 8$

8 is the difference.

My Word Cards

Use what you know to complete the sentences.
Extend learning by writing your own sentence using each word.

The following ten after a number is the

_____

_____ .

A _____

_____

shows how many groups of ten are in a number.

_____

_____

is math you do in your head.

The answer in a subtraction sentence is called the

_____ .

Name _____

Solve & Share

What strategy can you use to add 44 + 20? Explain. Use your strategy to find the sum.

 TEKS 2.4B Add up to four two-digit numbers ... using mental strategies and algorithms based on knowledge of place value and properties of operations. **Mathematical Process Standards** 2.1C, 2.1F, 2.1G.

 Digital Resources at SavvasTexas.com

Solve Learn Glossary Check Tools Games

44 + 20 = _____

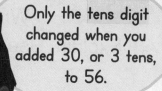

Find 56 + 30.

You can use mental math to find the sum.

One way is to count on by tens.

Start at 56. Count on 66, 76, 86.

$56 + 30 = 86$

You can also add the tens. Then add the ones to the sum.

Think 50 + 30 = 80. 80 + 6 = 86

$56 + 30 = 86$

Look at the sum, 86.

Only the tens digit changed when you added 30, or 3 tens, to 56.

Guided Practice Add using mental math.

Do You Understand?

Show Me! Explain how to add 22 + 30 using mental math.

1. $28 + 20 = \underline{48}$

2. $33 + 30 = \underline{\hphantom{00}}$

3. $\underline{\hphantom{00}} = 18 + 20$

4. $56 + 40 = \underline{\hphantom{00}}$

5. $45 + 20 = \underline{\hphantom{00}}$

6. $\underline{\hphantom{00}} = 17 + 40$

Topic 5 | Lesson 1

Name _____

☆ Independent ☆ Practice

Add using mental math.

7. $83 + 10 = $ _____

8. $38 + 30 = $ _____

9. _____ $ = 21 + 50$

10. $57 + 40 = $ _____

11. $64 + 30 = $ _____

12. $28 + 60 = $ _____

13. _____ $ = 23 + 30$

14. $19 + 50 = $ _____

15. $61 + 20 = $ _____

16. $12 + 40 = $ _____

17. _____ $ = 42 + 20$

18. $53 + 30 = $ _____

19. $16 + 60 = $ _____

20. $35 + 40 = $ _____

21. _____ $ = 28 + 70$

22. **Extend Your Thinking** Jane added 6 tens to find each sum.
Show the addition sentences Jane wrote.

$15 + $ _____ $ = $ _____

$2 + $ _____ $ = $ _____

Topic 5 | Lesson 1

one hundred eighty-seven **187**

Problem Solving   Use mental math to solve the problems below.

23. Beth has 14 ribbons. She buys a bag of 30 ribbons. How many ribbons does Beth have now?

_____ + _____ = _____

_____ ribbons

24. Carlos has 27 smooth rocks. He has 30 jagged rocks. How many rocks does Carlos have in all?

_____ + _____ = _____

_____ rocks

25. Miguel has 20 party hats in a pile. He has 43 party balloons. Miguel also has 25 party hats in a bag. Which number shows how many party hats Miguel has in all?

Think: What do I need to find out?

20 ○   25 ○

40 ○   45 ○

26. **Extend Your Thinking** Write an addition story using 40 and another two-digit number. Explain how you would find the sum.

Name _____

Another Look When you add tens, only the tens digit changes.

To add tens, you can count on by tens.

20 is 2 tens.
Think: Count on 2 tens.

🏠 **HOME CONNECTION**
Your child used models and a mental math strategy to add multiples of ten to a two-digit number.

HOME ACTIVITY Ask your child to count on by tens to find the sum for 54 + 20.

Add: 35 and 20.

35, _45_ , _55_

So, 35 + 20 = _55_.

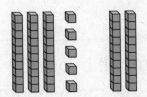

Add tens. Use mental math.

1.
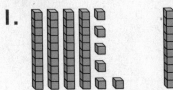

46 and 30 = ___

Count on 3 tens:

46, ____, ____, ____

46 + 30 = ___

2.
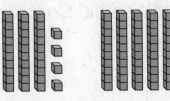

34 + 50 = ___

Circle the tens that make each addition sentence true. Then write the number.

3. $28 + \underline{\quad} = 68$

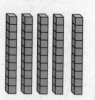

4. $42 + \underline{\quad} = 72$

5. $53 + \underline{\quad} = 63$

6. Nellie had 14 rubber bands. Then she bought a pack of 30 rubber bands. How many rubber bands does Nellie have now?

_____ rubber bands

7. A squirrel has 26 acorns. It brings 50 more acorns into the nest. How many acorns does the squirrel have in all?

_____ acorns

8. Caitlyn picked 10 tulips. Then she picked some daisies. Now Caitlyn has 33 flowers in all. How many daisies did Caitlyn pick?

13
○

23
○

33
○

43
○

9. **Extend Your Thinking** Write the digit that makes the number sentence true. Explain your thinking.

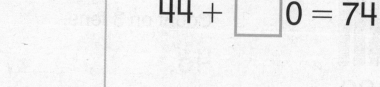

$44 + \boxed{}0 = 74$

Name _____

Solve & Share

Pick one number card from each pile. Find the sum of your numbers. What strategy can you use? Explain.

TEKS 2.4B Add up to four two-digit numbers ... using mental strategies and algorithms based on knowledge of place value and properties of operations. **Mathematical Process Standards** 2.1C, 2.1E, 2.1F.

Digital Resources at SavvasTexas.com

Solve   Learn   Glossary   Check   Tools   Games

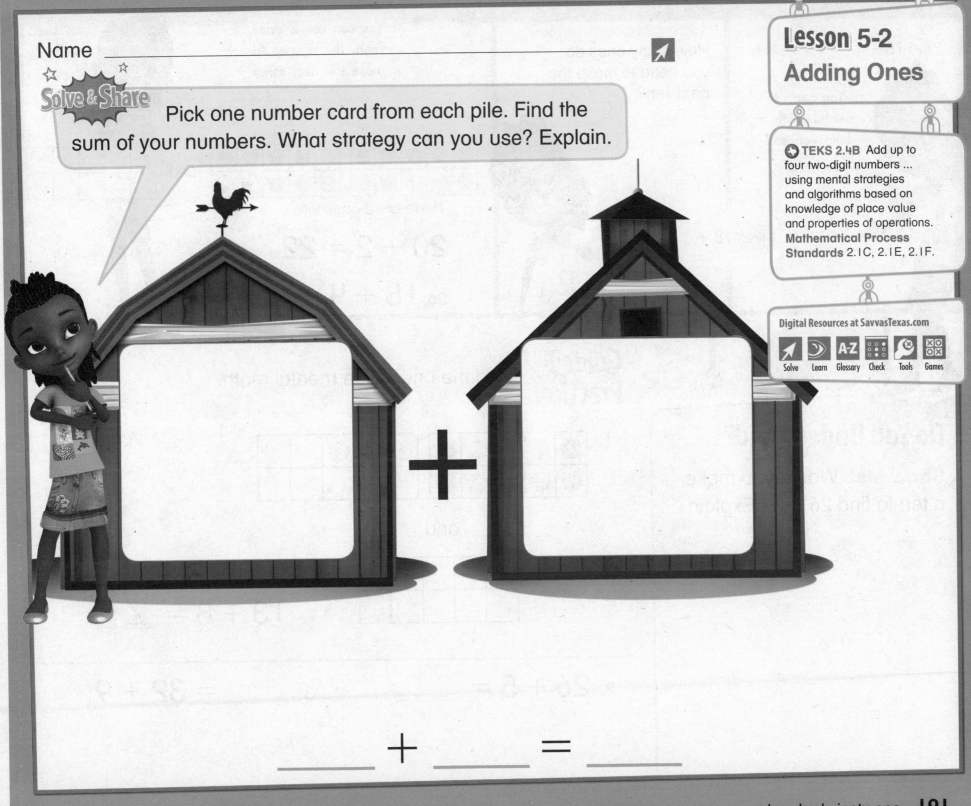

____ + ____ = ____

Find 18 + 4.

You can use mental math to help you add.

How many ones do you need to make the **next ten**?

Think: $18 + 2 = 20$.

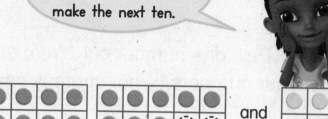

You can use 2 ones from the 4 ones to make the next ten.

There are 2 ones left.

and

$20 + 2 = 22$

So, $18 + 4 = 22$.

Do You Understand?

Show Me! Would you make a ten to find $26 + 3$? Explain.

☆ **Guided Practice** ☆ Add the ones. Use mental math.

1.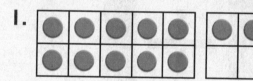

and

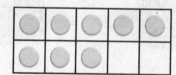

$13 + 8 = 21$

2. $26 + 5 = \underline{}$

3. $\underline{} = 32 + 9$

☆ Independent ☆ Practice

Add the ones. Use mental math.

4. 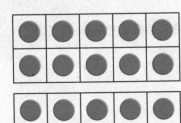 and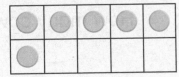

17 + 6 = _____

5. 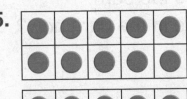 and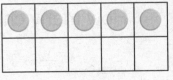

19 + 5 = _____

6. 52 + 6 = _____

7. _____ = 48 + 7

8. 39 + 4 = _____

9. 73 + 2 = _____

10. 67 + 3 = _____

11. _____ = 56 + 6

12. **Extend Your Thinking** Find the missing number that will make the next ten. Explain your thinking.

44 + ☐ = 50

13. There are 27 chicks in the barn.
5 more chicks go into the barn.
How many chicks are in the barn now?

_____ + _____ = _____

_____ chicks

14. A farmer has 36 cows.
He buys 9 cows.
How many cows does he have in all?

_____ + _____ = _____

_____ cows

15. 41 apples are in a crate. A worker
puts 8 more apples into the crate.
Now how many apples are in the crate?

_____ apples

16. ⭐ 16 pigs and 3 hens are in a pen. 8 pigs are
in the barn. How many pigs are there in all?

8
○

19
○

24
○

27
○

17. **Extend Your Thinking** A herd
has 19 elephants. More
elephants join the herd.
Now the herd has 25 elephants.
How many elephants joined the
herd? Explain your thinking.

Another Look

$36 + 7 =$?

Circle the ones to make the next ten.

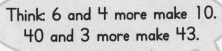

Think: 6 and 4 more make 10.
40 and 3 more make 43.

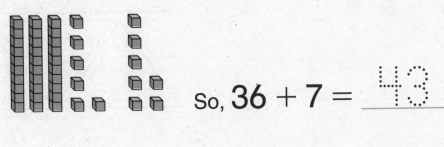

So, $36 + 7 = \underline{43}$.

🏠 **HOME CONNECTION**
Your child added a one-digit number to a two-digit number by making the next ten and adding the extra ones.

HOME ACTIVITY Ask your child to tell you how to add $12 + 9$ by making a ten.

Circle the ones to make the next ten.
Add the ones to the tens.

1.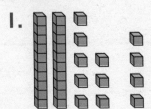

$28 + 4 =$ ____

2.

$47 + 8 =$ ____

3.

$66 + 8 =$ ____

Circle the number of balls needed to fill the last triangle to make 10. Then add all the balls and write the sum.

4.

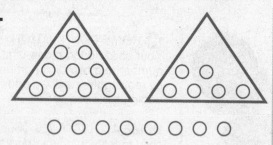

$16 + 8 =$ _____

5.

$22 + 8 =$ _____

6.

$45 + 9 =$ _____

7. Which is the missing number that will make the next ten?

$53 +$ _____ $= 60$

○ 6   ○ 7   ○ 8   ○ 9

8. Extend Your Thinking Tyson has 14 pears. Dan has 9 pears. Judy has 8 pears. How many pears do they have in all?

_____ pears

9. Extend Your Thinking Janna and Leah made necklaces. They used 27 beads in all. Janna used 18 beads. How many beads did Leah use? Explain your thinking.

_____ beads

Name _____

Solve & Share

Monica has 24 crayons. Paul has 64 crayons. How many crayons do they have in all? Explain.

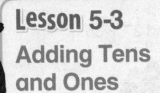

TEKS 2.4B Add up to four two-digit numbers ... using mental strategies and algorithms based on knowledge of place value and properties of operations. **Mathematical Process Standards** 2.1B, 2.1C, 2.1G.

Digital Resources at SavvasTexas.com

Solve   Learn   Glossary   Check   Tools   Games

$$24 + 64 = \underline{\qquad}$$

_____ crayons

Topic 5 | Lesson 3
Digital Resources at SavvasTexas.com
one hundred ninety-seven **197**

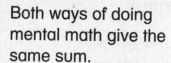

Find 27 + 35.

You can use mental math to find the sum.

One way is to add the tens.

$$20 + 30 = 50$$

Then add the ones.

$$7 + 5 = 12$$

Then add the sums.

$$50 + 12 = 62$$

So, 27 + 35 = _62_.

Another way is to add just the tens of the second number.

$$27 + 30 = 57$$

Then add the ones from the second number.

$$57 + 5 = 62$$

You can use either way!

So, 27 + 35 = _62_.

Both ways of doing mental math give the same sum.

Do You Understand?

Show Me! Can you also find the sum of 20 + 14 + 32 + 10 using mental math? Explain.

Guided Practice Add using mental math. Use ten-frames if needed.

1. $17 + 42 = $ 59

2. _____ $= 53 + 23$

3. $43 + 22 = $ _____

4. _____ $= 51 + 47$

5. $68 + 24 = $ _____

6. $25 + 32 = $ _____

Topic 5 | **Lesson 3**

Name _____

Add using mental math.

7. $23 + 26 =$ _____

8. $39 + 43 =$ _____

9. $51 + 16 =$ _____

10. $56 + 15 =$ _____

11. _____ $= 76 + 11$

12. $33 + 49 =$ _____

13. $44 + 17 =$ _____

14. $34 + 25 =$ _____

15. _____ $= 57 + 26$

16. $26 + 62 =$ _____

17. _____ $= 62 + 25$

18. $43 + 36 =$ _____

19. _____ $= 56 + 25$

20. $37 + 21 =$ _____

21. $17 + 52 =$ _____

Add tens and ones to solve.

$17 + \boxed{} = 28$

$\boxed{} + 28 = 39$

22. **Extend Your Thinking** One number makes both sentences true. Find the missing number.

The missing number is _____.

23. Billy puts 24 skateboard wheels in a pile. He puts 24 more in another pile. How many wheels does Billy have in all?

_____ wheels

24. Lily has 56 songs on her music player. Taina has 43 songs on her music player. How many songs do the girls have in all?

_____ songs

25. ⭐ Cindy has some toy planes. She buys 12 more toy planes. Now she has 27 toy planes. How many toy planes did Cindy start with?

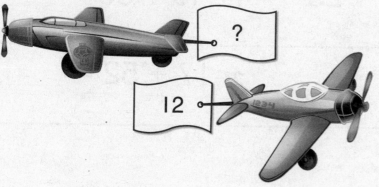

12
○

13
○

14
○

15
○

26. **Extend Your Thinking** Write a story about 14 + 41. Then solve.

$14 + 41 = \underline{\qquad}$

Name _____

Another Look

Find 25 + 34.

25 and

Think: 25 and 3 tens

First add just the tens from the second number.

25, 35, 45, 55

Then add the ones from the second number.

$$55 + 4 = 59$$

So, $25 + 34 = 59$.

🏠 **HOME CONNECTION**
Your child learned to mentally add tens and ones.

HOME ACTIVITY Ask your child to describe how to add 23 + 46 in his or her head.

Add. Use mental math.

1. 34 + 23   34 and

34, ____, ____

____ + ____ = ____

So, 34 + 23 = ____.

2. 52 + 33   52 and

52, ____, ____, ____

____ + ____ = ____

So, 52 + 33 = ____.

Look at each number pattern. Write the numbers for the addition sentences that come next.

3. $32 + 12 = 44$

   $42 + 12 = 54$

   $52 + \boxed{} = 64$

   $\boxed{} + \boxed{} = 74$

4. $17 + 22 = 39$

   $27 + 22 = 49$

   $37 + \boxed{} = 59$

   $\boxed{} + \boxed{} = 69$

5. $30 + 27 = 57$

   $40 + 27 = 67$

   $50 + \boxed{} = 77$

   $\boxed{} + \boxed{} = 87$

6. Tad has 72 seashells.
   He finds 15 more seashells.
   How many seashells does
   Tad have in all?

   _____ seashells

7. Toby has three bunches of grapes.
   ⭐ One bunch has 31 grapes.
   Another bunch has 11 grapes.
   The last bunch has 28 grapes.
   How many grapes does Toby have in all?

   ○ 42   ○ 60   ○ 70   ○ 75

8. **Extend Your Thinking** Carla bought
   49 pens in all in two packages. Which
   color pens did she buy? Show how you
   found your answer.

Pen Packages	
Pen Color	**Number of Pens**
Blue	25
Black	12
Red	24
Green	33

Name _____

Solve & Share

How can you use the hundred chart to help you solve 32 + 43? Explain. Write an addition sentence to show the sum.

TEKS 2.4B Add up to four two-digit numbers ... using mental strategies and algorithms based on knowledge of place value and properties of operations. Also, 2.4. **Mathematical Process Standards** 2.1A, 2.1D, 2.1E, 2.1F.

Digital Resources at SavvasTexas.com

Solve   Learn   Glossary   Check   Tools   Games

1	2	3	4	5	6	7	8	9	10
11	12	13	14	15	16	17	18	19	20
21	22	23	24	25	26	27	28	29	30
31	32	33	34	35	36	37	38	39	40
41	42	43	44	45	46	47	48	49	50
51	52	53	54	55	56	57	58	59	60
61	62	63	64	65	66	67	68	69	70
71	72	73	74	75	76	77	78	79	80
81	82	83	84	85	86	87	88	89	90
91	92	93	94	95	96	97	98	99	100

_____ + _____ = _____

You can add on a hundred chart. Find $54 + 18$.

Start at 54. You need to add the tens from 18. Move down 1 row to show 1 ten.

51	52	53	54	55	56	57	58	59	60
61	62	63	64	65	66	67	68	69	70
71	72	73	74	75	76	77	78	79	80

Now add the ones.

You're already at 64. Now move ahead 8 to show 8 ones. You need to go to the next row to add them all. So, $54 + 18 = 72$.

51	52	53	54	55	56	57	58	59	60
61	62	63	64	65	66	67	68	69	70
71	72	73	74	75	76	77	78	79	80

Do You Understand?

Show Me! How can you use a hundred chart to add 35 and 24?

☆ Guided Practice ☆

Add using the hundred chart. Draw arrows on the chart if needed.

11	12	13	14	15	16	17	18	19	20
21	22	23	24	25	26	27	28	29	30
31	32	33	34	35	36	37	38	39	40
41	42	43	44	45	46	47	48	49	50

1. $17 + 32 = \underline{49}$

2. $28 + 21 = \underline{}$

3. $\underline{} = 19 + 20$

4. $18 + 23 = \underline{}$

Name _____

☆ **Independent** ☆
☆ **Practice**

Add using the hundred chart.

1	2	3	4	5	6	7	8	9	10
11	12	13	14	15	16	17	18	19	20
21	22	23	24	25	26	27	28	29	30
31	32	33	34	35	36	37	38	39	40
41	42	43	44	45	46	47	48	49	50
51	52	53	54	55	56	57	58	59	60
61	62	63	64	65	66	67	68	69	70
71	72	73	74	75	76	77	78	79	80
81	82	83	84	85	86	87	88	89	90
91	92	93	94	95	96	97	98	99	100

5. $33 + 34 =$ _____

6. _____ $= 12 + 73$

7. $38 + 21 =$ _____

8. $56 + 42 =$ _____

9. $47 + 28 =$ _____

10. $39 + 17 =$ _____

11. _____ $= 61 + 19$

12. **Extend Your Thinking** Write the digit that makes each number sentence true.

$34 + 2\boxed{} = 57$ | $1\boxed{} + 51 = 67$ | $62 + \boxed{}1 = 83$

Problem Solving
Use the hundred chart to solve the problems.

13. Sara has 48 buttons. Luis has 32 buttons. How many buttons do they have in all?

_____ buttons

31	32	33	34	35	36	37	38	39	40
41	42	43	44	45	46	47	48	49	50
51	52	53	54	55	56	57	58	59	60
61	62	63	64	65	66	67	68	69	70
71	72	73	74	75	76	77	78	79	80
81	82	83	84	85	86	87	88	89	90
91	92	93	94	95	96	97	98	99	100

14. Mika has 70 buttons. Thom has 19 more buttons than Mika. How many buttons does Thom have?

_____ buttons

15. Which weights will balance the weights already on the scale?

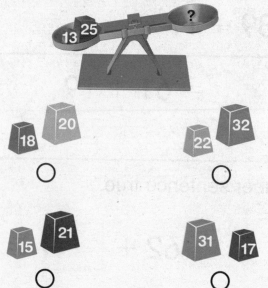

○   ○

○   ○

16. Extend Your Thinking Write the steps you take to add 43 and 39 on a hundred chart.

206 two hundred six

Topic 5 | Lesson 4

Name _____

Another Look

Find 16 + 23.

1	2	3	4	5	6	7	8	9	10
11	12	13	14	15	16	17	18	19	20
21	22	23	24	25	26	27	28	29	30
31	32	33	34	35	36	37	38	39	40
41	42	43	44	45	46	47	48	49	50
51	52	53	54	55	56	57	58	59	60
61	62	63	64	65	66	67	68	69	70
71	72	73	74	75	76	77	78	79	80
81	82	83	84	85	86	87	88	89	90
91	92	93	94	95	96	97	98	99	100

1. Start on square 16.

2. Move down 2 rows to show the tens in ⬛2⬛ 3.

3. Move 3 squares to the right to add the ones in 2 ⬛3⬛ .

4. Where did you stop? _39_

So, _16_ + _23_ = _39_ .

> The numbers increase by 10 as you move down each row.

HOME CONNECTION
Your child learned to add tens and ones on a hundred chart.

HOME ACTIVITY Ask your child to describe how to add 37 and 16 on a hundred chart.

> Add using the hundred chart.

1. 12 + 11 = ____

2. 31 + 45 = ____

3. 81 + 14 = ____

Write the digits that make each number sentence true.

4. $\boxed{}4 + 1\boxed{} = 39$
5. $4\boxed{} + \boxed{}9 = 82$
6. $74 + \boxed{}4 = 8\boxed{}$

7. Arthur did 49 sit-ups on Monday.
He did 20 sit-ups on Tuesday.
He did 25 sit-ups on Wednesday.
How many sit-ups did Arthur do
on all three days?

_____ sit-ups

8. Kenji threw two bean
bags at the target.
He scored 79 points. One
bean bag landed on 61.
Which number did the
other bean bag land on?

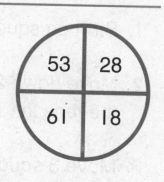

The other bean bag landed on _____.

9. ★ Choose the two shapes that answer
the question. Which weights can you
put on the scale to make it balance?

10. **Extend Your Thinking** Explain how you
could use a hundred chart to find the
missing number.

$$63 + \boxed{?} = 87$$

The missing number is _____.

Name _____

Solve & Share

Suppose you have 98 balloons.
Choose a number below to be the number of balloons you give away.
How many balloons do you have left? Explain.

10 30 40 20

⭐ **TEKS 2.4B** ... subtract two-digit numbers using mental strategies and algorithms based on knowledge of place value and properties of operations. **Mathematical Process Standards** 2.1C, 2.1D, 2.1E, 2.1F.

Digital Resources at SavvasTexas.com

Solve Learn Glossary Check Tools Games

98 − _____ = _____

Topic 5 | Lesson 5
Digital Resources at SavvasTexas.com
two hundred nine **209**

You can subtract tens mentally.

Find 63 − 20.

One way is to count back by tens.

Start at 63. Count back 53, 43.

$$63 - 20 = 43$$

You can also subtract using ten-frame cards.

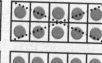

The 3 does not change, so $63 - 20 = 43!$

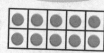

When you subtract tens, the ones stay the same.

Do You Understand?

Show Me! Explain why only the tens digit changes when you subtract 20 from 81.

Guided Practice

Subtract. Use mental math or ten-frame cards.

1.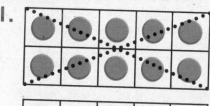

$$38 - 20 = \underline{18}$$

2. $64 - 30 = \underline{\hspace{1cm}}$

3. $\underline{\hspace{1cm}} = 29 - 10$

Name _____

Independent Practice

Subtract. Use mental math or ten-frame cards.

4.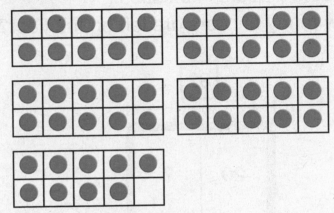

$$49 - 30 = \underline{\hspace{1cm}}$$

5.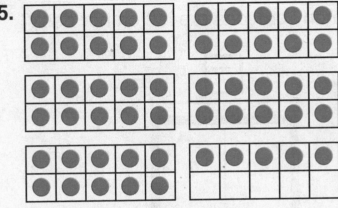

$$55 - 40 = \underline{\hspace{1cm}}$$

---

6. $35 - 20 = \underline{\hspace{1cm}}$

7. $76 - 50 = \underline{\hspace{1cm}}$

8. $43 - 10 = \underline{\hspace{1cm}}$

---

9. $\underline{\hspace{1cm}} = 87 - 40$

10. $95 - 40 = \underline{\hspace{1cm}}$

11. $52 - 30 = \underline{\hspace{1cm}}$

---

12. $76 - 40 = \underline{\hspace{1cm}}$

13. $94 - 60 = \underline{\hspace{1cm}}$

14. $\underline{\hspace{1cm}} = 65 - 10$

---

15. **Extend Your Thinking** Write each missing number.

$34 - \boxed{} = 14$

$87 - \boxed{} = 77$

$61 - \boxed{} = 31$

16. Shandra has 77 crayons on her desk.
She puts 40 crayons into boxes.
How many crayons are left on her desk?

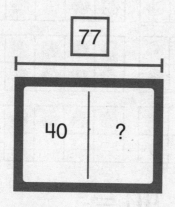

77

40 | ?

_____ crayons

17. Walter has 32 toy cars on the floor.
He puts 20 cars into cases.
How many toy cars are left on the floor?

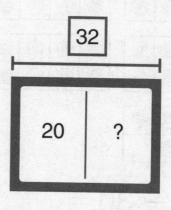

32

20 | ?

_____ toy cars

18. Robin made 34 rings. She sold some rings.
Now Robin has 14 rings.
How many rings did Robin sell?

○ 54   ○ 34   ○ 20   ○ 14

19. Extend Your Thinking Write a
subtraction story about 42 − 20.
Solve your story.

$42 - 20 = \underline{\hspace{2cm}}$

Name _____

Another Look Here are two ways you can find 57 − 30.

1. Count back 3 tens, or 30.

57, <u>47</u>, <u>37</u>, <u>27</u>

When you subtract tens, only the tens digit changes.

2. Use models to subtract the tens.

50 − 30 = <u>20</u>

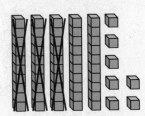

Then subtract the ones.

7 − 0 = <u>7</u>

So, 57 − 30 = <u>27</u>.

🏠 **HOME CONNECTION**
Your child subtracted tens from a two-digit number.

HOME ACTIVITY Ask your child to subtract 37 − 20 mentally and explain how he or she found the answer.

Count back to subtract tens.

1. 64 − 30 = ?

64, ___, ___, ___

64 − 30 = ___

2. 62 − 40 = ___

3. 76 − 20 = ___

Topic 5 | Lesson 5

Digital Resources at SavvasTexas.com

two hundred thirteen **213**

4. Algebra Write the missing number.

$$47 - \boxed{} = 17$$

5. Algebra Write the missing number.

$$61 - \boxed{} = 21$$

6. Algebra Write the missing number.

$$22 = \boxed{} - 30$$

Use mental math to solve.

7. A box holds 48 crackers. Austin eats 10 of them. How many crackers are left in the box?

_____ crackers

8. Luz had 87 books. She gave 40 of them to the library. How many books does Luz have left?

_____ books

9. Allie had 36 dolls. On Thursday she gave 10 dolls away. On Friday she gave away 10 more dolls. How many dolls does Allie have now?

46 ○   36 ○

26 ○   16 ○

Think: What do I know about this problem?

10. Extend Your Thinking You and a partner are playing a game. Each player starts at 93. Each player subtracts the number the spinner lands on. The first player to reach 3 wins.

You spin three times and win. The first number you spin is 20.

The third number you spin is 40. What is the second number you spin?

_____

Name _____

Solve & Share

A juggler has a box that holds 100 balls.
There are 68 balls in the box already.
How many balls will the juggler need to fill the box?
Use models and an addition sentence to solve.

TEKS 2.4B Add up to four two-digit numbers and subtract two-digit numbers using mental strategies and algorithms based on knowledge of place value and properties of operations. **Mathematical Process Standards** 2.1C, 2.1E, 2.1F, 2.1G.

Parts of 100

Digital Resources at SavvasTexas.com

Solve   Learn   Glossary   Check   Tools   Games

_____ + _____ = _____

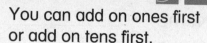

To find the other part of 100, add on.

$37 + ? = 100$

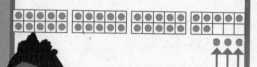

> You can start by adding on ones to make the next ten.
> $37 + 3 = 40$

Then add on tens to make 100.

$40 + 60 = 100$

> You added on 3 and 60.
> $3 + 60 = 63$
> So, $37 + 63 = 100$.

You can also add on tens first.

$37 + 60 = 97$

> Then add on 3 more to make 100.

You can add on ones first or add on tens first.

> Either way,
> $37 + 63 = 100$.

Do You Understand?

Show Me! Josh shows 56 with his ten-frame cards. He says the other part of 100 is 44. How can you tell if he is correct?

★ **Guided Practice** ★ Add on to find the other part of 100. Use ten-frame cards if needed.

1.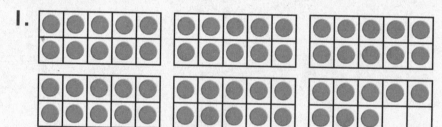

$$\underline{58} + \underline{42} = \underline{100}$$

2.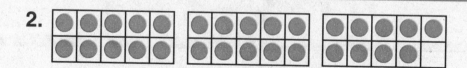

$$\underline{} + \underline{} = \underline{}$$

Topic 5 | Lesson 6

Name _____

Add on to find the other part of 100.

3. $62 + \underline{} = 100$ | 4. $51 + \underline{} = 100$ | 5. $100 = 36 + \underline{}$

6. $88 + \underline{} = 100$ | 7. $72 + \underline{} = 100$ | 8. $48 + \underline{} = 100$

9. $100 = 91 + \underline{}$ | 10. $22 + \underline{} = 100$ | 11. $29 + \underline{} = 100$

12. $43 + \underline{} = 100$ | 13. $100 = 14 + \underline{}$ | 14. $89 + \underline{} = 100$

15. $100 = 18 + \underline{}$ | 16. $37 + \underline{} = 100$ | 17. $61 + \underline{} = 100$

Complete the number sentences.

18. **Extend Your Thinking** Find two parts to make 100 in each number sentence.

$37 + \boxed{} + \boxed{} = 100$ | $54 + \boxed{} + \boxed{} = 100$

19. Jorge has a puzzle with 100 pieces.
He has already put together 38 pieces.
How many more pieces does he need
to put together?

_____ pieces

20. Ann has a puzzle with 100 pieces.
She needs to put together 17 more pieces.
How many pieces has she already put
together?

_____ pieces

21. Sharla has 100 pictures.
⭐ She put 43 pictures in an album.
The rest are in a pile.
Which number shows how many
pictures are in the pile?

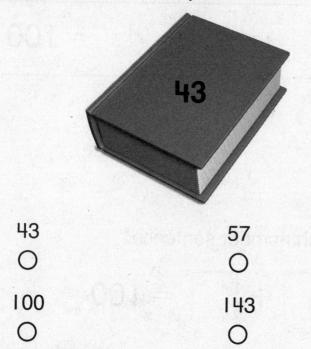

43
○

57
○

100
○

143
○

22. **Extend Your Thinking** Nelida wants
to fill a crate with 100 oranges.
She has already put 24 oranges in
the crate.
Describe how Nelida can find how many
more oranges she needs to put in the crate.

Topic 5 | Lesson 6

Name _____

Another Look You can find parts of 100.

Add on tens to make 100.

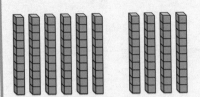

60 and _40_ is 100.

$$60 + \underline{40} = 100$$

Add on tens and ones to make 100.

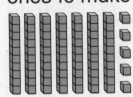

75 and _25_ is 100.

$$75 + \underline{25} = 100$$

You can add on tens first or ones first!

🏠 **HOME CONNECTION**
Your child used models to find parts of 100.

HOME ACTIVITY Ask your child to describe how to find the other part of 100 when one part is 29.

Find the other part of 100.

1. Draw tens to find the other part of 100.

50 and _____ is 100.

$$50 + \underline{} = 100$$

2. Draw tens and ones to make 100. Add on.

45 and _____ is 100.

$$45 + \underline{} = 100$$

3. Algebra Find the missing part to make 100.

$$61 + 20 + \underline{} = 100$$

4. Algebra Find the missing part to make 100.

$$100 = 40 + \underline{} + 35$$

5. Algebra Find the missing part to make 100.

$$\underline{} + 27 + 27 = 100$$

Circle the basket that makes the other part of 100. Complete the sentence.

6.

25 and 25 and _____ is 100.

7.

30 and 30 and _____ is 100.

8. ⭐ Latisha had a box of 100 birthday cards. So far, she has sent out 47 cards. She plans to send out 3 cards today.
How many cards will be left in the box?

50
○

52
○

53
○

54
○

9. Extend Your Thinking A store had 100 class rings. They sold 37 rings. Taina says there are 73 rings left. Is Taina correct? Explain.

Name _____

Solve & Share

How can you use the hundred chart to help you solve 57 − 23? Explain. Write a subtraction sentence.

1	2	3	4	5	6	7	8	9	10
11	12	13	14	15	16	17	18	19	20
21	22	23	24	25	26	27	28	29	30
31	32	33	34	35	36	37	38	39	40
41	42	43	44	45	46	47	48	49	50
51	52	53	54	55	56	57	58	59	60
61	62	63	64	65	66	67	68	69	70
71	72	73	74	75	76	77	78	79	80
81	82	83	84	85	86	87	88	89	90
91	92	93	94	95	96	97	98	99	100

⭐ **TEKS 2.4B** ... subtract two-digit numbers using mental strategies and algorithms based on knowledge of place value and properties of operations. Also, 2.4. **Mathematical Process Standards** 2.1B, 2.1C, 2.1F.

Digital Resources at SavvasTexas.com

Solve   Learn   Glossary   Check   Tools   Games

_____ − _____ = _____

Find 43 − 28 using a hundred chart.

I need to find the difference between 28 and 43.

Start at 28. Count to the next number that matches the ones in 43.

21	22	23	24	25	26	27	28	29	30
31	32	33	34	35	36	37	38	39	40
41	42	43	44	45	46	47	48	49	50

Count by ones! I counted 5 ones to get from 28 to 33.

Count by tens to 43.

21	22	23	24	25	26	27	28	29	30
31	32	33	34	35	36	37	38	39	40
41	42	43	44	45	46	47	48	49	50

That's 1 ten, or 10 more.

I added 5 and 10. That makes 15.

28 + 15 = 43
So, 43 − 28 = 15.

Do You Understand?

Show Me! How can you use a hundred chart to find the difference between 18 and 60?

Subtract using the hundred chart. Draw arrows if you need to.

21	22	23	24	25	26	27	28	29	30
31	32	33	34	35	36	37	38	39	40
41	42	43	44	45	46	47	48	49	50
51	52	53	54	55	56	57	58	59	60
61	62	63	64	65	66	67	68	69	70

1. 69 − 36 = 33

2. 54 − 24 = ___

3. ___ = 65 − 34

4. 47 − 22 = ___

Name _____

Subtract using the hundred chart. Draw arrows if you need to.

1	2	3	4	5	6	7	8	9	10
11	12	13	14	15	16	17	18	19	20
21	22	23	24	25	26	27	28	29	30
31	32	33	34	35	36	37	38	39	40
41	42	43	44	45	46	47	48	49	50
51	52	53	54	55	56	57	58	59	60
61	62	63	64	65	66	67	68	69	70
71	72	73	74	75	76	77	78	79	80
81	82	83	84	85	86	87	88	89	90
91	92	93	94	95	96	97	98	99	100

5. $59 - 28 =$ _____

6. _____ $= 96 - 63$

7. $45 - 22 =$ _____

8. $82 - 61 =$ _____

9. $65 - 21 =$ _____

10. _____ $= 79 - 47$

11. $84 - 41 =$ _____

12. **Extend Your Thinking** Write the digit that makes each number sentence true.

$73 - \boxed{}2 = 41$

$46 - \boxed{}1 = 15$

$53 - \boxed{}2 = 31$

$5\boxed{} - 32 = 26$

$78 - 36 = \boxed{}2$

$99 - \boxed{}3 = 16$

13. Darren's puzzle has 98 pieces.
Darren fits 55 pieces together.
How many more pieces does Darren still
need to fit to complete the puzzle?

_____ − _____ = _____

_____ pieces

41	42	43	44	45	46	47	48	49	50
51	52	53	54	55	56	57	58	59	60
61	62	63	64	65	66	67	68	69	70
71	72	73	74	75	76	77	78	79	80
81	82	83	84	85	86	87	88	89	90
91	92	93	94	95	96	97	98	99	100

14. A test has 86 questions.
Glenda needs to answer 23 more
questions to finish the test.
How many test questions has
Glenda answered already? _____

15. Lu has 75 buttons.
29 of the buttons are blue.
16 buttons are green.
The rest of the buttons are red.
How many of the buttons are red?

13 ○   30 ○

46 ○   59 ○

16. Extend Your Thinking Chris wants to
subtract 76 − 42. Write the steps Chris
can take to subtract 42 from 76 on the
hundred chart.

Name _____

Another Look A hundred chart can help you subtract.

Find 36 − 24.

1. Start at 24.

2. Move down to 34.
   This is the row that 36 is in.
   One row down makes __10__.

3. Move right from 34 to 36 to
   count __2__ ones.

4. Count the tens down and
   ones across.

1	2	3	4	5	6	7	8	9	10
11	12	13	14	15	16	17	18	19	20
21	22	23	24	25	26	27	28	29	30
31	32	33	34	35	36	37	38	39	40
41	42	43	44	45	46	47	48	49	50
51	52	53	54	55	56	57	58	59	60
61	62	63	64	65	66	67	68	69	70
71	72	73	74	75	76	77	78	79	80
81	82	83	84	85	86	87	88	89	90
91	92	93	94	95	96	97	98	99	100

🏠 **HOME CONNECTION**
Your child learned to subtract two-digit numbers on a hundred chart.

HOME ACTIVITY Ask your child to subtract 58 − 23 on a hundred chart and explain how he or she subtracted.

__10__ + __2__ = __12__, so 36 − 24 = 12.

Subtract using the hundred chart.

1. 87 − 72 = _____

2. 79 − 48 = _____

3. 65 − 41 = _____

4. 99 − 52 = _____

5. 35 − 13 = _____

6. _____ = 84 − 33

Write the digits that make each number sentence true.

7. $\boxed{}3 - 2\boxed{} = 71$ 8. $5\boxed{} - \boxed{}1 = 14$ 9. $78 - \boxed{}5 = 4\boxed{}$

---

10. A pan holds 36 biscuits.
⭐ Kiana put 12 biscuits on the pan.
How many more biscuits will fit on the pan?

  ○ 24   ○ 23   ○ 22   ○ 21

11. A garden has room for 22 flowers.
⭐ Dan needs to plant 11 more flowers.
How many flowers did Dan already plant?

  ○ 10   ○ 11   ○ 12   ○ 13

---

12. **Extend Your Thinking** A treasure is hidden under one of the rocks. Follow the clues to find the treasure. Color the rocks you land on.

1. Start at 55.

2. Subtract 20.

3. Add 5.

4. Add 20.

5. Add 10.

6. Subtract 5.

7. Subtract 20.

8. Add 5.

9. Subtract 20.

10. Subtract 5.

The treasure is hidden under the last rock that you colored. What is the number of that rock? _____
Write the pattern you see in the numbers you colored. _____

1	2	3	4	5	6	7	8	9	10
11	12	13	14	15	16	17	18	19	20
21	22	23	24	25	26	27	28	29	30
31	32	33	34	35	36	37	38	39	40
41	42	43	44	45	46	47	48	49	50
51	52	53	54	55	56	57	58	59	60
61	62	63	64	65	66	67	68	69	70
71	72	73	74	75	76	77	78	79	80
81	82	83	84	85	86	87	88	89	90
91	92	93	94	95	96	97	98	99	100

Name _____

Solve & Share

3 bees land on some flowers. 10 more bees join them. Then 4 bees fly away. How many bees are left?
What number sentences can you write to solve this problem?

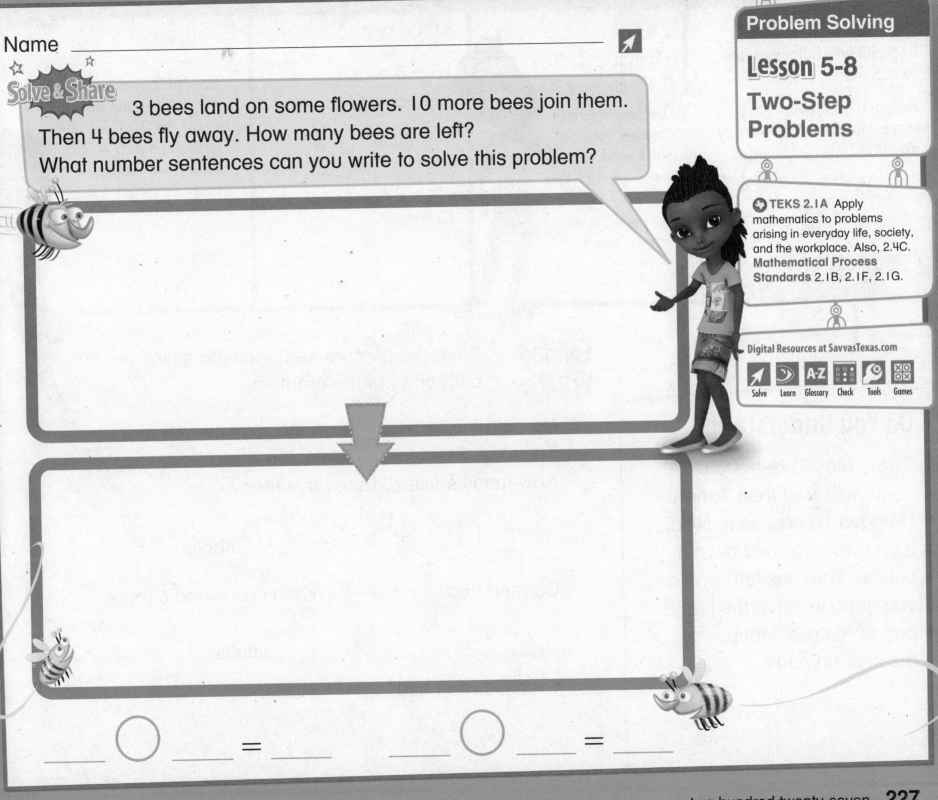

TEKS 2.1A Apply mathematics to problems arising in everyday life, society, and the workplace. Also, 2.4C. **Mathematical Process Standards** 2.1B, 2.1F, 2.1G.

Digital Resources at SavvasTexas.com

Solve   Learn   Glossary   Check   Tools   Games

_____ ◯ _____ = _____   _____ ◯ _____ = _____

Analyze

Bop picked 18 flowers and then 5 more.

He gave 10 flowers to Buzz. How many flowers are left?

Plan

$18 + 5 = ?$

This problem has a hidden question that I need to solve first. I need to find how many flowers Bop picked in all before I can solve the problem.

Solve and Justify

$18 + 5 = \underline{23}$

Bop picked 23 flowers.

$\underline{23} - \underline{10} = \underline{13}$

Bop gave 10 flowers to Buzz. Now he has 13 flowers.

Evaluate

I added 2 ones to make the next ten and then added the 3 leftover ones to find $18 + 5 = 23$. Then I subtracted 10 from 23 to get 13.

Do You Understand?

Show Me! Tom bought 15 pencils and then 7 more. He gave 10 pencils to Nyla. If you want to find how many pencils Tom has left, why do you need to solve the first part of the problem before the second part?

Guided Practice

Write the number sentences to solve both parts of the problem.

1. Carmen found 14 shells on Monday and 15 more on Tuesday. She found 6 more shells on Wednesday. How many shells did she have then?

$$\underline{14} \underbrace{+} \underline{15} = \underline{29} \text{ shells}$$

Carmen had $\underline{29}$ shells. Then she found 6 more.

$$\underline{} \bigcirc \underline{} = \underline{} \text{ shells}$$

Then Carmen had $\underline{}$ shells.

Topic 5 | Lesson 8

Name _____

Write the number sentences to solve both parts.

2. Val swims 18 laps on Monday and 11 laps on Tuesday. Val swims 20 laps on Friday. How many laps is that in all?

___ ◯ ___ = ___ laps

___ ◯ ___ = ___ laps

That is ___ laps in all.

3. There are 23 birds in a tree. 6 birds are red. The rest are brown. If 8 more brown birds come, how many brown birds will there be in all?

___ ◯ ___ = ___ brown birds

___ ◯ ___ = ___ brown birds

There will be ___ brown birds.

4. Erika saw 16 frogs on a lily pad and 8 frogs in the mud. If 7 frogs hop away, how many will be left?

___ ◯ ___ = ___ frogs

___ ◯ ___ = ___ frogs

___ frogs will be left.

5. Reuben has 100 pennies. He spends 65 pennies at the store. Then he finds 43 pennies. How many pennies does Reuben have now?

___ ◯ ___ = ___ pennies

___ ◯ ___ = ___ pennies

Reuben has ___ pennies.

6. Extend Your Thinking Kevin has 15 photos in his scrapbook. He adds 21 photos. Then he takes out some photos. Now he has 28 photos in the scrapbook. How many photos did Kevin take out?

___ ◯ ___ = ___ photos

___ ◯ ___ = ___ photos

Kevin took out ___ photos.

7. 24 children are walking by the pond. 14 adults go with them. 5 more adults join the walkers. How many people are walking now?

___ ◯ ___ = ___ people

___ ◯ ___ = ___ people

There are ___ people walking now.

8. There are 35 questions on a test. Kareem answers 10 of the questions. Then he answers 12 more questions. How many more questions must he answer?

___ ◯ ___ = ___ questions

___ ◯ ___ = ___ questions

Kareem needs to answer ___ more questions.

9. Find the missing numbers.

$$35 + \blacksquare = 100 \qquad \blacksquare = \underline{\quad}$$

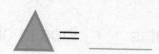

$$100 - \triangle = 18 \qquad \triangle = \underline{\quad}$$

10. Bill caught 22 fish and threw 6 back. He caught 8 more. How many does he have now? Which number sentences match the story?

◯ $22 + 6 = 28, 28 - 8 = 20$

◯ $22 - 6 = 16, 8 - 6 = 2$

◯ $22 - 6 = 16, 16 + 8 = 24$

◯ $22 + 6 = 28, 28 + 8 = 36$

11. Extend Your Thinking There are 25 friends at a party. Another 20 friends arrive. Then some friends leave the party. Only 7 friends stay. How many friends leave the party? Write two number sentences to solve the problem.

_____

_____ friends leave the party.

Name _____

Another Look Write number sentences to solve both parts of the problem.

Jenna had 13 red markers and 15 blue markers. Then Jenna lost 12 markers. How many markers did she have left?

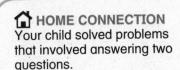

HOME CONNECTION Your child solved problems that involved answering two questions.

HOME ACTIVITY Make up story problems that take two questions, or steps, to solve. Ask your child to solve both parts of each problem.

Part 1
Add to find out how many markers Jenna had in all.

_____ ◯ _____ = _____

Part 2
Subtract the number of markers Jenna lost.

_____ ◯ _____ = _____

Jenna had _____ markers left.

Write the number sentences to solve both parts of the problem.

1. There were 15 red apples and 6 green apples in a bowl. Eric ate 2 of the apples. How many apples are in the bowl now?

Part 1 _____ ◯ _____ = _____

Part 2 _____ ◯ _____ = _____

There are _____ apples in the bowl now.

2. Brad buys 35 ride tickets at the carnival. He uses 23 tickets. Then he buys 15 more tickets. How many tickets does Brad have now?

Part 1 _____ ◯ _____ = _____

Part 2 _____ ◯ _____ = _____

Brad has _____ tickets now.

Write addition or subtraction sentences for each part. Then solve.

3. Kendra drew 26 stars. She erased 12 stars. Then Kendra drew 15 more stars. How many stars are there in all?

____ ◯ ____ = ____

____ ◯ ____ = ____

There are _____ stars in all.

4. ★ Ken needs to buy 100 nails. He buys 25 nails at one store and 36 nails at another store. How many more nails does Ken need to buy?

○ 75

○ 64

○ 61

○ 39

5. **Extend Your Thinking** Three students recorded how many jumping jacks they did each day. Use the table to answer the questions and fill in the missing numbers.

Jumping Jacks				
	Wednesday	Thursday	Friday	Total
Emma	30	_____	15	88
Hank	33	32	_____	85
Tana	_____	35	25	100

How many jumping jacks did Hank do on Friday?

Hank did _____ jumping jacks on Friday.

How many jumping jacks did Emma do on Thursday?

Emma did _____ jumping jacks on Thursday.

How many jumping jacks did Tana do on Wednesday?

Tana did _____ jumping jacks on Wednesday.

Topic 5 | Lesson 8

Name _____

Roll along to add and subtract. **Use tools** or **mental math!**

1. Pick a number from the roller coaster. Write it to start the number sentence. Then add 20. Write the sum.

29 42 58 71

_____ + 20 = _____

2. Ride to 100! Pick two numbers from the roller coaster. Make sure they add to 100.

_____ + _____ = 100

3. Use this part of a hundred chart.

51	52	(53)	54	55	56	57	58	59	60
61	62	63	64	65	66	67	68	69	70
71	72	73	74	75	76	77	78	(79)	80

Find the difference between the numbers in circles. Write the number sentence.

_____ − _____ = _____

4. Explain which tool you would select to find the sum of 29 and 42 — real objects, manipulatives, paper and pencil, or technology.

What Comes Next?

1. Look at each set of numbers.
   Write the number that comes next.

14	34	54	74	_____
16	32	48	64	_____
99	77	55	33	_____
98	75	52	29	_____
63	60	57	54	_____
52	54	56	58	_____
35	40	45	50	_____
41	48	55	62	_____

You can use addition and subtraction to help you find the number that comes next!

What's Wrong?

11	12	13	14	15	16	17	18	19	20
21	22	23	24	25	26	27	28	29	30
31	32	33	34	35	36	37	38	39	40
41	42	43	44	45	46	47	48	49	50

2. Trent says he can't subtract 50 − 25.
   "Fifty has no ones."

   Use the number chart to show how to subtract 25 from 50.

Code Math

3. Use the code to solve the number sentences.

   $$37 + \square = 77$$

   $$\square + 63 = 93$$

   $$61 - \square = 41$$

   $$\square - \square = 30$$

   | $\square$ = 20 | $\blacksquare$ = 30 |
   | $\bigcirc$ = 40 | $\bullet$ = 50 |

Name _____

Set A

Use mental math to add tens.

$$34 + 20 = ?$$

Way 1

Count on by tens.
Start at 34.
Count on 44, 54.

Way 2

Add the tens. $30 + 20 = 50$
Then add the ones to the sum.
$$50 + 4 = 54$$

$$34 + 20 = \underline{54}$$

Add. Use mental math.

Reteaching

1.
$$69 + 30 = \underline{}$$

2.
$$26 + 50 = \underline{}$$

Set B

You can use a hundred chart to help you add.
Find $62 + 12$.

Start at 62.
Move down
1 row to add
the tens in 12.
Now move
ahead 2 to show
the 2 ones in 12.

51	52	53	54	55	56	57	58	59	60
61	62	63	64	65	66	67	68	69	70
71	72	73	74	75	76	77	78	79	80
81	82	83	84	85	86	87	88	89	90
91	92	93	94	95	96	97	98	99	100

So, $62 + 12 = \underline{74}$.

Use a hundred chart to solve the problems.

3.
$$85 + 15 = \underline{}$$

4.
$$60 + 23 = \underline{}$$

You can add on to make 100.

$$46 + \underline{\quad} = 100$$

Add ones to the nearest ten.
Then add tens to 100.

$46 + 4 = 50$

$50 + 50 = 100$

So, $46 + \underline{54} = 100$.

Or add tens.
Then add ones.

$46 + 50 = 96$

$96 + 4 = 100$

So, $46 + \underline{54} = 100$.

Add on to find the other part of 100.

5.

$$27 + \underline{\quad} = 100$$

6.

$$34 + \underline{\quad} = 100$$

You can use a hundred chart to help you subtract.

$$65 - 31 = ?$$

31	32	33	34	35	36	37	38	39	40
41	42	43	44	45	46	47	48	49	50
51	52	53	54	55	56	57	58	59	60
61	62	63	64	65	66	67	68	69	70

Down 3 spaces is 3 tens.
Across 4 spaces is 4 ones.
3 tens and 4 ones is 34.

$$65 - 31 = \underline{34}$$

Subtract. Use a hundred chart to help.

7.

$$50 - 14 = \underline{\quad}$$

8.

$$70 - 28 = \underline{\quad}$$

Name _____

1. Lisa has 18 markers.
Adam has 22 markers.

How many markers are there in all?

11	12	13	14	15	16	17	18	19	20
21	22	23	24	25	26	27	28	29	30
31	32	33	34	35	36	37	38	39	40
41	42	43	44	45	46	47	48	49	50

43   42   41   40
○   ○   ○   ○

2. Mrs. Wu has 48 math cards.
Then she opens a pack of
20 math cards.

Which number sentence
shows how many math
cards Mrs. Wu has now?

○ $48 + 20 = 68$

○ $48 + 2 = 50$

○ $20 + 20 = 40$

○ $48 - 20 = 28$

3. 42 people went to the park.
Then 9 more people went
to the park.

How many people went
to the park in all?

○ 49

○ 50

○ 51

○ 52

4. Tyler has 100 cards.
52 cards are in a box.
The rest are in a stack.

How many cards are
in the stack?

○ 46

○ 48

○ 50

○ 58

5. Katrina has 53 balloons.
30 of them pop.

How many balloons are left?

- ○ 23
- ○ 33
- ○ 53
- ○ 83

6. Rick picks up 42 sticks.
Troy picks up 54 sticks.

How many sticks are there in all?

- ○ 86
- ○ 92
- ○ 94
- ○ 96

7. Emma has 66 rocks.
She gives 23 rocks to Gus.

How many rocks does Emma have now?

_____ — _____ = _____

_____ rocks

41	42	43	44	45	46	47	48	49	50
51	52	53	54	55	56	57	58	59	60
61	62	63	64	65	66	67	68	69	70
71	72	73	74	75	76	77	78	79	80

8. Write the number sentences to solve both parts.
Cameron has 45 stamps.
He uses 20 stamps.
Then he buys 7 more stamps.

How many stamps does he have now?

_____ ○ _____ = _____

_____ ○ _____ = _____

Cameron has _____ stamps.

Adding 2-Digit Numbers

Essential Question: What are ways to add 2-digit numbers?

It's fun to fly kites when the weather is windy.

The weather changes from day to day.

Wow! Let's do this project and learn more.

Math and Science Project: Weather

Find Out Look at the weather section in the newspaper. Read the forecast for today's weather. Record the different parts of the forecast, including the temperature, wind speed, and amounts of rain or snow. See if the forecast is correct.

Journal: Make a Book Draw pictures to show different kinds of weather. In your book, also:

- Describe things you like to do in each kind of weather.
- Make up and solve addition problems about kites or sailboats on windy days, or about umbrellas on rainy days.

Name _____

Review What You Know

Vocabulary

1. Circle the **tens digit** in the number below.

    38

2. Circle the **addition sentence.**

    $24 - 3 = 21$

    $12 + 5 = 17$

3. Circle the **addends.**

    $10 + 20 + 40 = 70$

Writing Addition Sentences

4. Write an addition sentence to solve the problem.

    Ben had 7 comic books. Then he bought 7 more comic books. How many comic books does Ben have now?

    _____ + _____ = _____

    _____ comic books

5. Write an addition sentence to solve the problem. Then change the order of the addends.

    Pablo builds a tower with 7 blocks. Meg adds 4 more blocks to the tower. How many blocks are in the tower in all?

    _____ + _____ = _____

    _____ + _____ = _____

Using Models

6. What number is shown in the model below?

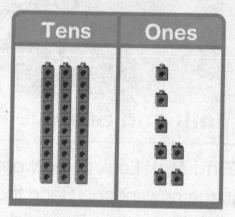

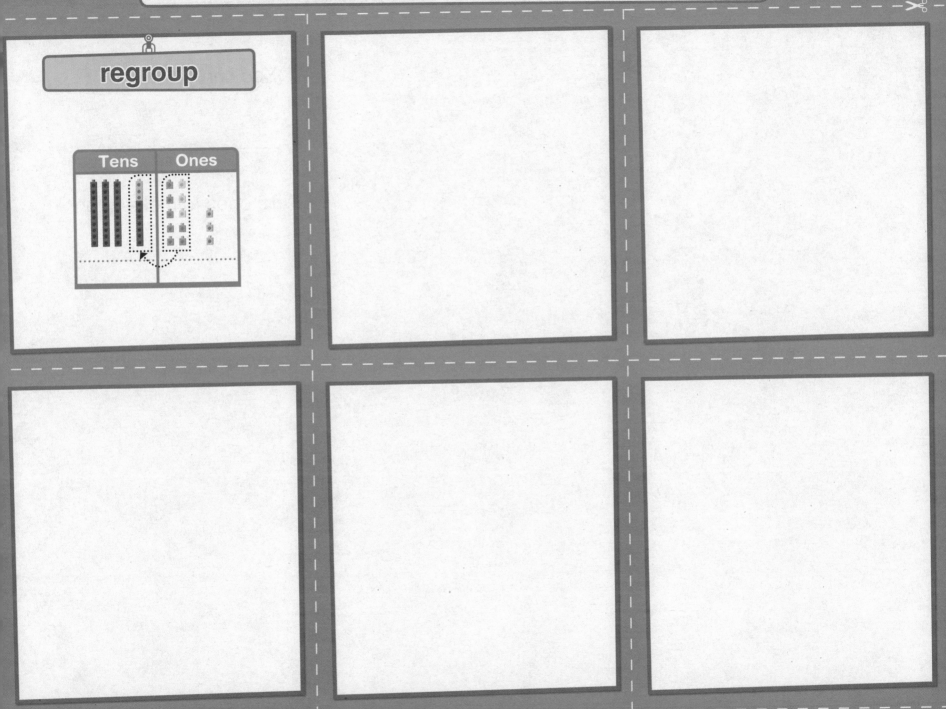

regroup

Tens	Ones

My Word Cards

Use what you know to complete the sentences.
Extend learning by writing your own sentence using each word.

You can

_____

10 ones to make 1 ten.

Name ______________________

Solve & Share

How can you use groups of 10 to help you add 25 + 8? Show your work.

Lesson 6-1
Regrouping 10 Ones for 1 Ten

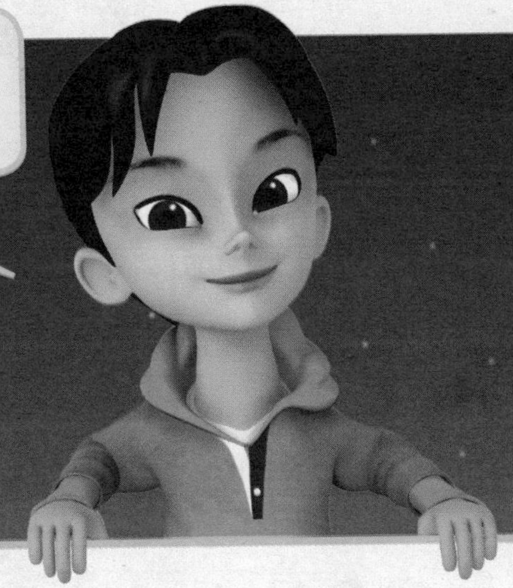

TEKS 2.4B Add up to four two-digit numbers ... using mental strategies and algorithms based on knowledge of place value and properties of operations. **Mathematical Process Standards** 2.1C, 2.1D, 2.1F.

Digital Resources at SavvasTexas.com

Solve Learn Glossary Check Tools Games

____ + ____ = ____

You can use models to add 37 + 6.

First show 37. Then show 6.

Tens	Ones

Show how to add. Put the ones together.

6 ones plus 7 ones is 13 ones. You need to regroup.

Tens	Ones
3 tens	13 ones

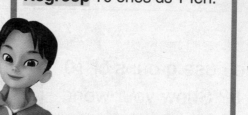

Regroup 10 ones as 1 ten.

Tens	Ones

There are 4 tens and 3 ones.

$$37 + 6 = 43$$

Tens	Ones
4 tens	3 ones

Do You Understand?

Show Me! When you add two numbers, how do you know if you need to regroup?

☆ Guided Practice ☆

Add. Use connecting cubes and your workmat. Regroup if you need to.

	Show	Add	Do you need to regroup?	Find the sum.
1.	24	6	(Yes) No	24 + 6 = 30
2.	54	8	Yes No	___ + ___ = ___
3.	65	2	Yes No	___ + ___ = ___
4.	36	9	Yes No	___ + ___ = ___

Topic 6 | Lesson 1

Name _____

Add. Use connecting cubes and your workmat. Regroup if you need to.

	Show	Add	Do you need to regroup?	Find the sum.
5.	17	7	Yes No	____ + ____ = ____
6.	32	4	Yes No	____ + ____ = ____
7.	42	8	Yes No	____ + ____ = ____
8.	29	5	Yes No	____ + ____ = ____
9.	38	3	Yes No	____ + ____ = ____

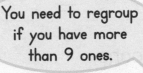

You need to regroup if you have more than 9 ones.

Extend Your Thinking Write the missing numbers. Use models if you need to.

10. $23 + \boxed{} = 32$

11. $35 + \boxed{} = 40$

12. Molly bought 18 balloons. Then she bought 8 more balloons. How many balloons did Molly buy in all?

_____ + _____ = _____

_____ balloons

13. 31 boys wore hats. 9 girls wore hats. How many students wore hats?

_____ + _____ = _____

_____ students

14. Ben counted 24 cars in a parking lot. He saw 5 cars drive away. Next, Ben watched 7 more cars park. How many cars were in the parking lot then?

12
○

26
○

29
○

31
○

Did the cars come or go?

15. **Extend Your Thinking** Find the sum of 26 + 7. Explain how you used regrouping to solve.

_____

_____

_____

_____

_____

_____

_____

Name _____

Another Look You can use models to find 24 + 8.

Regroup 10 ones as 1 ten.

There are ⋯3⋯ tens and ⋯2⋯ ones

$24 + 8 = 32$

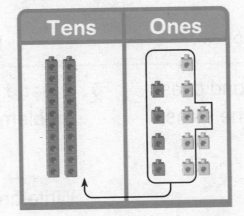

🏠 **HOME CONNECTION**
Your child added a two-digit number and a one-digit number using models.

HOME ACTIVITY Ask your child to use pennies to find the sum of 26 + 5. Have your child make groups of 10 to explain the answer.

Regroup 10 ones as 1 ten. Circle the group of 10.
Then write the sum.

1.

Tens	Ones

$28 + 3 =$ ____

2.

Tens	Ones

$47 + 7 =$ ____

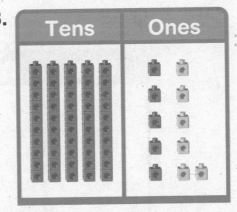

3.

Tens	Ones

$55 + 6 =$ ____

Topic 6 | Lesson 1
Digital Resources at SavvasTexas.com
two hundred forty-seven **247**

4. Pat has 9 beads. She finds 12 more beads.
⭐ Then Jill gives her some beads.
Now Pat has 28 beads.
How many beads does Jill give Pat?

○ 7   ○ 9   ○ 24   ○ 26

5. Tai counted 69 red plates.
Then he counted 8 blue plates.
How many plates did Tai count
in all?

_____ plates

6. Solve each problem. Draw tens and ones
in the place-value charts. Write the sums.

$48 + 5 =$ _____

Tens	Ones

$25 + 9 =$ _____

Tens	Ones

7. **Extend Your Thinking** Write an addition
problem for which you need to regroup.

_____

Write an addition problem for which you
do NOT need to regroup.

_____

Explain how you chose each problem.

_____

_____

_____

_____

_____

Name _____

Solve & Share

Use cubes and the workmat to help you solve 16 + 8. Show the tens and ones you have.

Tens	Ones

TEKS 2.4B Add up to four two-digit numbers ... using mental strategies and algorithms based on knowledge of place value and properties of operations. **Mathematical Process Standards** 2.1C, 2.1D, 2.1E, 2.1F.

Digital Resources at SavvasTexas.com

Solve   Learn   Glossary   Check   Tools   Games

____ tens   ____ ones

16 + 8 = ____

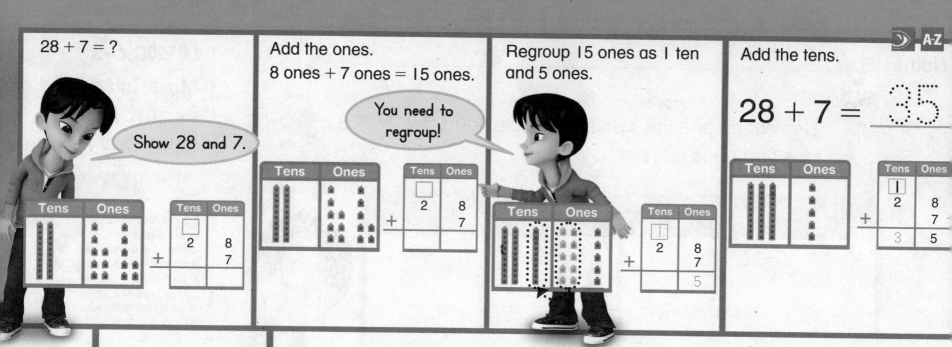

28 + 7 = ?

Show 28 and 7.

Add the ones.
8 ones + 7 ones = 15 ones.

You need to regroup!

Regroup 15 ones as 1 ten and 5 ones.

Add the tens.

28 + 7 = 35

Do You Understand?

Show Me! Suppose the sum of the ones is 10. What do you write in the ones place of the sum? Why?

☆ **Guided Practice** ☆ Add. Use connecting cubes and your workmat. Do you need to regroup? Circle **Yes** or **No**.

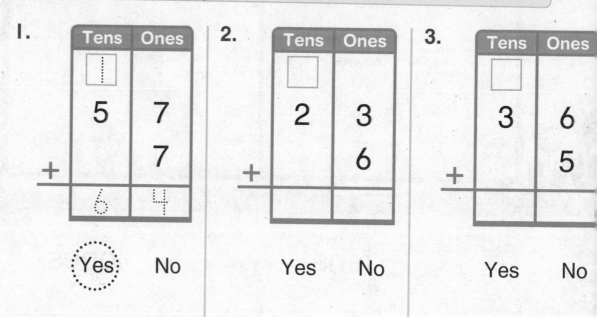

1.

Tens	Ones
1	
5	7
+	7
6	4

Yes   No

2.

Tens	Ones
2	3
+	6

Yes   No

3.

Tens	Ones
3	6
+	5

Yes   No

Name _____

☆Independent ☆Practice

Add. Use connecting cubes and your workmat.
Do you need to regroup? Circle **Yes** or **No**.

4.

Tens	Ones
☐	
4	1
	7
+	

Yes   No

5.

Tens	Ones
☐	
6	6
	3
+	

Yes   No

6.

Tens	Ones
☐	
3	5
	7
+	

Yes   No

7.

Tens	Ones
☐	
5	2
	8
+	

Yes   No

8.

Tens	Ones
☐	
4	8
	5
+	

Yes   No

9. **Extend Your Thinking** Jon said he regrouped when he solved 82 + 7. Is Jon correct? Explain.

_____

_____

_____

_____

Think: When can you regroup?

10. Mia has 32 white roses.
She has 4 pink roses.
How many roses does Mia have in all?

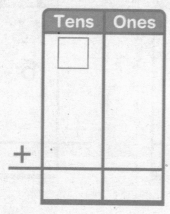

_____ roses

11. Juan found 29 rocks. Luz found 5 rocks.
⭐ Which shows how many they found in all?

$$\begin{array}{r} 29 \\ +\ 5 \\ \hline 24 \end{array}$$
○

$$\begin{array}{r} 29 \\ +\ 4 \\ \hline 33 \end{array}$$
○

$$\begin{array}{r} 29 \\ +\ 5 \\ \hline 34 \end{array}$$
○

$$\begin{array}{r} 29 \\ +\ 5 \\ \hline 44 \end{array}$$
○

12. Extend Your Thinking Write an addition story. Use a two-digit number and a one-digit number. Solve your number story.

Topic 6 | Lesson 2

Name _____

Another Look You can use models to add 35 + 7.

Step 1:
How many ones?

$5 + 7 = \underline{12}$

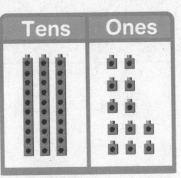

Tens	Ones

Step 2:
Regroup. Write 2 ones.
Write 1 ten.

Tens	Ones

Tens	Ones
$\boxed{1}$	
3	5
+	7
4	2

$35 + 7 = \underline{42}$

HOME CONNECTION
Your child modeled how to add a 2-digit number and 1-digit number and then recorded the addition.

HOME ACTIVITY Write 57 + 6 vertically. Have your child model the addition with dimes and pennies, and then write the sum.

Add. Use connecting cubes and the workmat.
Do you need to regroup? Circle **Yes** or **No**.

1.
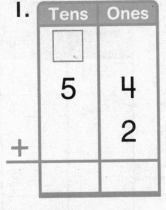

Tens	Ones
$\square$	
5	4
+	2

Yes   No

2.
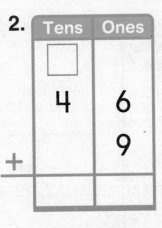

Tens	Ones
$\square$	
4	6
+	9

Yes   No

3.
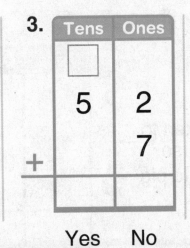

Tens	Ones
$\square$	
5	2
+	7

Yes   No

4.
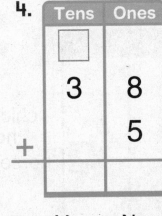

Tens	Ones
$\square$	
3	8
+	5

Yes   No

5.
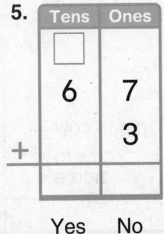

Tens	Ones
$\square$	
6	7
+	3

Yes   No

6. Algebra Write the missing numbers in the boxes.

```
    4   9
+   [ ]
    5   2
```
[ ]

7. A crow ate some kernels of corn. Then it ate 4 more kernels. It ate 26 kernels in all. How many kernels did the crow eat first?

18 ○   20 ○

22 ○   26 ○

Use the map to solve each problem. Use connecting cubes if needed.

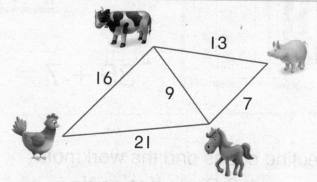

13

16

9

7

21

8. How long is the path from the pig to the cow to the horse?

Tens	Ones
[ ]	

pig to cow →
cow to horse →
+

9. How long is the path from the chicken to the horse to the pig?

Tens	Ones
[ ]	

chicken to horse →
horse to pig →
+

10. Extend Your Thinking Use the map to write and solve your own problem.

_____ to
_____ →

_____ to
_____ →

Tens	Ones
[ ]	

+

Name _____

☆ ☆
Solve & Share

Aiden has 24 stamps.
He gets 9 more stamps.
How many stamps does Aiden have now?
Add using only paper and pencil. Explain.

⊕ TEKS 2.4B Add up to
four two-digit numbers ...
using mental strategies
and algorithms based on
knowledge of place value
and properties of operations.
**Mathematical Process
Standards** 2.1A, 2.1C, 2.1D,
2.1F.

Tens	Ones
+	

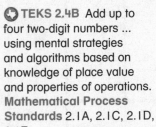

Digital Resources at SavvasTexas.com

Solve   Learn   Glossary   Check   Tools   Games

Find 48 + 4.
Use paper and pencil to add.

Tens	Ones
☐	
4	8
	4
+	

Look at the ones.

Do you need to regroup?

Tens	Ones
☐	
4	8
	4
+	

Add the ones.
Regroup if you need to.

Tens	Ones
1	
4	8
	4
+	
	2

Add the tens.

48 + 4 = 52

Tens	Ones
1	
4	8
	4
+	
5	2

Do You Understand?

Show Me! What do you write to show regrouping 10 ones as 1 ten?

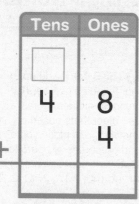

☆ Guided Practice ☆ Add. Regroup if you need to.

1.

Tens	Ones
1	
2	2
	9
+	
3	1

2.

Tens	Ones
☐	
3	6
	7
+	

3.

Tens	Ones
☐	
1	7
	2
+	

2 + 9 = ? Do I need to regroup?

Independent Practice

Add. Regroup if you need to.

4.

Tens	Ones
☐	
4	5
	5
+	

5.

Tens	Ones
☐	
9	3
	6
+	

6.

Tens	Ones
☐	
7	7
	7
+	

7.

Tens	Ones
☐	
5	8
	4
+	

8.

Tens	Ones
☐	
2	3
	6
+	

9.

Tens	Ones
☐	
3	6
	5
+	

10.

Tens	Ones
☐	
4	1
	7
+	

11.

Tens	Ones
☐	
6	5
	6
+	

12.

Tens	Ones
☐	
8	2
	4
+	

13.

Tens	Ones
☐	
5	1
	9
+	

Extend Your Thinking Write the missing numbers. Use models if needed.

14. $4 + \boxed{} = 43$

15. $\boxed{} + 7 = 64$

16. $4 + \boxed{} = 84$

17. Jody has 17 cans to recycle. She collects 5 more. How many cans does Jody have in all?

Tens	Ones
1	7
	5

+

_____ cans

Do you need to regroup?

18. Dana has 45 marbles.
She buys 8 more.
She also buys 3 rubber balls.
How many marbles does Dana have in all?

52 ○   53 ○

54 ○   56 ○

19. Ming collected 33 state quarters.
He gave 2 to his brother.
Then he collected 9 more.
How many state quarters does Ming have now?

11 ○   31 ○

40 ○   42 ○

20. Extend Your Thinking Write an addition story about something you collect. Add. Regroup if you need to.

_____

_____

_____

_____

Tens	Ones

+

Name _____

Another Look Remember these steps for adding.

Step 1: Add the ones.

Step 2: Regroup if there are 10 or more ones.

Step 3: Add the tens.

$37 + 6 = ?$

There are more than 9 ones.

Regroup 13 as 1 ten and 3 ones. Add.

$37 + 6 = \underline{43}$

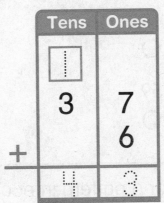

🏠 **HOME CONNECTION**
Your child used paper and pencil to add two-digit numbers and one-digit numbers with and without regrouping.

HOME ACTIVITY Write $23 + 9$ in vertical form on a sheet of paper. Have your child use paper and pencil to solve.

Use paper and pencil to add.

1. Do you need to regroup?

Yes   No

Tens	Ones
	2	8
+		4

2. Do you need to regroup?

Yes   No

Tens	Ones
	3	6
+		9

3. Do you need to regroup?

Yes   No

Tens	Ones
	3	4
+		5

4. Bessie has 25 flowers. Then she picks more flowers. Now she has 34 flowers. How many more flowers did Bessie pick?

8 ○   9 ○

35 ○   59 ○

5. Tell how you know when to regroup.

_____

_____

_____

Extend Your Thinking Look for a pattern in each row. Then write the missing numbers.

6.

$$\begin{array}{r} 56 \\ +\boxed{} \\ \hline 62 \end{array} \qquad \begin{array}{r} 66 \\ +\boxed{} \\ \hline 72 \end{array} \qquad \begin{array}{r} 76 \\ +\boxed{} \\ \hline 82 \end{array}$$

7.

$$\begin{array}{r} 31 \\ +\boxed{} \\ \hline 36 \end{array} \qquad \begin{array}{r} 41 \\ +\boxed{} \\ \hline 46 \end{array} \qquad \begin{array}{r} 51 \\ +\boxed{} \\ \hline 56 \end{array}$$

8.

$$\begin{array}{r} 45 \\ +\boxed{} \\ \hline 54 \end{array} \qquad \begin{array}{r} 55 \\ +\boxed{} \\ \hline 64 \end{array} \qquad \begin{array}{r} 65 \\ +\boxed{} \\ \hline 74 \end{array}$$

9.

$$\begin{array}{r} 68 \\ +\boxed{} \\ \hline 75 \end{array} \qquad \begin{array}{r} 78 \\ +\boxed{} \\ \hline 85 \end{array} \qquad \begin{array}{r} 88 \\ +\boxed{} \\ \hline 95 \end{array}$$

Name _____

Solve & Share

Leslie collects 36 rocks. Her brother collects 27 rocks. How many rocks do they collect in all? Use cubes to help you solve. Draw your cubes. Tell if you need to regroup.

⊕ **TEKS 2.4B** Add up to four two-digit numbers ... using mental strategies and algorithms based on knowledge of place value and properties of operations. **Mathematical Process Standards** 2.1B, 2.1C, 2.1F, 2.1G.

Digital Resources at SavvasTexas.com

Solve   Learn   Glossary   Check   Tools   Games

Tens	Ones
+	

Regroup?

Yes   No

Let's add!

37 + 19 = ?

Show 37.
Then show 19.

Tens	Ones
	3	7
+	1	9

Add the ones.

7 ones + 9 ones = 16 ones

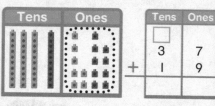

Tens	Ones
	3	7
+	1	9

There are 16 ones. Regroup 16 ones as 1 ten and 6 ones.

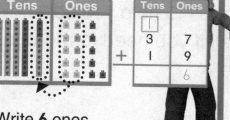

Tens	Ones
1		
	3	7
+	1	9
		6

Write **6** ones.
Write **1** to show 1 ten.

Add the tens.

3 tens + 1 ten = 4 tens
4 tens + 1 ten = 5 tens

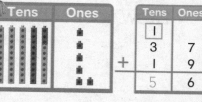

Tens	Ones
1		
	3	7
+	1	9
	5	6

Write **5** to show 5 tens.

Do You Understand?

Show Me! When do you have to regroup when adding?

☆ **Guided Practice** ☆ Add. Use connecting cubes and your workmat. Did you need to regroup? Circle **Yes** or **No**.

1.

Tens	Ones
1	
3	2
+ 2	9
6	1

(Yes)　No

2.

Tens	Ones
☐	
2	4
+ 5	2

Yes　No

3.

Tens	Ones
☐	
1	5
+ 3	8

Yes　No

262 two hundred sixty-two

Topic 6 | Lesson 4

Name _____

Add. Use connecting cubes and your workmat.

4.

Tens	Ones
☐	
5	6
2	9
+	

5.

Tens	Ones
☐	
2	7
2	3
+	

6.

Tens	Ones
☐	
5	9
1	3
+	

7.

Tens	Ones
☐	
2	4
3	5
+	

8.

Tens	Ones
☐	
3	6
4	7
+	

9.

Tens	Ones
☐	
5	8
4	1
+	

10.

Tens	Ones
☐	
4	5
1	6
+	

11.

Tens	Ones
☐	
3	4
4	6
+	

12.

Tens	Ones
☐	
3	9
1	9
+	

13.

Tens	Ones
☐	
2	2
5	3
+	

14. Extend Your Thinking Draw the second addend.

First Addend   Second Addend   Sum

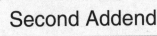
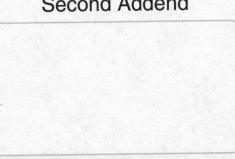

15. Rico builds a fort with 36 blocks.
Tony uses 38 blocks to make it bigger.
How many blocks are used in all?

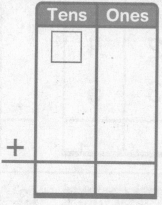

Tens	Ones
☐	
+	

_____ blocks

16. Chen counts 47 buttons. Then he counts
20 more. How many buttons does Chen
count altogether?

Tens	Ones
☐	
4	7
2	0
+	

_____ buttons

17. ⭐ Jenny has 22 pennies. Her mom gives
her 29 pennies and 7 nickels. How many
pennies does Jenny have now?

41 ◯   42 ◯

51 ◯   58 ◯

18. Extend Your Thinking Write an addition
story about the desks and chairs in your
classroom. Use pictures, numbers, or words.

Another Look You can use steps to add. Add $46 + 18$.

Step 1:
How many ones?

$6 + 8 = \underline{14}$

Tens	Ones

Step 2:
Write 4 ones.
Write 6 tens.

Tens	Ones

Tens	Ones
1	
4	6
1	8
+ 6	4

$46 + 18 = \underline{64}$

🏠 **HOME CONNECTION**
Your child used tens and ones models to show how to add two-digit numbers with and without regrouping.

HOME ACTIVITY Ask your child to show you how to add $27 + 34$. Have your child explain each step of the addition.

Follow the steps to add. Use connecting cubes and your workmat.

1.
Tens	Ones
2	4
2	9
+	

2.
Tens	Ones
5	2
1	7
+	

3.
Tens	Ones
3	8
4	5
+	

4.
Tens	Ones
1	7
6	3
+	

5.
Tens	Ones
5	1
4	7
+	

6. Lia has 38 red cups.
She has 25 blue cups.
How many cups does Lia have in all?

_____ cups

7. ⭐ Tom picks some apples. Ellen picks 27 apples. They pick 66 apples in all. How many apples did Tom pick?

39 ○   56 ○

58 ○   46 ○

Extend Your Thinking Write the missing numbers.
Use connecting cubes if needed.

8.

Tens	Ones
☐	
5	7
2	7
+	

9.

Tens	Ones
☐	
6	2
1	5
+	

10.

Tens	Ones
☐	
1	9
3	3
+	

Remember to write the regrouped numbers.

11.

Tens	Ones
☐	
2	7
○	8
+	
4	5

12.

Tens	Ones
☐	
2	○
5	7
+	
8	0

13.

Tens	Ones
☐	
3	8
○	4
+	
6	2

Topic 6 | Lesson 4

Name ______________________

Solve & Share

How can you add 46 + 26 without using cubes? Explain.

Tens	Ones
+	

____

____

____

Lesson 6-5
Adding 2-Digit Numbers

TEKS 2.4B Add up to four two-digit numbers ... using mental strategies and algorithms based on knowledge of place value and properties of operations. **Mathematical Process Standards** 2.1C, 2.1F, 2.1G.

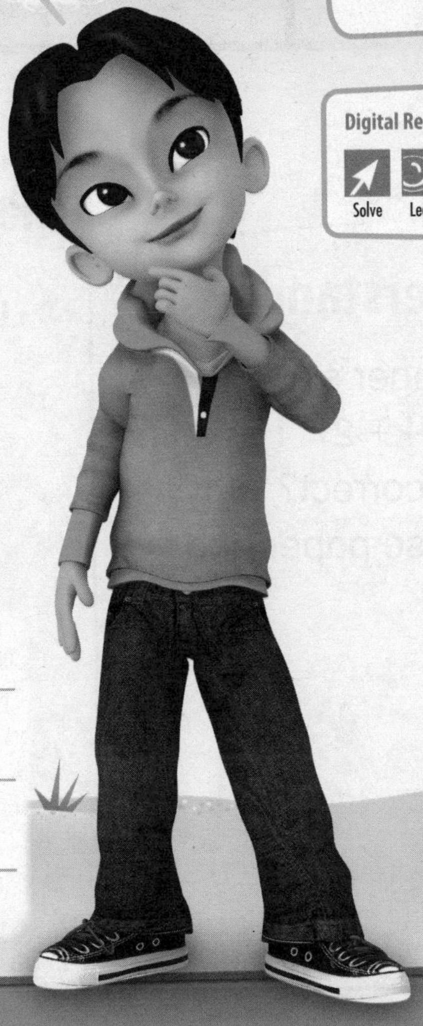

Digital Resources at SavvasTexas.com
Solve Learn Glossary Check Tools Games

Find 56 + 38.

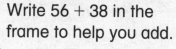

You can use paper and pencil to add.

Write 56 + 38 in the frame to help you add.

Tens	Ones
□	
+	

Write the ones in the ones column. Write the tens in the tens column.

Tens	Ones
5	6
+ 3	8

Add. Regroup if you need to.

94!

Tens	Ones
1	
5	6
+ 3	8
9	4

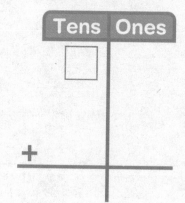

Do You Understand?

Show Me! Roger solved the problem 54 + 27. His sum was 71. Is he correct? Why or why not? Use paper and pencil to check.

☆ **Guided Practice** ☆ Write the addition problem. Find the sum.

1. **34 + 17**

Tens	Ones
1	
3	4
+ 1	7
5	1

2. **52 + 31**

Tens	Ones
□	
+	

3. **35 + 26**

Tens	Ones
□	
+	

Name _____

☆ **Independent**
☆ **Practice**   Write the addition problem. Find the sum.

4. 15 + 28

Tens	Ones
☐	

+

5. 29 + 20

Tens	Ones
☐	

+

6. 63 + 29

Tens	Ones
☐	

+

7. 37 + 48

Tens	Ones
☐	

+

8. 67 + 17

Tens	Ones
☐	

+

9. 15 + 18

Tens	Ones
☐	

+

10. 43 + 49

Tens	Ones
☐	

+

11. 62 + 28

Tens	Ones
☐	

+

Extend Your Thinking Write the missing numbers.

12. 27 + 2☐ = 50

13. 3☐ + 16 = 48

14. ☐4 + 49 = 93

Problem Solving Solve each problem.

15. Amir planted 25 trees. Juan planted 27 trees. How many trees did they plant in all?

Tens	Ones
☐	
+	

_____ trees

16. On Monday, Sasha put 32 pennies in her bank. On Tuesday, she put 57 more pennies in her bank. How many pennies did she put in her bank on both days?

Tens	Ones
☐	
+	

_____ pennies

17. ⭐ 52 acorns fell from the tree. Then 37 more acorns fell. Some squirrels ran away with 9 acorns. How many acorns were left?

70 ◯   80 ◯

90 ◯   98 ◯

18. **Extend Your Thinking** Write an addition story using 2 two-digit numbers. Then solve the problem for your story.

_____

_____

Tens	Ones
☐	
+	

_____

_____

Name _____

Another Look Remember the steps for adding.

Step 1:	**Step 2:**	**Step 3:**
Add the ones.	Regroup if you need to.	Add the tens.

$34 + 27 = ?$

Regroup
11 ones as
1 ten and
1 one.

Tens	Ones
[1]	
3	4
+ 2	7
6	1

$12 + 36 = ?$

You do
not need
to regroup
8 ones.

Tens	Ones
[ ]	[ ]
1	2
+ 3	6
4	8

🏠 **HOME CONNECTION**
Your child used paper and pencil to add 2 two-digit numbers with and without regrouping.

HOME ACTIVITY Write $28 + 45$ on a sheet of paper. Have your child find the sum using paper and pencil. Once finished, have your child explain why regrouping was needed.

Write the addition problem. Find the sum.

1. $15 + 26$

Tens	Ones
[ ]	
1	5
+ 2	6

2. $32 + 24$

Tens	Ones
[ ]	
3	2
+ 2	

3. $28 + 15$

Tens	Ones
[ ]	
2	8
+	

4. $49 + 13$

Tens	Ones
[ ]	
+	

5. $75 + 13$

Tens	Ones
+	

Topic 6 | Lesson 5

6. Paul has a stack of 43 cards.
He also has a stack of 36 cards.
How many cards does Paul have in all?

_____ cards

7. One box has 38 blue paper clips.
⭐ Another box has 43 green paper clips.
A third box has 6 red paper clips.
How many paper clips are in all the boxes?

77 ○   81 ○

87 ○   97 ○

Extend Your Thinking Read the sum. Circle all of the number pairs in the box that match that sum.

8. Sum 22

10	4	18
12	15	14
20	21	13

9. Sum 55

25	30	14
18	14	45
15	21	10

10. Sum 83

30	45	30
56	19	64
27	29	20

Name _____

Solve & Share

Amelia walked 18 blocks on Monday and 5 blocks on Tuesday. How many blocks did she walk in all? Use the number line to show how many blocks Amelia walked. Write a number sentence to solve.

⭐ TEKS 2.9C Represent whole numbers as distances from any given location on a number line. Also, 2.2F, 2.4B. Mathematical Process Standards 2.1C, 2.1D, 2.1E, 2.1F.

Digital Resources at SavvasTexas.com

Solve   Learn   Glossary   Check   Tools   Games

+——————+————0————5————10————15————20————25————30

_____ + _____ = _____

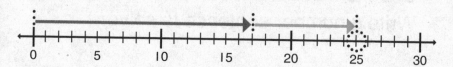
Amelia walked 17 blocks before dinner.
She walked 8 blocks after dinner.
How many blocks did she walk in all?

You can show the problem on a number line.
First show the 17 blocks Amelia walked
before dinner.

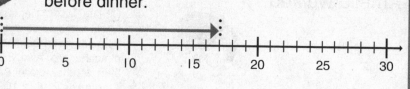

Then show the 8 blocks she walked after dinner.
The two lines together stretch to 25.
Amelia walked 25 blocks in all.

$$17 + 8 = 25$$

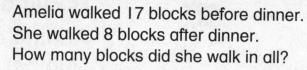

Do You Understand?

Show Me! Explain how to show adding $7 + 11$ on a number line.

✰ Guided Practice ✰

Show these addition problems on the number lines.

1. $21 + 7 = \underline{28}$

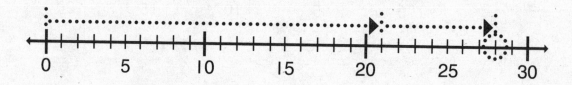

2. $14 + 9 = \underline{}$

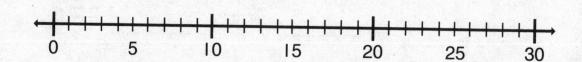

Name _____

Solve each problem.

Show these addition problems on the number lines.

3. $16 + 5 =$ _____

4. $8 + 14 =$ _____

What addition problems do these number lines show?

5. _____ $+$ _____ $=$ _____

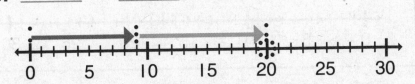

6. _____ $+$ _____ $=$ _____

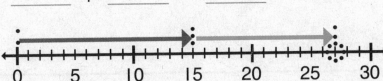

7. **Extend Your Thinking** You show an addition problem on a number line. Will the sum always be farther along the number line than the first number you show? Use the number line to help explain your answer.

What could be your first and second addends?

_____

_____

_____

Problem Solving — Solve each problem using the number lines.

8. Lakisha draws 15 blue horses. Liam draws green horses. Together they drew 25 horses. How many horses did Liam draw? Use the number line to help.

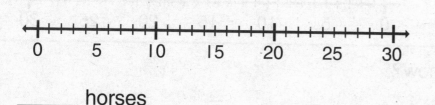

_____ horses

9. Steve has some tomatoes. He buys 12 more tomatoes. Steve now has 20 tomatoes. How many tomatoes did Steve have to begin with?

8 ⚪   20 ⚪

24 ⚪   32 ⚪

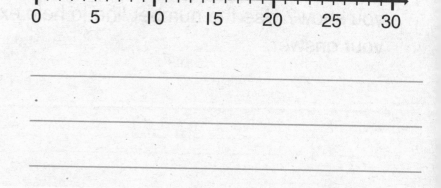

10. **Extend Your Thinking** The runners on the track team ran 12 miles on Monday. On Tuesday, they ran 6 more miles than they ran on Monday. How many miles did they run on both days? Explain.

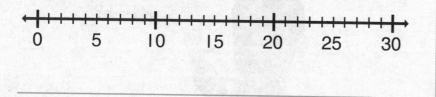

_____

_____

_____

11. **Extend Your Thinking** Explain how to solve 9 + 13 using a number line.

_____

_____

_____

_____

Topic 6 | Lesson 6

Name _____

Another Look You can show addition on a number line.

$10 + 29 = ?$

Start at 0. Move 10 spaces to the right.

Then move 29 spaces to the right.

When adding on a number line, the arrow for the second addend starts where the first arrow ended.

🏠 **HOME CONNECTION**
Your child used a number line to add two-digit numbers.

HOME ACTIVITY Create a number line and use it to count the number of steps from one place to the next. Then count the number of steps from the last place to a different place. Add that number to the original number of steps using the number line.

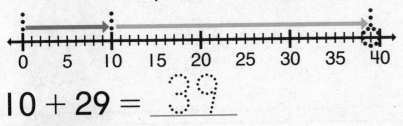

0 5 10 15 20 25 30 35 40

$10 + 29 = $ _39_

Show the addition problems on the number line.

1. $24 + 7 = $ _____

0 5 10 15 20 25 30 35 40

2. $18 + 23 = $ _____

0 5 10 15 20 25 30 35 40 45 50

3. What addition problem does the number line show? Write the number sentence.

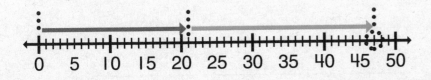

0 5 10 15 20 25 30 35 40 45 50

_____ + _____ = _____

4. One box has 15 crayons. Another box has 14 crayons. How many crayons are in both boxes? Use the number line to solve.

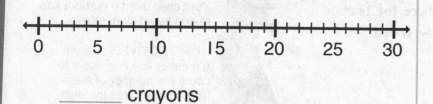

_____ crayons

5. Dave put 19 red apples in a basket. His mom took 4 red apples out. Then she put 7 yellow apples in the basket. How many apples were left in the basket?

11 ○   15 ○

22 ○   26 ○

Which numbers do I add? Which do I subtract?

6. Extend Your Thinking A class has 12 girls and 12 boys. How many girls and boys are in the class in all? Draw a number line to solve. Explain why you do not begin at 0 to show the second number.

_____

_____

_____

_____

7. Extend Your Thinking Write an addition sentence with a sum less than 50. Explain how to show the addition sentence on a number line.

_____ + _____ = _____

_____

_____

_____

_____

Name _____

Solve & Share

Use mental math to find $20 + 18 + 22 + 30$. Think about how place value or adding in any order can help you.

Show and explain your work.

★ **TEKS 2.4B** Add up to four two-digit numbers ... using mental strategies and algorithms based on knowledge of place value and properties of operations. **Mathematical Process Standards** 2.1C, 2.1F, 2.1G.

Digital Resources at SavvasTexas.com

Solve Learn Glossary Check Tools Games

Use place value. Start by adding the ones.

$$\begin{array}{r} 2\ 4 \\ 1\ 6 \\ 1\ 4 \\ +1\ 5 \\ \hline \end{array}$$

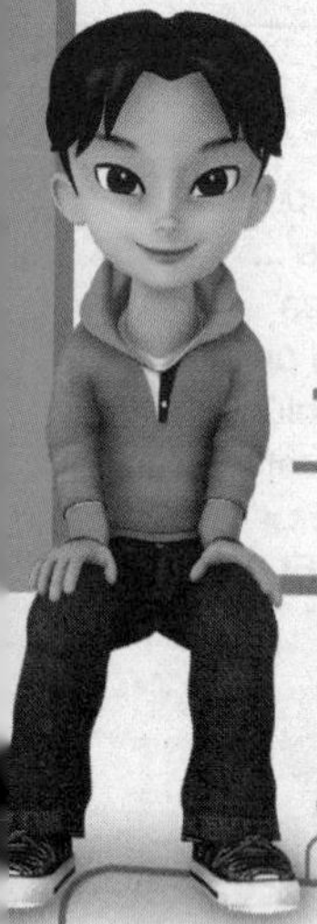

Add in any order. You can use doubles.

$$\begin{array}{r} 2\ 4 \\ 1\ 6 \\ 1\ 4 \\ +1\ 5 \\ \hline 9 \end{array}$$

4 + 4 = 8
6 + 5 = 11
11 + 8 = 19

Or you can make 10.

$$\begin{array}{r} 2\ 4 \\ 1\ 6 \\ 1\ 4 \\ +1\ 5 \\ \hline 9 \end{array}$$

6 + 4 = 10
4 + 5 = 9
10 + 9 = 19

Then add the tens.

$$\begin{array}{r} 1 \\ 2\ 4 \\ 1\ 6 \\ 1\ 4 \\ +1\ 5 \\ \hline 6\ 9 \end{array}$$

The sum is 69!

Do You Understand?

Show Me! In the second box above, why can you add 4 + 4 first? Can you always change the order of the numbers that you are adding? Explain.

Guided Practice

Add. Circle the two numbers you added first.

1.
$$\begin{array}{r} 18 \\ 12 \\ +\ 15 \\ \hline 45 \end{array}$$

2.
$$\begin{array}{r} 14 \\ 11 \\ +\ \ 9 \\ \hline \end{array}$$

3.
$$\begin{array}{r} 21 \\ 14 \\ 41 \\ +\ \ 2 \\ \hline \end{array}$$

4.
$$\begin{array}{r} 21 \\ 15 \\ 32 \\ +\ 25 \\ \hline \end{array}$$

Add. Circle the two numbers you added first.

5.
```
   22
   14
 + 22
_____
```

6.
```
   16
   23
 + 26
_____
```

7.
```
   27
   13
 + 21
_____
```

8.
```
   13
   33
 + 25
_____
```

9.
```
   25
   21
 + 32
_____
```

10.
```
   55
    7
 + 24
 +  2
_____
```

11.
```
   32
   16
   18
 + 31
_____
```

12.
```
   16
   42
   12
 + 22
_____
```

13.
```
   17
   41
   27
 + 13
_____
```

14.
```
   37
   11
   15
 + 28
_____
```

Extend Your Thinking Find the missing numbers.

15. $8 + 3 + \boxed{} + 2 = 18$

16. $5 + \boxed{} + 6 + 5 = 19$

17. $7 + 27 + 23 + \boxed{} = 61$

18. $\boxed{} + 24 + 18 + 4 = 52$

Problem Solving
Solve each problem.

19. Cody and Jill play with toy trucks. 28 trucks are blue. 32 trucks are yellow. 17 trucks are green. 11 trucks are pink. How many trucks are there in all?

_____ trucks

20. Julia has 15 flower stickers. She has 23 animal stickers. She has 35 smiley face stickers and 18 star stickers. How many stickers does Julia have in all?

_____ stickers

21. ⭐ Henry is adding the numbers 24, 36, and 18. If he makes a ten to add, which ones digits would Henry add first?

3 and 8
○

4 and 6
○

4 and 8
○

8 and 6
○

22. **Extend Your Thinking** Find the sum. Explain how you solved the problem.

$$
\begin{array}{r}
25 \\
16 \\
15 \\
+\ 8 \\
\hline
\end{array}
$$

_____

_____

_____

_____

Topic 6 | Lesson 7

Name _____

Another Look You can add three or four numbers in any order. Remember to add the ones first.

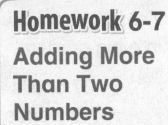

Look for doubles.

$$14$$
$$35$$
$$+24$$
$$73$$

$4 + 4 = 8$
$8 + 5 = 13$

Make a ten.

$$13$$
$$26$$
$$24$$
$$+12$$
$$75$$

$6 + 4 = 10$
$3 + 2 = 5$
$10 + 5 = 15$

Count on.

$$53$$
$$19$$
$$+22$$
$$94$$

Add 9 and 3.

$9 + 3 = 12$

Count on from 12, 13, 14.

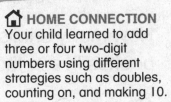
HOME CONNECTION Your child learned to add three or four two-digit numbers using different strategies such as doubles, counting on, and making 10.

HOME ACTIVITY Ask your child to find the sum of $16 + 14 + 6$ using two different strategies.

Add. Circle the numbers you add first.

I. Look for doubles.

$$21$$
$$10$$
$$34$$
$$+24$$

2. Count on.

$$12$$
$$17$$
$$+24$$

3. Make a ten.

$$15$$
$$28$$
$$+22$$

4. Choose a way to add.

$$26$$
$$22$$
$$+36$$

5. These animals live in a big garden:

Do I count all of these?

37 snails

49 worms

12 moths

11 beetles

How many snails, worms, and beetles live in the garden?

○ 86　　○ 97　　○ 98　　○ 101

6. Mac's family donates clothes to charity. Mac donates 16 shirts. His brother donates 14 shirts and his mother donates 25 shirts. How many shirts do Mac's family give to charity?

$$\begin{array}{r} 16 \\ 14 \\ + 25 \\ \hline \end{array}$$

_____ shirts

Extend Your Thinking Look at the sum. Read the clues. Circle the three numbers that add up to that sum. Show the addition you used to find the sum.

---

7. Sum: 83

5　　44　　12　　19　　10　　20

One number is the sum of 22 + 22.
One number is one less than 20.
One number is greater than 19 and less than 44.

_____ + _____ + _____

---

8. Sum: 72

36　　12　　25　　7　　33　　14

One number has two of the same digits.
One number is greater than 12 and less than 25.
One number is 20 more than 5.

_____ + _____ + _____

Name _____

Solve & Share

Kim puts 15 toys in the toy box. Then she puts 17 more toys in the toy box. How many toys are in the toy box in all? Use a model and a number sentence to solve.

★TEKS 2.1D Communicate mathematical ideas, reasoning, and their implications using ... symbols, diagrams, graphs, and language ... Also, 2.4C. Mathematical Process Standards 2.1B, 2.1C, 2.1E, 2.1F, 2.1G.

Digital Resources at SavvasTexas.com

Solve   Learn   Glossary   Check   Tools   Games

____ + ____ = ____

Analyze

Eric has 29 crayons.
He buys a box of 16 crayons.

How many crayons does he have in all?

Plan

I know I need to add 29 and 16. I can use a strip diagram.

?

| 29 | 16 |

Solve and Justify

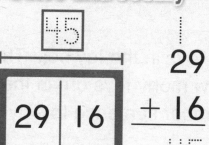

45

| 29 | 16 |

$$29$$
$$+\ 16$$
$$45$$

$$29 + 16 = 45$$

Evaluate

I needed to regroup to add. My answer makes sense.

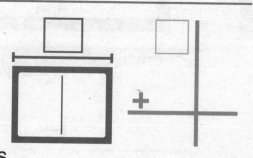

Do You Understand?

Show Me! How does writing a number sentence help you solve a problem?

Guided Practice

Write a number sentence and use a strip diagram to solve each problem.

1. Flora has 24 books about birds. She has 18 books about bugs. How many books does Flora have in all?

42

| 24 | 18 |

$$\begin{array}{r} 1 \\ 2\ 4 \\ +\ 1\ 8 \\ \hline 4\ 2 \end{array}$$

$$24 + 18 = 42 \text{ books}$$

2. Barb saw 14 cars on one street. She saw 15 cars on another street. How many cars did Barb see on both streets?

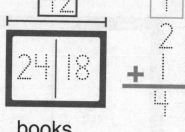

____ + ____ = ____ cars

Name _____

Write a number sentence and solve the problem.

3. Avi takes 16 pictures.
   Then he takes 17 more pictures.
   How many pictures does Avi take?   _____ + _____ = _____ pictures

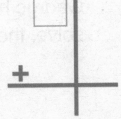

4. Tina picks 39 blueberries.
   She picks 14 strawberries.
   How many berries does Tina pick in all?   _____ + _____ = _____ berries

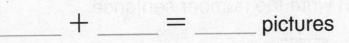

5. Raj finds 47 acorns in his front yard.
   He finds 29 acorns in his backyard.
   How many acorns does Raj find in all?   _____ + _____ = _____ acorns

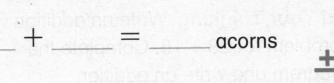

Extend Your Thinking Write the missing numbers.

6.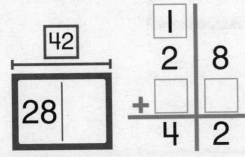

```
        1   8
  42    2
 28   +     
        4   2
```

7.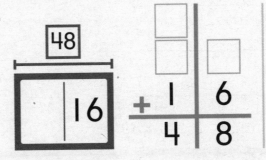

```
  48
        1   6
 16   +     
        4   8
```

8.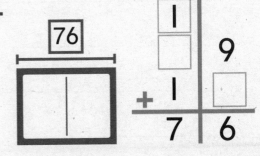

```
        1   9
  76    
      +1    
        7   6
```

Problem Solving
Solve each problem.

9. George has 19 daisies. He plants 14 more daisies and 12 roses. How many daisies does George have in all? Use the strip diagram to solve, then write the number sentence.

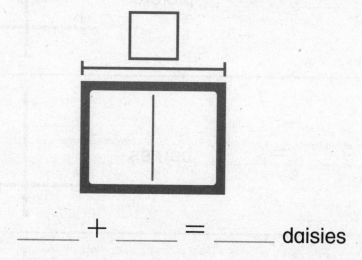

_____ + _____ = _____ daisies

10. Joy plants 59 seeds in all. She plants 37 bean seeds and some carrot seeds. Which number sentence shows how many seeds Joy plants?

○　59 + 37 = 96

○　59 + 22 = 81

○　37 − 22 = 15

○　37 + 22 = 59

11. Extend Your Thinking Write an addition story problem for 23 + 18. Complete the strip diagram and write an addition sentence to solve your problem.

_____

_____

_____

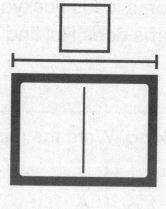

_____ + _____ = _____

Name _____

Another Look Read the story problem carefully. Then decide if you need to add or subtract to solve.

Tina has 23 counters.
She gets 27 more counters.
How many counters does Tina have in all?

"How many in all" tells you to add.

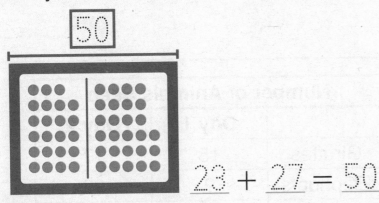

$$23 + 27 = 50$$

Tens	Ones
1	
2	3
+ 2	7
5	0

Write a number sentence to solve the problem. Use the strip diagram if needed.

1. Jordan had 19 yo-yos. Then he got 17 more.
   How many yo-yos does Jordan have now?

   _____ + _____ = _____ yo-yos

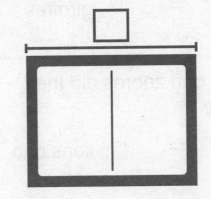

Tens	Ones
+	

2. Curt made some blue paper cranes. He made 17 green cranes. In all, Curt made 62 paper cranes. Which number sentence shows how many cranes he made?

$45 - 17 = 28$
○

$17 + 17 = 34$
○

$45 + 17 = 62$
○

$45 + 45 = 90$
○

3. Tamara needs 45 muffins for her party. She has made 27. How many more muffins does Tamara need to make? Write a number sentence.

_____ − _____ = _____ muffins

Extend Your Thinking Mr. and Mrs. Santos went on an African safari. Use the information in the chart to answer the questions. Write a number sentence.

Number of Animals Seen		
	Day 1	Day 2
Giraffes	15	17
Elephants	9	22
Lions	16	25
Zebras	11	19

4. How many giraffes did Mr. and Mrs. Santos see in all on Day 1 and on Day 2?

_____ + _____ = _____ giraffes

5. How many elephants did they see in all on Day 1 and on Day 2?

_____ + _____ = _____ elephants

6. How many lions and zebras did they see in all on Day 1?

_____ + _____ = _____ lions and zebras

7. How many elephants and zebras did they see in all on Day 2?

_____ + _____ = _____ elephants and zebras

290 two hundred ninety

Topic 6 | Lesson 8

Name _____

Take a closer look at two-digit numbers!
Explain and **show the math** you use to add.

1. Pick a number from the round lens.
   Draw cubes to show it.

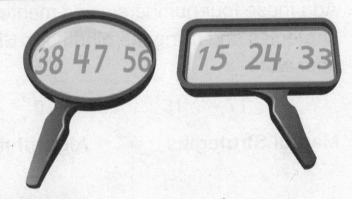

38 47 56   15 24 33

2. Pick a number from the other lens.
   Write it in the workmat.
   Then write the number in expanded form.

Tens	Ones

3. Write an addition sentence with your
   two numbers. Find the sum.

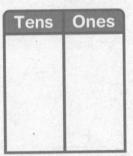

   ___ + ___ = ___

4. Pick any three numbers from the lenses.
   Aim for a sum less than 99. Write the
   numbers below. Then explain how
   you added them.

   ___ + ___ + ___ = ___

   _____

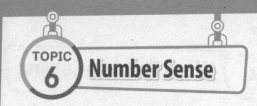
Making Sense

1. Add these four numbers using mental strategies and using the algorithm. Show your work.

| 17 | 15 | 23 | 10 |

Mental Strategies | **Algorithm**

$+$ _____

2. Tell how you used place value and adding in any order in Exercise 1.

What's Wrong?

3. Rowan got this problem wrong. Solve the problem. Explain Rowan's mistake.

$$\begin{array}{r} 3 \\ 37 \\ + 26 \\ \hline 81 \end{array}$$

Complete It!

4. Make addition sentences with numbers from each shape. Then find each sum.

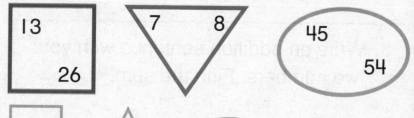

13 26   7   8   45 54

[square] $+$ [triangle] $+$ [oval] $=$ _____

[triangle] $+$ [oval] $+$ [square] $=$ _____

[oval] $+$ [square] $+$ [triangle] $=$ _____

Name _____

Set A

You can show numbers as tens and ones to add.
Find 46 + 8.

> 6 ones + 8 ones = 14 ones
> Regroup 10 ones as 1 ten.
> Now there are 5 tens and 4 ones.
> 5 tens + 4 ones = 54 ones

46 + 8 = **54**

Add. Regroup if you need to.
Use connecting cubes and your workmat.

1. 67 + 6 = _____
Do you need to regroup?

Yes   No

2. 56 + 3 = _____
Do you need to regroup?

Yes   No

Set B

You can regroup to find a sum.
Add the ones. Regroup if you need to. Then add the tens.
Find 34 + 7.

> 4 ones + 7 ones = 11 ones
> So regroup.

Tens	Ones
[1]	
3	4
+	7
4	1

Add. Regroup if you need to.

3.

Tens	Ones
[ ]	
5	1
+	9

4.

Tens	Ones
[ ]	
2	8
+	6

When you add two-digit numbers, line up the tens and the ones.

$45 + 29 = ?$

Now the tens and ones are lined up. I can add.

Tens	Ones
1	
4	5
+ 2	9
7	4

$45 + 29 = \underline{74}$

Write the addition problem. Find the sum.

5. $67 + 26$

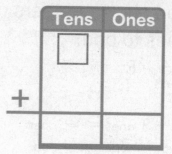

Tens	Ones
☐	
+	

6. $38 + 25$

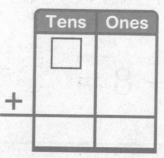

Tens	Ones
☐	
+	

You can show $10 + 13$ on a number line.

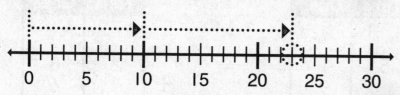

Draw a line to 10. Then draw a line that is 13 more.

$10 + 13 = \underline{23}$

Show this addition problem on the number line.

7. $15 + 9 = \underline{}$

Name _____

1. Miles had 23 comic books, 14 books of fiction, 17 of poetry, and 10 of nonfiction. Use an algorithm to find how many books he has in all.

○ 74

○ 64

○ 54

○ 53

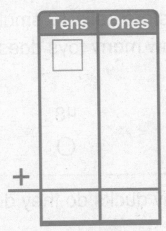

2. Sara read 34 pages in a book on Friday. She read some more pages on Saturday. She read 55 pages in all on both days. How many pages did she read on Saturday?

○ 21

○ 31

○ 34

○ 89

3. Jackson swam 28 laps on Monday, 24 laps on Tuesday, 11 laps on Wednesday, and 14 laps on Thursday. How many laps did he swim in all 4 days? Use mental strategies to solve.

○ 63

○ 67

○ 75

○ 77

4. Jerry spent 34 dollars at the store. Matt spent 15 dollars at the store. How many dollars did both boys spend in all?

○ 59 dollars

○ 55 dollars

○ 54 dollars

○ 49 dollars

5. Jaleel had 23 yo-yos in his collection. His sister gave him 9 more. How many yo-yos does Jaleel have now?

22　　　　30　　　　32　　　　40
○　　　　○　　　　○　　　　○

---

6. Leo drove 66 miles yesterday. He drove 29 miles today. How many miles did he drive on both days?

84　　　85　　　94　　　95
○　　　○　　　○　　　○

7. A store sells 19 small toys and 29 large toys. How many toys does the store sell in all?

39　　　48　　　55　　　58
○　　　○　　　○　　　○

---

8. Zora draws 12 ducks. Liam draws 8 ducks. How many ducks do they draw in all? Show the problem on the number line.

_____ + _____ = _____

0　　5　　10　　15　　20　　25　　30

---

9. Circle the problem you need to regroup. Explain how you know.

$$71 + 8 \qquad 55 + 2 \qquad 34 + 8$$

Subtracting 2-Digit Numbers

Essential Question: What are ways to subtract 2-digit numbers?

Long ago, sailing ships spent months on ocean voyages.

Sailors often brought fresh water with them to drink.

Wow! Let's do this project and learn more.

Math and Science Project: Water

Find Out Ask an adult to peel a potato and then cut it in half. Fill 2 cups with water. Place a half potato in each cup. Mix 3 spoonfuls of salt in one of the cups. Wait one day. Then compare the two potatoes.

Journal: Make a Book Draw pictures to show the results of the potato experiment. In your book, also:

• Describe how you use water every day.

• Make up and solve subtraction problems about the supply of fresh water on a ship.

Name _____

Review What You Know

Vocabulary

1. Circle the **tens digit** in each number.

    $48 + 30 = 78$

2. Circle the **difference** in the subtraction sentence.

    $73 - 20 = 53$

3. Circle the problem in which you need to **regroup** to solve.

    $18 + 4$

    $22 + 7$

Subtraction Strategies

4. Use addition facts to help you subtract.

    $13 - 8 = $ _____

    $8 + $ _____ $ = 13$

Subtracting Tens

5. Use the cubes to subtract.

    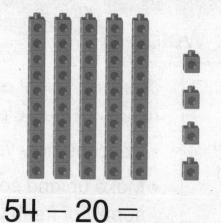

    $54 - 20 = $ _____

6. Use mental math to solve.

    Luke has 78 marbles. He gives 50 marbles to Lily. How many marbles does Luke have now?

    _____ marbles

Name _____

Solve & Share

How can you use tens and ones to solve 23 − 6? Use cubes to help you. Show your work.

⭐ TEKS 2.4B Add up to four two-digit numbers and subtract two-digit numbers using mental strategies and algorithms based on knowledge of place value and properties of operations. Mathematical Process Standards 2.1C, 2.1F, 2.1G.

Digital Resources at SavvasTexas.com

Solve   Learn   Glossary   Check   Tools   Games

_____ − _____ = _____

Find 34 − 6. Show 34. There are not enough ones to subtract 6.

Tens | Ones

You need to regroup.

Regroup 1 ten as 10 ones.

Tens | Ones

Subtract 6.

Tens | Ones

Now there are 2 tens and 8 ones.

34 − 6 = 28

Do You Understand?

Show Me! Do you need to regroup when you subtract 5 from 44? Explain why or why not.

☆ **Guided Practice** ☆ Use your workmat and connecting cubes. Subtract. Regroup if you need to.

Show.	Subtract.	Do you need to regroup?		Find the difference.
1. 35	8	Yes	No	35 − 8 = 27
2. 46	3	Yes	No	46 − 3 = ___
3. 62	4	Yes	No	62 − 4 = ___
4. 50	7	Yes	No	50 − 7 = ___

Name _____

Use your workmat and connecting cubes. Subtract. Regroup if you need to.

	Show.	Subtract.	Do you need to regroup?		Find the difference.
5.	81	2	Yes	No	$81 - 2 =$ _____
6.	29	1	Yes	No	$29 - 1 =$ _____
7.	60	4	Yes	No	$60 - 4 =$ _____
8.	24	9	Yes	No	$24 - 9 =$ _____
9.	75	3	Yes	No	$75 - 3 =$ _____
10.	43	5	Yes	No	$43 - 5 =$ _____

11. **Extend Your Thinking** Which one-digit numbers can you subtract from 74 without first regrouping? Explain how you know.

Think about what each digit stands for in 74.

_____

_____

Solve the problems below.

12. There are 21 snails in a garden.
6 snails leave.
How many snails are still in the garden?

_____ snails

13. Kate has 45 marbles.
She gives 3 marbles to her brother.
How many marbles does Kate have now?

_____ marbles

14. ⭐ Malcolm has 38 seeds.
Juan has 4 fewer seeds than Malcolm.
Juan gives 8 seeds to his friend.
How many seeds does Juan have now?

○ 22

○ 26

○ 36

○ 46

15. Extend Your Thinking Sammie has 9 fewer rings than Emilio.
Sammie has 7 more rings than Sara.
Emilio has 34 rings.
Complete the sentences below.
Draw a picture to help.

Sammie has _____ rings.

Sara has _____ rings.

Name _____

Another Look Use connecting cubes to subtract 7 from 42.

Show 42.

Tens	Ones

Regroup.

Tens	Ones

Subtract 7 ones.

Tens	Ones

 HOME CONNECTION
Your child modeled subtraction with connecting cubes and found the difference between two numbers, with and without regrouping.

HOME ACTIVITY Ask your child to show you how to subtract 26 − 7 using small objects such as buttons, marbles, or paper clips. Have your child explain and show you how to regroup.

12 − 7 = 5 ones

42 − 7 = __35__

Subtract. Use the pictures to help.

1. Subtract 5 from 31.

Show 31.

Tens	Ones

Regroup.

Tens	Ones

Subtract _____ ones.

Tens	Ones

11 − 5 = _____ ones

31 − 5 = _____

2. Algebra What number is missing?

$$42 - \underline{\hspace{1cm}} = 35$$

3. Algebra What number is missing?

$$\underline{\hspace{1cm}} - 5 = 20$$

4. Algebra What number is missing?

$$37 - \underline{\hspace{1cm}} = 28$$

Solve the problems below.

5. Maria buys 36 beads.
She uses 9 of the beads.
How many beads does Maria have left?

_____ beads

6. Luke buys 7 new pencils.
Now he has 21 pencils.
How many pencils did Luke have at first?

_____ pencils

7. An old building has 48 big windows.
The building has 12 small windows.
There are 9 broken windows.
How many windows are **NOT** broken?

○　51

○　48

○　41

○　37

8. **Extend Your Thinking** A flag pole is 30 feet tall. A bug crawls 14 feet up the pole. Then it crawls another 4 feet up the pole. How much farther must the bug crawl to get to the top?

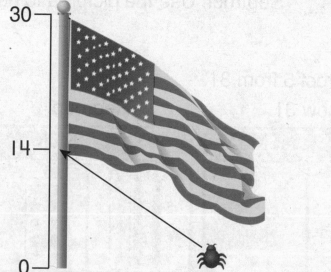

_____ feet

Name _____

☆ **Solve & Share** ☆

There are 22 students drawing pictures.
4 of them finish drawing. How many students are still drawing?
Use cubes to help you solve. Show the tens and ones you have.

⭐ **TEKS 2.4B** Add up to four two-digit numbers and subtract two-digit numbers using mental strategies and algorithms based on knowledge of place value and properties of operations. **Mathematical Process Standards 2.1A, 2.1C, 2.1D.**

Digital Resources at SavvasTexas.com

Solve   Learn   Glossary   Check   Tools   Games

Tens	Ones

_____ tens   _____ ones

22 − 4 = _____

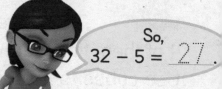

Find 32 − 5.

Tens	Ones
3	2
	5

There are not enough ones to subtract.

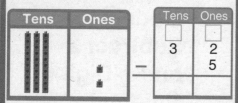

Regroup!

Regroup 1 ten as 10 ones.

Write 2 to show 2 tens. Write 12 to show 12 ones.

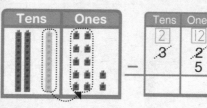

Tens	Ones
2	12
3̶	2̶
	5

Subtract the ones.

Tens	Ones
2	12
3̶	2̶
	5
	7

Then subtract the tens.

So, 32 − 5 = 27.

Tens	Ones
2	12
3̶	2̶
	5
2	7

Do You Understand?

Show Me! Why do you need to regroup when you subtract 32 − 5?

☆ **Guided Practice** ☆ Use connecting cubes and your workmat. Subtract. Regroup if you need to.

1.

Tens	Ones
3̶	1̶4̶
4	4̶
	9
3	5

2.

Tens	Ones
2	3
	5

3.

Tens	Ones
3	8
	0

4.

Tens	Ones
3	5
	8

5.

Tens	Ones
4	2
	2

6.

Tens	Ones
5	0
	9

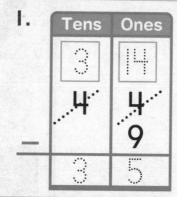
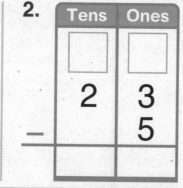
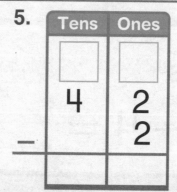

Name _____

Independent Practice

Use connecting cubes and your workmat. Subtract. Regroup if you need to.

7.

Tens	Ones
☐	☐
6	3
−	2

8.

Tens	Ones
☐	☐
9	1
−	7

9.

Tens	Ones
☐	☐
6	6
−	9

10.

Tens	Ones
☐	☐
5	7
−	5

11.

Tens	Ones
☐	☐
6	5
−	6

12.

Tens	Ones
☐	☐
3	2
−	4

13.

Tens	Ones
☐	☐
8	0
−	1

14.

Tens	Ones
☐	☐
7	4
−	5

15.

Tens	Ones
☐	☐
9	4
−	8

16.

Tens	Ones
☐	☐
2	4
−	5

Draw a picture to solve. Write the missing number in the box.

17. Extend Your Thinking What numbers will complete the subtraction sentences?

$\boxed{} - 8 = 17$ $34 - \boxed{} = 29$

18. There are 23 students playing tag. 9 students go home. How many students are still playing tag?

Tens	Ones
☐	☐
−	

_____ students

19. There are 67 books on the shelf. Dion takes 5 of them. How many books are left on the shelf?

Tens	Ones
☐	☐
−	

_____ books

20. ⭐ Maria collected 41 leaves. She put some of them in a book. She had 8 leaves left. How many leaves did she put in the book?

33 ○   34 ○

43 ○   49 ○

21. **Extend Your Thinking** What mistake did Alia make when she subtracted 72 − 4? Show how to fix her mistake.

$$\begin{array}{r} 72 \\ -\ \ 4 \\ \hline 72 \end{array}$$

Tens	Ones
☐	☐
−	

_____

_____

_____

Another Look Regroup when there are not enough ones. Subtract 52 − 8.

Step 1
Think: There are not enough ones to subtract 8.

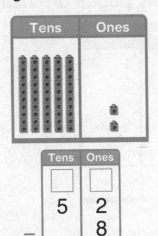

Tens	Ones
5	2
−	8

Step 2
Regroup 1 ten as 10 ones.

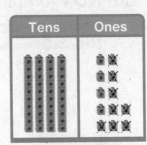

Tens	Ones
4	12
5̸	2̸
−	8

Step 3
Subtract the ones. Then subtract the tens.

Tens	Ones
4	12
5̸	2̸
−	8
4	4

So, 52 − 8 = 44.

🏠 **HOME CONNECTION**
Your child used connecting cubes to model subtracting a one-digit number from a two-digit number, with and without regrouping. Then your child recorded the subtraction.

HOME ACTIVITY Write 22 − 6 in vertical form on a piece of paper. Ask your child to show you how to subtract 22 − 6 using small objects such as paper clips, buttons, or marbles. Have your child write the difference.

 Subtract. Decide if you need to regroup.

1.
Tens	Ones
1	16
2̸	6̸
−	7
1	9

2.
Tens	Ones
4	3
−	9

3.
Tens	Ones
6	9
−	3

4.
Tens	Ones
3	5
−	8

5.
Tens	Ones
7	6
−	7

Solve each problem.

6. Josh reads for 55 minutes. Steve reads for 5 fewer minutes than Josh. How many minutes does Steve read?

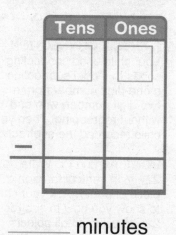

_____ minutes

7. There are 40 students in the gym. 9 students are jumping rope. How many students are **NOT** jumping rope?

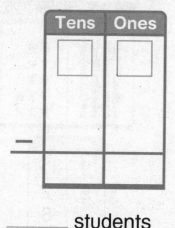

_____ students

8. Kate writes on 7 pages in her notebook. There are 34 pages in her notebook. How many pages are blank?

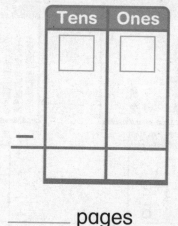

_____ pages

9. Juan needs 28 balloons. He has 6 balloons. How many more balloons does he need?

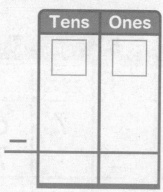

_____ balloons

10. A bakery makes 44 muffins. They sell some muffins. Now they have 9 muffins. How many muffins did the bakery sell?

○ 53

○ 48

○ 35

○ 34

11. **Extend Your Thinking** Write a subtraction story about 45 − 8. Then solve.

_____

_____

_____

_____

_____

Solve & Share

Ari has 31 stickers.
He puts 8 of his stickers in a scrapbook.
How many stickers does Ari have now?
Subtract using only paper and pencil.
Explain.

TEKS 2.4B Add up to four two-digit numbers and subtract two-digit numbers using mental strategies and algorithms based on knowledge of place value and properties of operations. **Mathematical Process Standards 2.1B, 2.1C, 2.1D, 2.1F.**

Digital Resources at SavvasTexas.com

| Solve | Learn | Glossary | Check | Tools | Games |

Tens	Ones
—	

_____

_____

_____

_____

_____

_____

You can use paper and pencil to subtract 9 from 42.	Look at the ones. There are not enough ones to subtract.	Subtract the ones.	Then subtract the tens.

Regroup!

Tens	Ones
☐	☐
4	2
	9

Tens	Ones
3	12
4̸	2̸
	9

Tens	Ones
3	12
4̸	2̸
	9
	3

Tens	Ones
3	12
4̸	2̸
	9
3	3

Do You Understand?

Show Me! Look at 42 − 9 in the boxes above. Why is 12 written above the 2 in the ones column?

☆ **Guided Practice** ☆ Subtract. Regroup if you need to.

1.

Tens	Ones
2	16
3̸	6̸
	8
2	8

2.

Tens	Ones
☐	☐
2	9
	4

3.

Tens	Ones
☐	☐
4	1
	4

4.

Tens	Ones
☐	☐
6	3
	5

5.

Tens	Ones
☐	☐
5	0
	1

6.

Tens	Ones
☐	☐
4	8
	7

Name _____

☆ Independent ☆ Practice

Subtract. Regroup if you need to.

7.

Tens	Ones
☐	☐
3	2
	6

8.

Tens	Ones
☐	☐
2	0
	3

9.

Tens	Ones
☐	☐
6	7
	6

10.

Tens	Ones
☐	☐
5	2
	4

11.

Tens	Ones
☐	☐
3	5
	0

12.

Tens	Ones
☐	☐
7	5
	3

13.

Tens	Ones
☐	☐
5	6
	7

14.

Tens	Ones
☐	☐
8	5
	5

15.

Tens	Ones
☐	☐
9	8
	9

16.

Tens	Ones
☐	☐
7	7
	9

Use words or a picture to solve.

17. Extend Your Thinking What is the missing number? Explain how to solve.

$$45 - 9 = 46 - \boxed{}$$

Problem Solving Solve the problems below.

18. There are 25 bikes at the store. The store owner sells 7 bikes. How many bikes are left?

Tens	Ones

_____ bikes

19. The bike store has 32 helmets. There are 9 red helmets. The rest are blue. How many blue helmets does the bike store have?

Tens	Ones

_____ blue helmets

---

20. ⭐ The store had 46 bike tires and 26 bike pumps. 7 of the tires and 2 of the bike pumps were sold. How many tires and pumps remain?

- ○ 55
- ○ 63
- ○ 72
- ○ 73

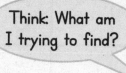
Think: What am I trying to find?

21. Extend Your Thinking A bike store sold 10 fewer locks on Wednesday than on Tuesday. How many more locks did the shop sell on Wednesday than on Monday?

Lock Sales	
Day	Number of Locks
Monday	9
Tuesday	33
Wednesday	

Tens	Ones

_____ locks

Name _____

Another Look Remember the steps for subtracting.

Subtract the ones first.

Think: Are there enough ones to subtract?

Subtract the tens next. Regroup if you need to.

There are enough ones to subtract.

Tens	Ones
2	7
	3
2	4

Regroup? Yes (No)

There are **NOT** enough ones to subtract.

Tens	Ones
3	12
4̸	2̸
	6
3	6

Regroup? (Yes) No

🏠 **HOME CONNECTION**
Your child used pencil and paper to subtract one-digit numbers from two-digit numbers, with and without regrouping.

HOME ACTIVITY Write 34 − 9 in vertical form on a sheet of paper. Have your child use pencil and paper to solve.

Remember the steps for subtracting.
Subtract. Regroup if you need to.

1.

Tens	Ones
2	5
−	4

2.

Tens	Ones
4	1
−	8

3.

Tens	Ones
6	5
−	7

4.

Tens	Ones
7	8
−	9

5.

Tens	Ones
8	3
−	6

Solve the problems. Regroup if you need to.

6. Aki had 48 marbles yesterday. Then he lost some marbles. Today he has 8 marbles. How many marbles did Aki lose?

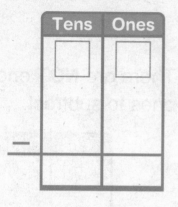

_____ marbles

7. Mandy has 32 stickers. There are 7 frog stickers. The rest are butterfly stickers. How many butterfly stickers does Mandy have?

Tens	Ones
☐	☐

_____ butterfly stickers

8. There are 53 grapes on the plate. Andrea eats 5 of them. How many grapes are on the plate now?

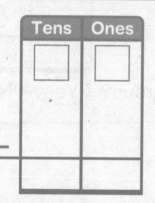

_____ grapes

9. Chato read 7 pages. There are 67 pages in the book. How many more pages does Chato have left to read?

Tens	Ones
☐	☐

_____ pages

10. Katara takes 7 more kites to the park than Luke. Katara takes 21 kites. How many kites does Luke take to the park?

○ 8

○ 11

○ 14

○ 30

11. Extend Your Thinking Complete the subtraction frame.

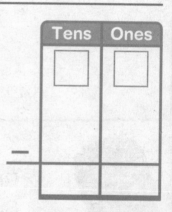

Name _____

Solve & Share

You have 42 pipe cleaners.
You use 19 of the pipe cleaners.
How many pipe cleaners do you have now?
Use cubes to help you solve.
Draw your cubes. Tell if you need to regroup.

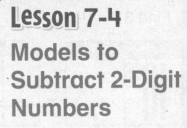

⊕ **TEKS 2.4B** Add up to four two-digit numbers and subtract two-digit numbers using mental strategies and algorithms based on knowledge of place value and properties of operations. **Mathematical Process Standards 2.1C, 2.1G.**

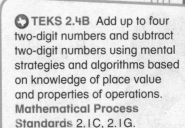

Digital Resources at SavvasTexas.com

Solve	Learn	Glossary	Check	Tools	Games

Tens	Ones
−	

Regroup?

Yes   No

Find 31 − 14.

There are not enough ones to subtract.

Regroup!

Regroup 1 ten as 10 ones.

Write 2 to show 2 tens.
Write 11 to show 11 ones.

Subtract the ones.

Subtract the tens.

So,
31 − 14 = __17__.

Do You Understand?

Show Me! Explain why you need to regroup to solve 65 − 17.

☆ **Guided Practice** ☆ Subtract. Use connecting cubes and your workmat. Regroup if you need to.

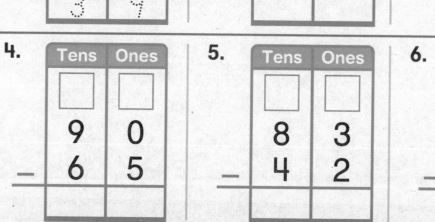

1.

Tens	Ones
4	12
5	2
− 1	3
3	9

2.

Tens	Ones
6	8
− 3	7

3.

Tens	Ones
4	1
− 2	6

4.

Tens	Ones
9	0
− 6	5

5.

Tens	Ones
8	3
− 4	2

6.

Tens	Ones
3	5
− 1	9

318 three hundred eighteen

Topic 7 | Lesson 4

Name _____

Subtract. Use connecting cubes and your workmat. Regroup if you need to.

7.

Tens	Ones
5	6
− 3	1

8.

Tens	Ones
7	2
− 2	7

9.

Tens	Ones
6	6
− 5	8

10.

Tens	Ones
2	3
− 1	7

11.

Tens	Ones
5	4
− 2	4

12.

Tens	Ones
4	8
− 2	5

13.

Tens	Ones
9	0
− 5	5

14.

Tens	Ones
8	5
− 7	6

15.

Tens	Ones
2	9
− 1	3

16.

Tens	Ones
5	7
− 3	8

17. Extend Your Thinking

Do the models show the same value? Explain.

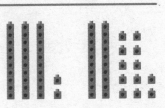

_____

_____

_____

18. Anita has $63. She spends $24 and saves the rest. How much does Anita save?

$ _____

Tens	Ones
☐	☐
−	

19. Esteban picked 68 blueberries. He ate 23 of the blueberries. How many blueberries does Esteban have now?

_____ blueberries

Tens	Ones
☐	☐
− 6	8
2	3

20. Sara has 70 beads. There are 11 beads that are NOT round. The rest are round. How many round beads does Sara have?

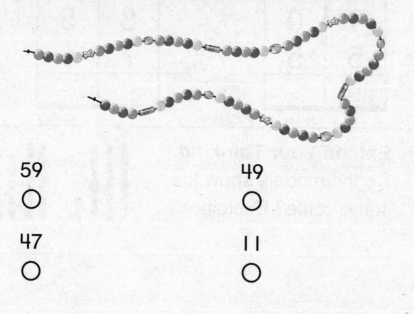

59 ○   49 ○

47 ○   11 ○

21. Extend Your Thinking Write a subtraction story about 36 − 17. Explain how to solve.

_____

_____

_____

_____

_____

_____

Name _____

Another Look Subtract 16 from 43.

Step 1

Think: There are not enough ones to subtract 6.

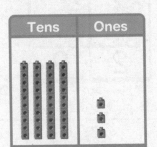

Tens	Ones
4	3

– 1 6

Step 2

Regroup 1 ten as 10 ones.

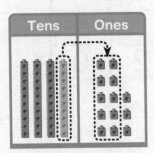

Tens	Ones
3	13
4̷	3̷

– 1 6

Step 3

Subtract the ones. Then subtract the tens.

Tens	Ones
3	13
4̷	3̷
– 1	6
2	7

So, 43 – 16 = _27_.

🏠 **HOME CONNECTION**
Your child used models to subtract two-digit numbers from two-digit numbers.

HOME ACTIVITY Ask your child to use paperclips or other small objects to find 25 – 16. Have your child explain how he or she regrouped.

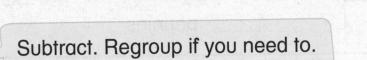

Subtract. Regroup if you need to.

1.

Tens	Ones
3	7
– 1	5

2.

Tens	Ones
5	0
– 1	3

3.

Tens	Ones
7	6
– 2	8

4.

Tens	Ones
4	5
– 2	7

Fill in the missing numbers to make the subtraction problem true.

5.

Tens	Ones
□ 7 ○	□ ○ 4
4	2

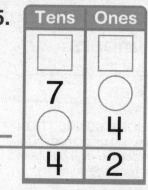

6.

Tens	Ones
□ ○ 2	□ 7 ○
3	5

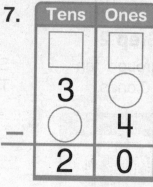

7.

Tens	Ones
□ 3 ○	□ ○ 4
2	0

8.

Tens	Ones
□ 4̷ ○	17 7̷ ○
2	9

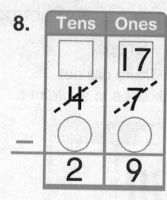

Solve. Show your work.

9. Jamal has 54 marbles. Lucas has 70 marbles. How many more marbles does Lucas have than Jamal?

Tens	Ones
□	□

_____ more marbles

10. Latoya had 95 pennies. She gave 62 pennies to her cousin. How many pennies does Latoya have now?

Tens	Ones
□	□

_____ pennies

11. To solve 36 − 17, how should the 36 be regrouped?

○ 2 tens and 6 ones

○ 2 tens and 16 ones

○ 3 tens and 16 ones

○ 4 tens and 16 ones

12. Extend Your Thinking

Fill in the missing numbers to make the subtraction problem true.

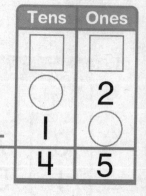

Tens	Ones
□ ○ 1	□ 2 ○
4	5

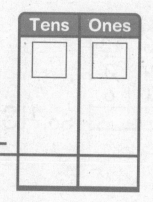

Name _____

Solve & Share

How is subtracting 23 from 71 like subtracting 3 from 71?
How is it different from subtracting 3 from 71? Explain.
Solve each problem using only paper and pencil.

TEKS 2.4B Add up to four two-digit numbers and subtract two-digit numbers using mental strategies and algorithms based on knowledge of place value and properties of operations. **Mathematical Process Standards** 2.1C, 2.1D, 2.1F, 2.1G.

Digital Resources at SavvasTexas.com

Solve   Learn   Glossary   Check   Tools   Games

Tens	Ones
7	1
−	3

Tens	Ones
−	

Digital Resources at SavvasTexas.com

Find 43 − 18.

A-Z

You can use paper and pencil to subtract.

You can use a frame to help you subtract 43 − 18.

Tens	Ones
4	3
−	

Write the ones in the ones column.

Write the tens in the tens column.

Tens	Ones
4	3
− 1	8

Subtract. Regroup if you need to.

$43 − 18 = \underline{25}$

Tens	Ones
3	13
4	8
− 1	8
2	5

Do You Understand?

Show Me! Do you need to regroup when you subtract 72 − 30? Explain.

☆ **Guided Practice** ☆ Write the subtraction problem. Find the difference.

1. 34 − 15

Tens	Ones
2	14
3	4
− 1	5
1	9

2. 52 − 31

Tens	Ones
−	

3. 67 − 48

Tens	Ones
−	

Sometimes you need to regroup. Sometimes you don't.

324 three hundred twenty-four

Name _____

Independent Practice

Write the subtraction problem. Find the difference.

4. 52 − 36

Tens	Ones
☐	☐

−

5. 94 − 54

Tens	Ones
☐	☐

−

6. 41 − 25

Tens	Ones
☐	☐

−

7. 33 − 28

Tens	Ones
☐	☐

−

8. 65 − 42

Tens	Ones
☐	☐

−

9. 70 − 48

Tens	Ones
☐	☐

−

10. 96 − 37

Tens	Ones
☐	☐

−

11. 87 − 45

Tens	Ones
☐	☐

−

Draw a model to help solve.

12. Extend Your Thinking Tia's basketball team scored
61 points. They won by 23 points. How many points
did the other team score?

_____ − _____ = _____ points

13. Don has 72 marbles. Josie has 56 marbles. How many more marbles does Don have than Josie?

Tens	Ones

_____ more marbles

$-$

14. Don has 72 marbles. Tariq has 98 marbles. How many more marbles does Tariq have than Don?

Tens	Ones

_____ more marbles

$-$

15. Eric can fit 90 cards in a scrapbook. He already put 46 cards into the scrapbook. How many more cards will fit?

44 ○

45 ○

46 ○

54 ○

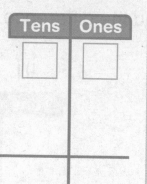

16. Extend Your Thinking Write a subtraction story using two two-digit numbers. Then solve the problem in your story.

_____

_____

_____

Tens	Ones

$-$

_____

_____

Name _____

Another Look Remember the steps for subtracting.

Step 1
Think: Are there enough ones to subtract?

Step 2
Regroup if you need to.

Step 3
Subtract the ones.
Subtract the tens.

Write the problems in the frames. Find the difference.

38 − 13

Tens	Ones
3	8
− 1	3
2	5

54 − 17

Tens	Ones
4	14
5̶	4̶
− 1	7
3	7

Be sure to cross out if you regroup.

🏠 **HOME CONNECTION**
Your child used paper and pencil to subtract a two-digit number from another two-digit number, with and without regrouping.

HOME ACTIVITY Have your child use paper and pencil to solve 65 − 37. Have your child explain the steps he or she takes to subtract.

Write each problem in a frame.
Find the difference.

1. 37 − 14

Tens	Ones
−	

2. 64 − 18

Tens	Ones
−	

3. 45 − 26

Tens	Ones
−	

4. 73 − 25

Tens	Ones
−	

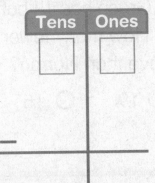

Decide what each child will buy.
Subtract to find how much money is left.

36¢

14¢

23¢

42¢

58¢

65¢

5. Bonnie has 47¢.
She buys the _____ .

Bonnie has _____ ¢ left.

Tens	Ones

__ — __

6. Ricky has 59¢.
He buys the _____ .

Ricky has _____ ¢ left.

Tens	Ones

__ — __

7. Lani has 63 grapes. She gives 36 grapes to Carla. How many grapes does Lani have left?

_____ grapes

Tens	Ones

__ — __

8. Write a number to make this a subtraction problem with regrouping. Then find the difference.

Tens	Ones

__ — 2 3

9. Norma has 48 buttons. Grace has 14 buttons. Connie has 29 buttons. How many fewer buttons does Connie have than Norma?

○ 34   ○ 29   ○ 19   ○ 15

10. **Extend Your Thinking** Use each number only once. Write the subtraction problem that has the greatest difference. Then solve.

1   2   4   5

Tens	Ones

__ — __

Name _____

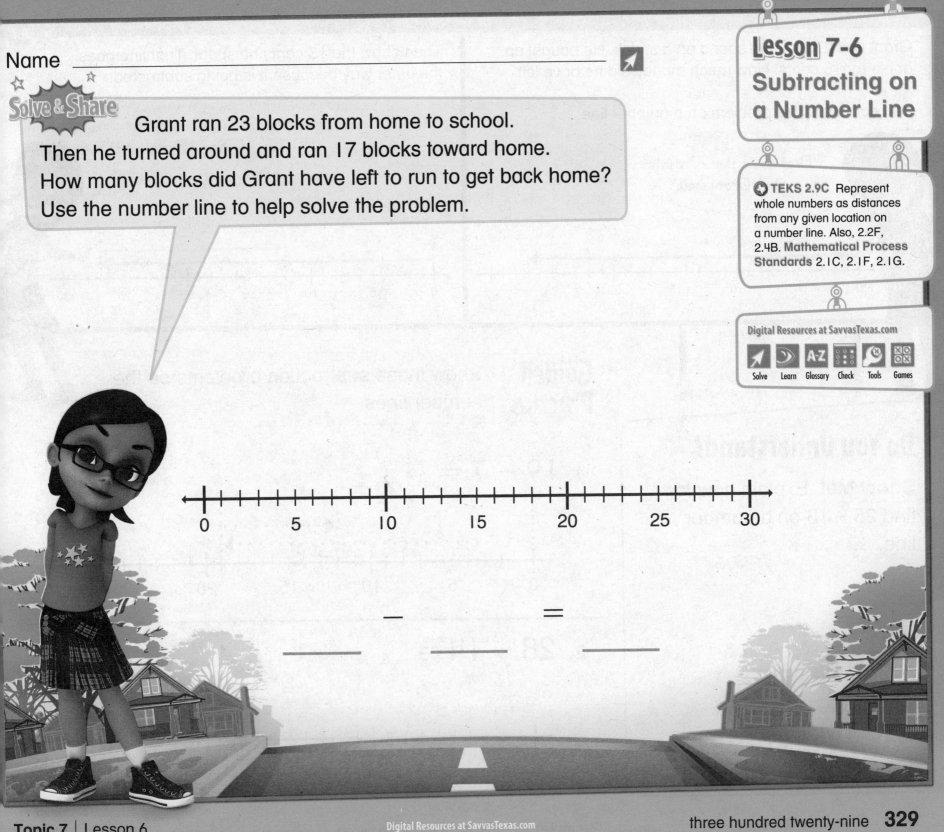

☆ Solve & Share

Grant ran 23 blocks from home to school.
Then he turned around and ran 17 blocks toward home.
How many blocks did Grant have left to run to get back home?
Use the number line to help solve the problem.

⊙ **TEKS 2.9C** Represent
whole numbers as distances
from any given location on
a number line. Also, **2.2F**,
**2.4B. Mathematical Process
Standards** 2.1C, 2.1F, 2.1G.

Digital Resources at SavvasTexas.com

Solve   Learn   Glossary   Check   Tools   Games

___ − ___ = ___

_____   _____   _____

Grant had 27 cents to spend on a snack. He bought an apple for 15 cents. How much money did he have left?

You can show this problem on a number line.

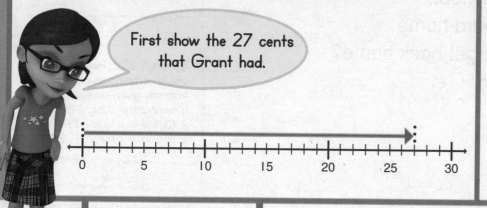

First show the 27 cents that Grant had.

Then show the 15 cents he spent. That line goes the other way because it is being subtracted.

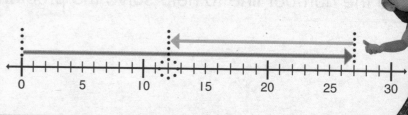

He has 12 cents left.

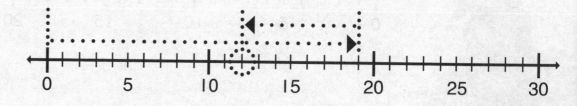

Do You Understand?

Show Me! Explain how to find 25 − 13 on a number line.

☆ Guided Practice ☆

Show these subtraction problems on the number lines.

1. $19 - 7 =$ _12_

2. $28 - 14 =$ _____

Name _____

Independent Practice

Show these subtraction problems on the number lines.

3. $26 - 5 =$ _____

4. $18 - 12 =$ _____

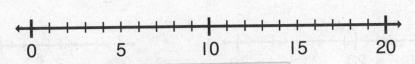

What subtraction problems do these number lines show?

5. _____ − _____ = _____

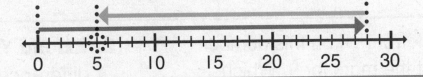

6. _____ − _____ = _____

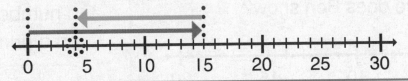

7. _____ − _____ = _____

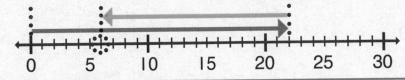

Draw a number line to solve.
Use words to explain.

8. Extend Your Thinking How do you show
$12 - 0$ on a number line?

9. All 29 students in Grant's class went to the school fair. 16 of the students are girls. How many students in the class are boys? Show your work on the number line.

_____ boys

10. Laila scored 26 points in a basketball game. Sondra scored 18 points in the game. How many more points did Laila score than Sondra? Show your work on the number line.

_____ more points

11. Ben counts back from 14 on this number line. He stops at the mark for 4. Which number sentence does Ben show?

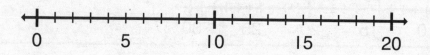

○ $14 - 4 = 10$

○ $14 - 5 = 9$

○ $14 - 10 = 4$

○ $14 + 4 = 18$

12. Extend Your Thinking Describe the difference between showing addition on a number line and showing subtraction on a number line.

_____

_____

_____

_____

Name _____

Another Look

Show $19 - 13 = 6$ on a number line. First find 19 on the number line.

Move 19 spaces to the right from zero.

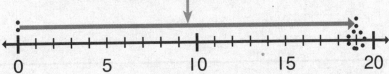

To subtract 13, count back 13 spaces on the number line.

Move 13 spaces to the left from 13.

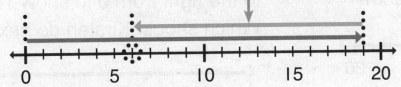

When you count back 13, you get to 6.
$19 - 13 = 6$

🏠 HOME CONNECTION
Your child used a number line
to subtract two-digit numbers.

HOME ACTIVITY Create a
number line at home and use
it to count the number of steps
from one room or place to the
next. Then count the number
of steps to a different room
or place and ask your child to
subtract that from the original
number using the number line.

Show these subtraction problems
on the number lines.

1. $16 - 12 = 4$

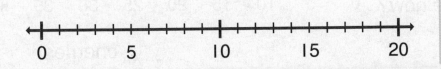

2. $17 - 6 = 11$

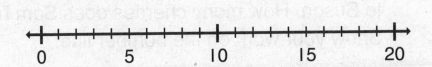

Draw the number lines to show the subtraction problems.

3. $15 - 12 =$ _____

4. $19 - 13 =$ _____

5. Jan counts back 5 spaces on this number line. She stops at the mark for 10.
Which number sentence does Jan show?

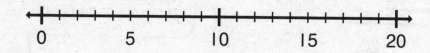

○ $10 + 5 = 15$

○ $15 + 10 = 25$

○ $10 - 5 = 5$

○ $15 - 5 = 10$

6. Kirsten wants to show $18 - 7$ on the number line. First, she moves 18 spaces to the right from 0 to show 18.
Which should Kirsten do next?

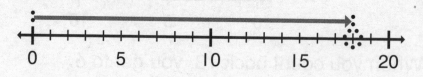

○ Move 7 spaces to the left from 18.

○ Move 7 spaces to the right from 18.

○ Move 11 spaces to the right from 18.

○ Move 18 spaces to the left from 18.

7. **Extend Your Thinking** Sam had 38 cherries. He gave 16 cherries to Lars. Then he gave 17 cherries to Susan. How many cherries does Sam have now? Show your work on the number line.

_____ cherries

Topic 7 | Lesson 6

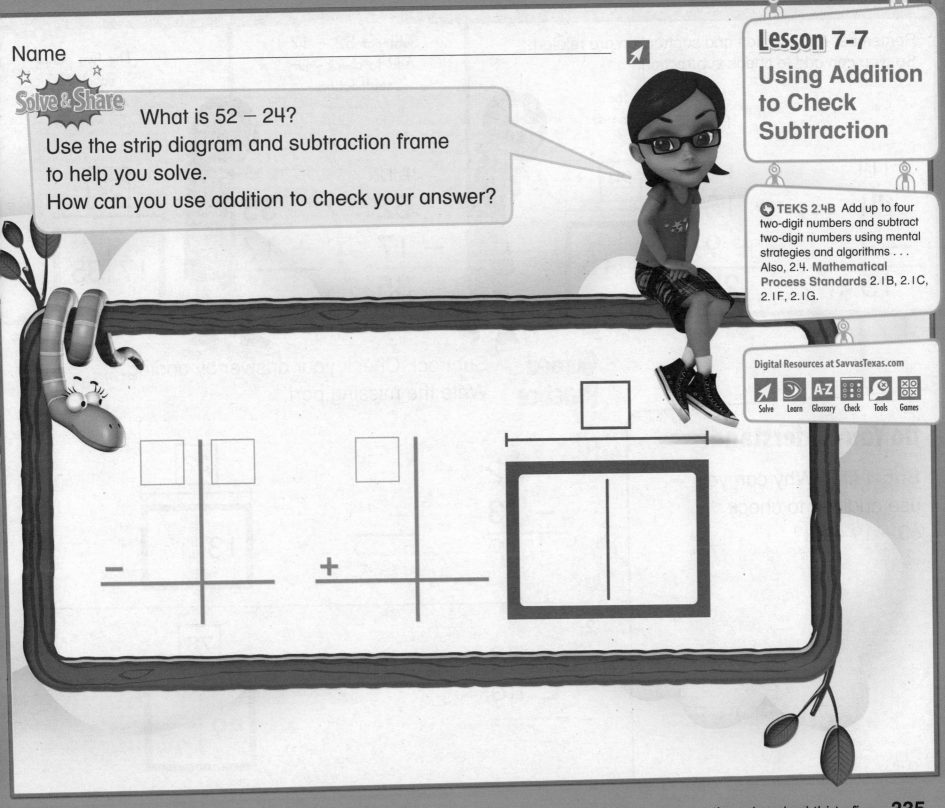

☆ Solve & Share

What is 52 − 24?
Use the strip diagram and subtraction frame
to help you solve.
How can you use addition to check your answer?

⊕ **TEKS 2.4B** Add up to four
two-digit numbers and subtract
two-digit numbers using mental
strategies and algorithms . . .
Also, 2.4. **Mathematical
Process Standards** 2.1B, 2.1C,
2.1F, 2.1G.

Digital Resources at SavvasTexas.com

Solve   Learn   Glossary   Check   Tools   Games

−

+

Remember that addition and subtraction are related. So, you can add to check subtraction.

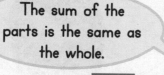

The sum of the parts is the same as the whole.

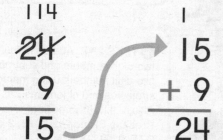

```
  114
  2̶4̶
-  9
―――
  15
```

```
   1
  15
+  9
―――
  24
```

24	
9	15

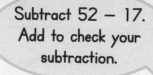

Subtract 52 – 17. Add to check your subtraction.

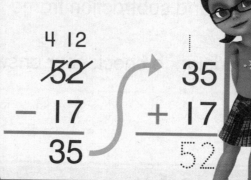

```
  4 12
  5̶2̶
- 17
―――
  35
```

```
   1
  35
+ 17
―――
  52
```

The two parts equal the whole again!

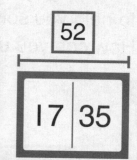

52	
17	35

Do You Understand?

Show Me! Why can you use addition to check 63 – 19 = 44?

Guided Practice

Subtract. Check your answer by adding. Write the missing part.

1.
```
  2 12
  3̶2̶
- 13
―――
  19
```

```
  19
+ 13
―――
  32
```

32	
13	19

2.
```
  78
- 49
```

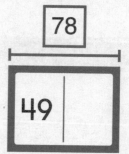

78	
49	

Topic 7 | Lesson 7

☆ Independent ☆ Practice

Subtract. Check your answer by adding. Write the missing part.

3.

$$\begin{array}{r} 52 \\ - 27 \\ \hline \end{array}$$

52
27	

4.

$$\begin{array}{r} 80 \\ - 14 \\ \hline \end{array}$$

80
14	

5.

$$\begin{array}{r} 54 \\ - 19 \\ \hline \end{array}$$

54
19	

6.

$$\begin{array}{r} 75 \\ - 62 \\ \hline \end{array}$$

75
62	

7.

$$\begin{array}{r} 83 \\ - 29 \\ \hline \end{array}$$

83
29	

8.

$$\begin{array}{r} 48 \\ - 21 \\ \hline \end{array}$$

48
21	

9. Extend Your Thinking Maria used $35 + 24$ to check her answer to a subtraction problem. Show two subtraction problems Maria could have solved.

Subtract. Check your answer by adding.

10. 62 students paint pictures. 48 students use red paint. The rest use blue paint. How many students use blue paint?

_____ ‒ _____

_____ students

11. 37 students make clay pots. 16 students use brown clay. The rest use green clay. How many students use green clay?

_____ ‒ _____

_____ students

12. Bill has 17 more craft sticks than Roger. Bill has 45 craft sticks. How many craft sticks does Roger have?

38 ○   32 ○

28 ○   22 ○

Think about how you can check your answer.

13. Extend Your Thinking Write a subtraction story about 65 − 41. Solve the story. Check your answer by adding.

_____

_____

_____

_____

_____

Another Look

When you subtract, you start with the whole. Then you take part away. The other part is left.

$$37 \quad \text{Whole}$$
$$-12 \quad \text{Part}$$
$$\overline{25} \quad \text{Part}$$

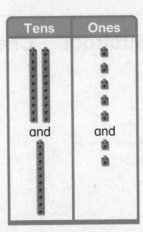

To check your work, add to put the parts back together. Your answer should be the whole.

$$25 \quad \text{Part}$$
$$+12 \quad \text{Part}$$
$$\overline{37} \quad \text{Whole}$$

🏠 **HOME CONNECTION**
Your child learned how to check subtraction problems by using addition.

HOME ACTIVITY Ask your child to solve 65 − 32. Then have him or her use addition to show you how to check the subtraction.

Subtract. Check your answer by adding.

1.
$$86$$
$$-9$$

2.
$$54$$
$$-19$$

3.
$$63$$
$$-37$$

Subtract. Check your answers by adding.

4. Mei Ling had 71 marbles. She lost 25. How many marbles does Mei Ling have left?

Subtract	Check
−	

_____ marbles

5. Eric had 62 crayons. He gave 33 to Mandy. How many crayons does Eric have left?

Subtract	Check
−	

_____ crayons

6. Denise had 51 beads. She used 32 beads for a bracelet. How many beads were **NOT** used?

Subtract	Check
−	

_____ beads

7. Raul had 99 craft sticks. He used 49. How many craft sticks were **NOT** used?

Subtract	Check
−	

_____ craft sticks

8. Lana had 39 moon stickers and 52 star stickers. She subtracted to find how many more star stickers than moon stickers she had. Which addition sentence could Lana use to check her answer?

13 + 26 = 39
○

13 + 39 = 52
○

39 + 52 = 91
○

52 + 13 = 65
○

9. Extend Your Thinking Write the number that makes each number sentence true.

63 − 20 = 20 + _____

58 − 40 = 18 + _____

75 − 30 = 15 + _____

89 − 46 = 30 + _____

In a number sentence, each side of the equal sign shows the same value.

Name _____

☆ Solve & Share

Draw a picture to show 18 + 14.
Then write a math story for your picture and solve.

⭐ **TEKS 2.1G** Display, explain, and justify mathematical ideas . . . using precise mathematical language. . . .
TEKS 2.4D Generate and solve problem situations . . . involving addition and subtraction. . . . **Mathematical Process Standards** 2.1B, 2.1E, 2.1F.

Digital Resources at SavvasTexas.com

Solve   Learn   Glossary   Check   Tools   Games

Analyze

Write a math story for 68 − 33.

You can start by drawing a strip diagram.

68

| 33 | ? |

Plan

Write a story about your diagram.

Harry found 68 acorns.
He gave 33 acorns to Joyce.
How many acorns did Harry have left?

Solve, Justify, and Evaluate

Solve your story.

$$
\begin{array}{r}
68 \text{ acorns} \\
- 33 \text{ acorns} \\
\hline
35 \text{ acorns}
\end{array}
$$

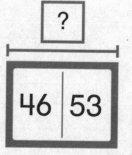

Harry had 35 acorns left.

Do You Understand?

Show Me! How does a strip diagram help you write a subtraction story?

☆ Guided Practice ☆

Write a math story for the number sentence. Then solve.

1. 47 − 18 = _____

47

| 18 | ? |

Greg picked 47 pears.

He gave 18 pears to Ana.

How many pears does

Greg have left?

2. 46 + 53 = _____

?

| 46 | 53 |

_____

_____

_____

☆ Independent ☆ Practice

Write a math story for the number sentence. Then solve.

3. 22 − 17 = _____

22

17 | ?

_____
_____

4. 84 − 62 = _____

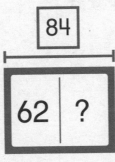

84

62 | ?

_____
_____
_____

5. 39 + 47 = _____

?

39 | 47

_____
_____

6. **Extend Your Thinking** Use the picture to write a comparing story. Then solve.

_____
_____
_____

_____ − _____ = _____

Problem Solving   Solve the problems below.

7. Write a story about the picture and solve the number sentence.

_____

_____

_____

_____

$16 + 24 =$ _____

8. José drew this picture to show $44 - 23$.

Write a story about the picture and solve the number sentence.

Tens	Ones

_____

_____

_____

_____

$44 - 23 =$ _____

9. Which number sentence matches the story below?

There are 25 birds in a tree. 7 birds fly away. How many birds are in the tree now?

$18 - 7 = 11$ ○ $25 + 7 = 32$ ○

$25 - 7 = 18$ ○ $25 + 32 = 57$ ○

10. **Extend Your Thinking** Write a math story for the number sentence and solve.

_____

_____

_____

_____

$75 +$ _____ $= 98$

Name _____

Another Look You can draw a picture and write a story to show 22 − 15.

Draw 22 red buttons in one box.
Draw 15 blue buttons in the other box.
Complete the story.

There are _22_ red buttons.

There are _15_ blue buttons.

How many more red buttons are there than
blue buttons? 22 − 15 = _7_

⌂ **HOME CONNECTION**
Your child drew pictures and
wrote math stories for addition
and subtraction sentences.

HOME ACTIVITY Ask your
child to draw a picture to show
41 − 28 = ?. Then have your
child use the picture to write
a subtraction story.

Finish the picture and the story for each number sentence. Then solve.

1. **31 − 8 =** _____

    [ ]   [ ]
    Kai   Pat

    There are _____ in Kai's crate.

    There are _____ in Pat's crate.

    How many more _____ are
    in Kai's crate than Pat's crate?

2. **23 + 37 =** _____

    [ ]   [ ]
    Jen   Bob

    There are _____ in Jen's jar.

    There are _____ in Bob's jar.

    How many _____ are there in all?

Dan, Pilar, and Max each bought some stickers. Use the pictures to write a story for each problem. Then solve.

Dan

Pilar

Max

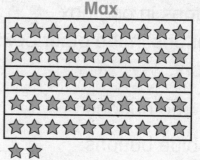

3. $36 + 18 =$ _____

_____

_____

_____

4. $52 - 18 =$ _____

_____

_____

_____

5. Which math story matches $40 - 14 = ?$

○ Kim has 40 dimes. Ted has 14 dimes. How many dimes do they have in all?

○ Al and Zoe have 54 pens in all. Al has 40 pens. How many pens does Zoe have?

○ There were 40 bees. 14 bees flew away. How many bees are left?

○ A box has 40 pencils. Mai added 14 pencils. How many pencils are there in all?

6. **Extend Your Thinking** Write a story for $43 -$ ___ $= 27$.

_____

_____

_____

_____

$43 -$ ___ $= 27$

Name _____

Solve & Share

You have 26 library books.
You return 14 books. Then you take out 15 more books.
How many books do you have now?
What number sentences can you write to solve this problem?

⭐ **TEKS 2.1A** Apply mathematics to problems arising in everyday life, society, and the workplace. **TEKS 2.4C** Solve one-step and multi-step word problems involving addition and subtraction. . . . **Mathematical Process Standards** 2.1B, 2.1F.

Digital Resources at SavvasTexas.com

Solve   Learn   Glossary   Check   Tools   Games

Analyze

Mia sees 15 yellow birds and 16 red birds.
Then 17 birds fly away.
How many birds are left?

Plan

I need to solve the first step in order to solve the second step.

Solve, Justify, and Evaluate

Mia sees __31__ birds in all.
There are __14__ birds left after 17 fly away.

I solved both steps. My answers make sense.

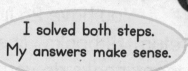

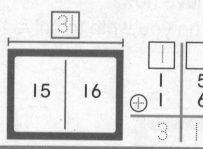

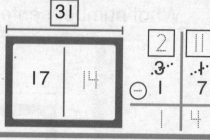

Do You Understand?

Show Me! Why do you need two steps to solve the problem above?

☆ Guided Practice ☆

Use the answer from the first step to solve the second step.

1. Alex bought 16 green peppers. He bought 11 red peppers. Alex uses 14 of the peppers. How many peppers are left?

$$16 \bigoplus 11 = 27$$
peppers in all

$$27 \bigodot 14 = 13$$
peppers left

2. Abby picks 15 red flowers. She picks 13 pink flowers. Then she picks 12 more flowers. How many flowers does Abby have now?

$$\underline{\quad} \bigcirc \underline{\quad} = \underline{\quad}$$
flowers in all

$$\underline{\quad} \bigcirc \underline{\quad} = \underline{\quad}$$
flowers now

 Topic 7 | Lesson 9

☆ Independent ☆ Practice

Use the answer from the first step to solve the second step.

3. There are 54 students in the park. 17 students go home. Then 9 more students go home. How many students are in the park now?

○ _____ = _____

○ _____ = _____

_____ students

4. Carlos pours 11 cups of apple juice. He pours 13 cups of grape juice. His friends drink 12 cups of juice. How many cups of juice are left?

○ _____ = _____

○ _____ = _____

_____ cups

5. Tracy has 41 potatoes in a basket. She uses 22 of the potatoes. She finds 18 potatoes in another basket. How many potatoes does she have in all?

○ _____ = _____

○ _____ = _____

_____ potatoes

Solve the problem.
Explain how to check your answer.

6. **Extend Your Thinking** Marcos had 80 stickers. He used 27 stickers. Then he used 25 more stickers. How many stickers are left?

_____ stickers

_____

_____

_____

_____

_____

Problem Solving Solve the two-step problems below.

7. Tim bakes 24 muffins.
Gina bakes 13 more muffins than Tim.
Lea bakes 5 fewer muffins than Gina.

How many muffins does Lea bake?

_____ muffins

8. In April, Hailey had 21 dance classes.
In May, she had 6 fewer dance classes
than she did in April. In June, she had 13
more dance classes than she did in May.

How many dance classes did Hailey have
in June?

_____ dance classes

9. There are 23 blue marbles
and 21 red marbles in a jar.
Julie adds 13 blue
marbles to the jar. Now
how many marbles are
in the jar?

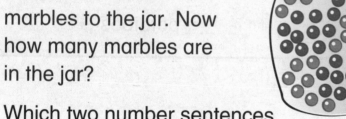

Which two number sentences
help solve the problem?

23 + 21 = 44
44 + 13 = 57
○

23 + 21 = 44
44 − 13 = 31
○

23 + 13 = 36
36 − 21 = 15
○

21 + 13 = 34
34 − 21 = 13
○

10. Extend Your Thinking Write a two-step
math story using the numbers 36, 65, and
16. Then solve the problem. Write number
sentences to show each step.

_____

_____

_____

____ ◯ ____ = ____

____ ◯ ____ = ____

Topic 7 | Lesson 9

Name _____

Another Look Use the answer from Step 1 to solve Step 2.

Tomas has 17 red toy cars and 8 blue toy cars. Tomas gives 6 cars to his brother. How many toy cars does Tomas have left?

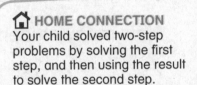

HOME CONNECTION
Your child solved two-step problems by solving the first step, and then using the result to solve the second step.

HOME ACTIVITY Ask your child to solve two-step problems. Use small objects found at home as props.

Step 1: Add to find out how many toy cars Tomas has in all.

$$17 + 8 = 25$$

Step 2: Subtract the number of cars Tomas gives his brother.

$$25 - 6 = 19$$

19 cars

Use the answer from Step 1 to solve Step 2.

1. Dani picked 12 red flowers and 9 pink flowers. Then Dani gave Will 5 flowers. How many flowers does Dani have left?

Step 1: Add to find out how many flowers Dani picked in all.

$$\_\_\_ + \_\_\_ = \_\_\_$$

Step 2: Subtract to find out how many flowers Dani has left.

$$\_\_\_ - \_\_\_ = \_\_\_$$

_____ flowers

2. Jim has 72 raisins. He gives 26 raisins to Ally. Ally gives 15 raisins back to Jim. How many raisins does Jim have now?

Step 1: Subtract to find out how many raisins Jim has left.

$$\_\_\_ - \_\_\_ = \_\_\_$$

Step 2: Add to find out how many raisins Jim has now.

$$\_\_\_ + \_\_\_ = \_\_\_$$

_____ raisins

Solve the problems below.

3. There are 21 students at the school picnic.
Then 42 more students join them.
Later, 30 students leave.

How many students are still at the picnic?

○ 21   ○ 63   ○ 33   ○ 72

4. A dam, made of rows of bricks, forms a lake.
18 rows of bricks are below water. After it
rains, 25 rows of bricks are below water.
After a second day of rain, 6 more rows of
bricks are below water.

How many more rows of bricks are below
water after two days of rain than at the start?

_____ rows of bricks

Mr. and Mrs. Morley picked their crops. Use the data in the chart to solve each problem.

Number of Fruits and Vegetables Picked				
Apples	Peaches	Pumpkins	Corn	Squash
35	23	47	25	17

5. Mr. Morley takes the apples and the
peaches to the fruit stand. He sells
13 peaches. How many apples and
peaches are at the stand now?

_____ apples and peaches

6. Extend Your Thinking Write and solve a
two-step problem about the data in the chart.

_____

_____

_____

_____

The number of stickers each friend has is shown under the albums.
Use math to **analyze** the albums!

 Trina **33**

 Katy **91**

 Drew **75**

 Ramon **18**

 Elena **60**

1. Who has the most stickers? _____

Who has the fewest stickers? _____

2. Find the difference between the greatest number of stickers and the least number of stickers.
Show your work.

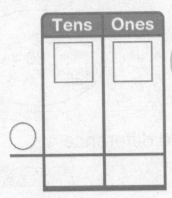

Tens	Ones

○ _____

The difference is _____ stickers.

Think about your answers to Exercise 1.

3. Trey has more stickers than Elena. Trey has fewer stickers than Drew. Write how many stickers Trey could have.

_____

4. Write a subtraction sentence to show how many more stickers Trey could have than Trina.

_____ − _____ = _____

5. Explain how to check your answer to Exercise 4.

_____

_____

What's Missing?

1. In the table below, the three numbers in every row and column add up to 72. But some numbers are missing. Add and subtract to find the missing numbers. Write the missing numbers where they belong. Check your work.

> Read across each row. Read up or down each column.

25	13	
13		25
	25	

What's Wrong?

2. Lena got this problem wrong. What happened? Redo the problem to make it right. Explain how you fixed it.

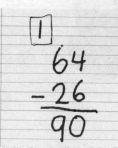

$$
\begin{array}{r}
\overset{1}{6}4 \\
-26 \\
\hline
90
\end{array}
$$

_____

_____

_____

Complete It!

3. Use a number from each shape. Make a subtraction problem so the difference fits each rule. Write the number sentence.

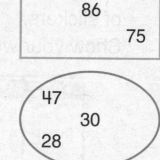

97
86
75

47
30
28

- It needs NO regrouping.

_____

- It has the greatest possible difference.

_____

- The difference is less than 35.

_____

Name _____

Set A

You can use cubes to subtract.

$46 - 8 =$ _____

There are not enough ones to subtract 8. So, regroup 1 ten as 10 ones.

Tens	Ones

$46 - 8 = 38$

Subtract. Use connecting cubes and your workmat.
Regroup if you need to.

1. $61 - 3 =$ _____

Did you need to regroup?

Yes   No

2. $57 - 5 =$ _____

Did you need to regroup?

Yes   No

Set B

You can use paper and pencil to subtract.

Subtract the ones. Then subtract the tens. Regroup if you need to.

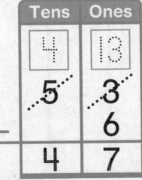

Tens	Ones
4	13
$\not5$	$\not3$
−	6
4	7

Subtract. Regroup if you need to.

3.

Tens	Ones
3	8
−	9

4.

Tens	Ones
6	1
−	4

Topic 7

You can use connecting cubes to help regroup.

$43 - 15 =$ _____

You can regroup 1 ten as 10 ones.

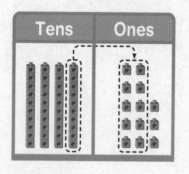

Tens	Ones
3̸ 4̸ 1	1̸3̸ 3̸ 5
−	
2	8

$43 - 15 =$ _28_

Use connecting cubes to subtract. Regroup if you need to.

5.

Tens	Ones
□	□
7	2
− 3	6

6.

Tens	Ones
□	□
4	9
− 2	3

You can write numbers in a frame to help you subtract.

Write the tens in the tens column.
Write the ones in the ones column.

$52 - 33$

Tens	Ones
4	12
5̸ 3	2̸ 3
−	
1	9

Write the subtraction problem in the frame. Find the difference.

7. $84 - 47$

Tens	Ones
□	□
−	

8. $62 - 36$

Tens	Ones
□	□
−	

Set E

You can show 15 − 10 = 5 on a number line.

Draw a line from 0 to 15.
Then draw a different line from 15 back 10 spaces to show the subtraction.

What subtraction problem does this number line show?

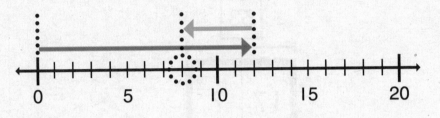

9. _____ − _____ = _____

Set F

You can check subtraction by adding. The sum of the parts is the same as the whole.

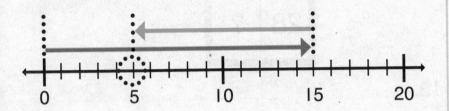

Subtract. Check your answer by adding.

10.
$$\begin{array}{r} 67 \\ -\ 48 \\ \hline \end{array}$$

11.
$$\begin{array}{r} 49 \\ -\ 27 \\ \hline \end{array}$$

You can write a math story for a number sentence.

$$53 - 17 = \underline{36}$$

Jake had 53 stamps. He used 17 stamps. How many stamps does Jake have left?

_____ stamps

Write a math story for this number sentence. Then solve.

$$45 - 28 = \underline{}$$

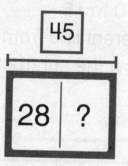

12. _____

_____

_____

You can solve two-step problems. Use the answer from Step 1 to solve Step 2.

Lena buys 28 peaches. She gives 12 to Ted. Then she buys 15 more. How many peaches does Lena have now?

Step 1: $28 - 12 = \underline{16}$

Step 2: $16 + 15 = \underline{31}$

Write number sentences to solve the problem.

13. James is playing a game. He scores 27 points. Next, he scores 33 points. Then he loses 14 points. How many points does James have at the end?

_____ + _____ = _____

_____ − _____ = _____

_____ points

1. Jason has 86 photos on his computer. He deletes 61 photos.

How many photos are left? Use the frame to help you.

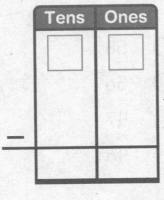

	Tens	Ones
−		

5 ○   15 ○

25 ○   35 ○

2. Ryan has 46 coins. He gives some away. Now he has 37 coins. How many coins does Ryan give away?

9 ○   19 ○

29 ○   39 ○

3. Sandy had some flowers. She gave 17 to her mother. She now has 41 flowers left. How many flowers did Sandy have at first?

42 ○   58 ○

62 ○   86 ○

4. There are 67 seats on the zoo tour bus. People are sitting in 24 seats.

How many seats are empty?

45 ○   44 ○

43 ○   33 ○

Subtract. Use cubes if you need to.

5. There are 92 students at the Wilson Street School.
On Monday, 7 students stay home.

How many students are at school on Monday?

- ○ 75
- ○ 85
- ○ 95
- ○ 99

6. Sam has 74 books.
He puts 28 books on a shelf in his bedroom.

How many books are not on the shelf?

- ○ 58
- ○ 56
- ○ 47
- ○ 46

7. Look at the subtraction situations. Which one does **NOT** need regrouping?

- ○ 32 − 7
- ○ 27 − 9
- ○ 25 − 4
- ○ 44 − 8

8. There are 31 students taking swimming lessons. 8 students are swimming at the deep end of the pool.

How many students are not at the deep end?

- ○ 25
- ○ 23
- ○ 13
- ○ 11

9. Alex collects 35 large shells and 23 small shells.

Then he gives 12 shells to his sister.

How many shells does he have now?

- ○ 70
- ○ 58
- ○ 46
- ○ 33

10. A book has 72 pages. Dan reads 38 pages on Monday and 26 pages on Tuesday.

How many pages does Dan have left to read?

Which two number sentences help solve the problem?

- ○ $38 + 26 = 64$
  $72 - 64 = 8$

- ○ $72 - 38 = 34$
  $34 + 26 = 60$

- ○ $72 + 26 = 98$
  $98 - 38 = 60$

- ○ $72 - 26 = 46$
  $46 + 38 = 84$

11. Which addition sentence can help you solve the subtraction problem?

- ○ $24 - 16 = 8$
- ○ $8 + 8 = 16$
- ○ $16 + 8 = 24$
- ○ $16 + 24 = 40$

$$\begin{array}{r} 24 \\ -\ 16 \\ \hline \end{array}$$

12. Use the strip diagram to write a math story. Then solve.

54

| 27 | ? |

_____

_____

_____

_____

_____ − _____ = _____

13. Check your answer by adding. Which shows the missing part?

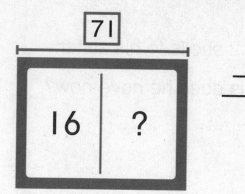

71

| 16 | ? |

$$\begin{array}{r} 71 \\ -\ 16 \\ \hline \end{array}$$

○ 55

○ 57

○ 65

○ 67

Make up your own subtraction problem.
Mark the number line to show how to solve your problem.

14. _____ − _____ = _____

TOPIC 8

3-Digit Addition and Subtraction

Essential Question: What are ways to add and subtract 3-digit numbers?

Yum! Leaves and twigs make a good meal for deer.

Forest animals eat lots of different kinds of food.

Wow! Let's do this project and learn more.

Math and Science Project: Math in the Forest

Find Out Find a library book or other reference source about forest plants and animals. Research the foods that the animals eat. Choose a mouse, deer, wolf, eagle, or other forest animal.

Journal: Make a Book Draw pictures to show different plants and animals. In your book, also:

• Draw arrows to connect each animal to its food.

• Make up and solve addition or subtraction problems about forest animals and the foods they eat.

Review What You Know

Vocabulary

1. Circle the addition problem in which you need to **regroup** 10 ones.

16 + 12   14 + 27

2. Circle the **hundreds digit** in the number below.

3 5 9

3. Circle the group with **fewer** cubes.

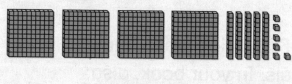

6

4

Knowing Place Value

4. Write how many hundreds, tens, and ones. Then write the number.

_____ hundreds _____ tens

_____ ones

Understanding Subtraction

5. Subtract. Regroup if you need to.

79
− 12

6. Subtract. Circle **Yes** or **No**.

You have 29 large bears. You also have some small bears. If you have 40 bears in all, do you have fewer than 10 small bears?

Yes   No

Name _____

Solve & Share

On Monday, 248 people visited the museum.

On Tuesday, 325 people visited the museum.

How many people visited the museum on Monday and Tuesday?

Add any way you choose.

⭐ **TEKS 2.4C** Solve ... word problems involving addition ... within 1,000 using a variety of strategies based on place value, including algorithms. **Mathematical Process Standards 2.1B, 2.1C, 2.1F.**

Digital Resources at SavvasTexas.com

Solve Learn Glossary Check Tools Games

_____ + _____ = _____

Find 365 + 196.

I'll try to think of numbers that are easier to work with to help me.

I'll add the hundreds first.

One way to add is to add the hundreds, the tens, and the ones.

$$
\begin{array}{ccc}
300 & 60 & 5 \\
+100 & +90 & +6 \\
\hline
400 & 150 & 11
\end{array}
$$

Then add the sums.

$$400 + 150 + 11 = \mathbf{561}$$

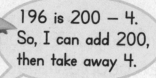

Another way to add is to use easier numbers.

196 is 200 − 4. So, I can add 200, then take away 4.

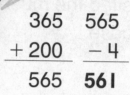

$$
\begin{array}{cc}
365 & 565 \\
+200 & -4 \\
\hline
565 & \mathbf{561}
\end{array}
$$

So, 365 + 196 = $\underline{561}$.

Both ways get the same answer!

☆ Guided Practice

Add any way you choose.
Use models if needed. Show your work.

Do You Understand?

Show Me! How could you use easier numbers to find 303 + 418?

1. $223 + 106 = \underline{329}$

2. $149 + 362 = \underline{}$

3. $171 + 202 = \underline{}$

4. $421 + 397 = \underline{}$

Topic 8 | Lesson 1

Name _____

Add any way you choose.
Use models if needed. Show your work.

5. $151 + 324 =$ ____

6. $250 + 298 =$ ____

7. $258 + 109 =$ ____

8. $187 + 246 =$ ____

9. $236 + 318 =$ ____

10. $432 + 365 =$ ____

11. **Extend Your Thinking** Jamal says that the sum of $183 + 198$ is less than 300. Is Jamal's answer reasonable? Why or why not?

Both numbers are close to 200.

_____

_____

_____

12. On Friday night, 156 people attend a play. On Saturday night, 148 people attend a play. How many people attend a play in all?

_____ people

13. Maria picked some berries. She put 208 berries in one jar and 375 berries in another jar. How many berries did Maria pick in all?

_____ berries

14. Maggie collects stickers for her album. She gives 129 stickers to her friend. Now she has 268 stickers left. How many stickers does Maggie have before she gives some away?

292 ○   294 ○

389 ○   397 ○

15. **Extend Your Thinking** Write an addition problem about stickers. Add 2 three-digit numbers. Solve the problem. Use pictures, numbers, or words.

Name _____

Another Look Find $358 + 213$. Add the hundreds, the tens, and the ones.

Add hundreds.

$$\begin{array}{r} 300 \\ + 200 \\ \hline 500 \end{array}$$

Add tens.

$$\begin{array}{r} 50 \\ + 10 \\ \hline 60 \end{array}$$

Add ones.

$$\begin{array}{r} 8 \\ + 3 \\ \hline 11 \end{array}$$

⌂ **HOME CONNECTION**
Your child explored different ways to add two 3-digit numbers with and without regrouping.

HOME ACTIVITY Ask your child to show you how to add $305 + 497$. Have your child explain each step of the addition.

Add the sums.

$$500 + 60 + 11 = 571$$

So, $358 + 213 = \underline{571}$.

You can also use easier numbers to find $358 + 213$.

 Add any way you choose.
Use models if needed. Show your work.

1. $248 + 455 =$ ___

2. $209 + 376 =$ ___

3. $597 + 122 =$ ___

Topic 8 | Lesson 1

Digital Resources at SavvasTexas.com

4. Extend Your Thinking The local theater wants to add 140 seats to its concert hall. This will give the hall a total of 375 seats. How many seats does the hall have now?

_____ seats

5. Rob collected 225 marbles. Jake collected 69 more marbles than Rob. How many marbles do they have in all?

419	519	509	529
○	○	○	○

Mrs. Jones is buying buttons for her school. Use the chart.
Add any way you choose.

Button	Number
animal	378
sport	142
fruit	296
holiday	455

6. Mrs. Jones buys all of the animal and fruit buttons.

____ + ____ = ____

_____ buttons

7. Mrs. Jones buys all of the sport and holiday buttons.

____ + ____ = ____

_____ buttons

---

8. Algebra Write the missing number.

$285 + 507 = $ _____

9. Algebra Write the missing number.

_____ $= 378 + 142$

10. Algebra Write the missing number.

$802 = $ _____ $+ 431$

Name _____

Solve & Share

One park has 565 trees.
Another park has 300 trees.
How can you use mental math to find the number of trees the two parks have in all?
Explain.

⭐ TEKS 2.4C Solve ... word problems involving addition ... within 1,000 using a variety of strategies based on place value, including algorithms. **Mathematical Process Standards 2.1B, 2.1C, 2.1D.**

Digital Resources at SavvasTexas.com

 Solve Learn Glossary Check Tools Games

$$565 + 300 = \underline{\qquad}$$

You can use mental math to add three-digit numbers. Find $243 + 200$.

How can I add 200 mentally?

Adding hundreds changes only the hundreds digit.

I know $2 + 2 = 4$. So, $243 + 200 = 443$.

Add these three-digit numbers.

$243 + 300 = 543$

$243 + 400 = 643$

$243 + 500 = 743$

Remember, only the hundreds digit changes.

Do You Understand?

Show Me! Explain how you can use mental math to add 100 to 567.

☆ **Guided Practice** ☆ Add using mental math. Use models if needed.

1.  plus 300

$325 + 300 = 625$

2.  plus 100

___ + ___ = ___

3.  $616 + 200 =$ _____

4. 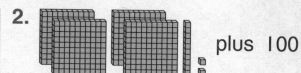 $342 + 400 =$ _____

Topic 8 | Lesson 2

Name _____

Add using mental math. Use models if needed.

5.  plus 200

___ + ___ = ___

6. 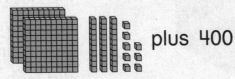 plus 400

___ + ___ = ___

7. 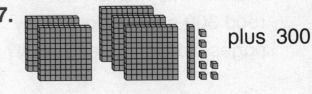 plus 300

___ + ___ = ___

8. 291 + 400 = ___

9. 693 + 200 = ___

10. 803 + 100 = ___

11. 460 + 400 = ___

12. 185 + 300 = ___

13. 761 + 200 = ___

Extend Your Thinking Find the missing numbers. Use mental math to solve.

14. 572 + ☐ = 972

15. 285 + ☐ = 485

16. 799 = 699 + ☐

17. 322 + ☐ = 622

18. 695 + 100 = ☐

19. ☐ + 508 = 708

20. Benita read 245 pages last month. This month she read 300 pages. How many pages did Benita read in all?

_____ + _____ = _____

_____ pages

21. Bob played a game. He scored 473 points. He played again and scored 200 points. How many points did Bob score in both games?

BOB'S SCORE
473 **points**

_____ + _____ = _____

_____ points

22. Together, Sharon and David have 756 marbles. Sharon counted 328 marbles. David counted 100 more marbles than Sharon. How many marbles did David count?

656 ○   428 ○

528 ○   228 ○

23. Extend Your Thinking Think of a three-digit number. Write a story about adding 100 to your number. Then complete the number sentence to show your addition.

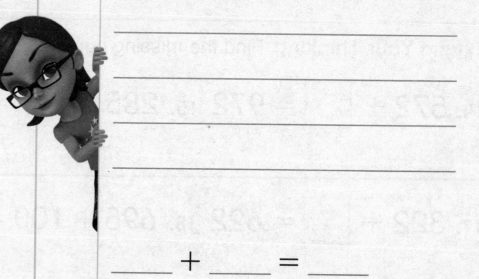

_____

_____

_____

_____

_____ + _____ = _____

Another Look Use mental math to add these three-digit numbers: 315 + 200.

You just need to add the hundreds.
Only the hundreds digit will change.

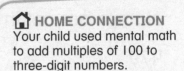
HOME CONNECTION
Your child used mental math to add multiples of 100 to three-digit numbers.

HOME ACTIVITY Choose a number between 200 and 300. Ask your child to add 100 to the number and tell you the sum.

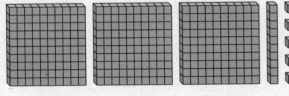

315   +   200   = $\underline{5}$15

Add using mental math.
Complete the addition sentences.

1. 281 + 400

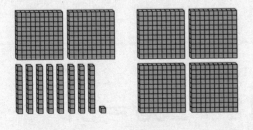

___ + 400 = ___

2. 193 + 500

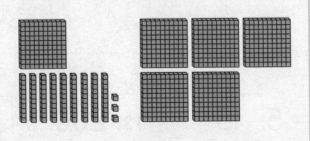

___ + 500 = ___

3. 487 + 300

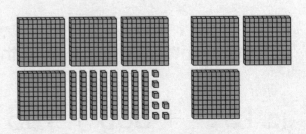

___ + 300 = ___

Use mental math to solve each story problem.

4. Tanner has 679 stamps. She has 179 stamps in her album. How many stamps are not in her album?

479 ○ 500 ○

579 ○ 679 ○

5. Darrin has 100 animal stickers. He has 274 basketball stickers and 300 football stickers. How many sports stickers does Darrin have in all?

274 ○ 374 ○

574 ○ 674 ○

Use mental math. Write the missing digit of each number.

6. $200 + 1\boxed{}2 = 342$

7. $400 + \boxed{}23 = 623$

8. $500 + 15\boxed{} = 651$

9. $3\boxed{}2 + 300 = 652$

10. $\boxed{}35 + 400 = 835$

11. $\boxed{}48 + 200 = 948$

Extend Your Thinking Write the missing digits.

12. $15\boxed{} + 300 + 105 = 5\boxed{}8$

13. $200 + \boxed{}12 + 205 = 51\boxed{}$

Name _____

Solve & Share

Oak School has 256 students. Pine School has 371 students. How many students do the schools have in all?
Use place-value blocks to help. Draw your blocks below and solve.

Hundreds	Tens	Ones
☐	☐	
+		

Hundreds	Tens	Ones

⚙ TEKS 2.4C Solve ... word problems involving addition ... within 1,000 using a variety of strategies based on place value, including algorithms. **Mathematical Process Standards** 2.1C, 2.1D, 2.1F.

Digital Resources at SavvasTexas.com

Solve | Learn | Glossary | Check | Tools | Games

You can use models to add three-digit numbers.

Find 173 + 244.
Add the ones.

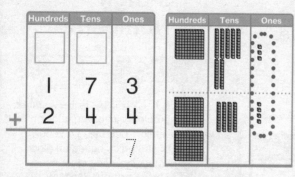

Hundreds	Tens	Ones
□	□	
1	7	3
+ 2	4	4
			7

Add the tens.

Regroup if needed!

Hundreds	Tens	Ones
□	□	
1	7	3
+ 2	4	4
	1	7

Add the hundreds.

So, 173 + 244 = 417.

Hundreds	Tens	Ones
1	□	
1	7	3
+ 2	4	4
4	1	7

Do You Understand?

Show Me! Do you have to regroup to find the sum of 268 + 351? Explain.

⭐ Guided Practice

Add. Regroup if needed. Use models and your workmat to help you.

1.

Hundreds	Tens	Ones
□	□	
2	3	6
+ 4	5	2
6	8	8

2.

Hundreds	Tens	Ones
□	□	
3	2	8
+ 1	2	4

3.

Hundreds	Tens	Ones
□	□	
1	6	5
+ 4	7	3

4.

Hundreds	Tens	Ones
□	□	
3	2	1
+ 1	9	9

5.

Hundreds	Tens	Ones
□	□	
2	1	7
+ 1	0	8

6.

Hundreds	Tens	Ones
□	□	
3	4	7
+ 2	4	2

Topic 8 | Lesson 3

Independent Practice

Add. Regroup if needed. Use models and your workmat to help you.

7.

Hundreds	Tens	Ones
3	7	2
+ 5	8	1

8.

Hundreds	Tens	Ones
6	4	9
+ 1	8	2

9.

Hundreds	Tens	Ones
2	7	3
+ 2	5	9

10.

Hundreds	Tens	Ones
1	6	5
+ 2	3	2

11.

Hundreds	Tens	Ones
2	4	3
+ 1	3	9

12.

Hundreds	Tens	Ones
7	0	9
+ 1	8	6

13.

Hundreds	Tens	Ones
3	5	7
+ 2	6	3

14.

Hundreds	Tens	Ones
2	7	5
+ 4	9	3

15.

Hundreds	Tens	Ones
4	8	1
+ 3	4	9

16.

Hundreds	Tens	Ones
3	2	8
+ 2	9	1

17. Extend Your Thinking Ben said that the sum of 157 and 197 is 254. Nikki said that Ben made a mistake. Who is correct? Explain.

_____

_____

Add 157 and 197. Did you get the same sum as Ben?

18. On Friday, 354 people went to the fair. On Saturday, 551 people went to the fair. How many people went to the fair in all?

Hundreds	Tens	Ones
□	□	
+ | | |

_____ people

19. Some squirrels gathered 187 nuts and put them in one pile. They gathered 239 nuts and put them in another pile. How many nuts did the squirrels gather in all?

Hundreds	Tens	Ones
□	□	
+ | | |

_____ nuts

20. Jessie has 262 beads. Nelly has 479 beads. Which shows the total number of beads they have in all?

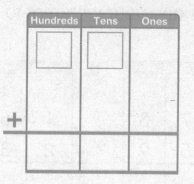

```
 1 1
 262
+479
 631
```
○

```
 1 1
 262
+479
 641
```
○

```
 1 1
 262
+479
 740
```
○

```
 1 1
 262
+479
 741
```
○

21. **Extend Your Thinking** Write an addition story. Use 2 three-digit numbers between 100 and 400. Then solve the problem.

Hundreds	Tens	Ones
□	□	
+ | | |

380 three hundred eighty

Topic 8 | Lesson 3

Name _____

Another Look Follow these steps to add 2 three-digit numbers.

$135 + 248 = $ _____

Step 1: Add the ones. Regroup if needed.
Step 2: Add the tens. Regroup if needed.
Step 3: Add the hundreds.

5 + 8 = 13 ones. Regroup 10 ones for 1 ten.

HOME CONNECTION Your child used place-value models to add three-digit numbers.

HOME ACTIVITY Have your child draw place-value blocks to model the addition of 158 + 146.

Hundreds	Tens	Ones

135

248

$135 + 248 = 383$

Add. Regroup if needed.

1.

Hundreds	Tens	Ones

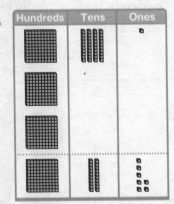

$341 + 127 = $ _____

2.

Hundreds	Tens	Ones

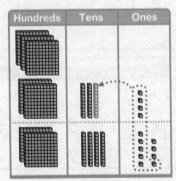

$524 + 249 = $ _____

3. In July, a fire truck traveled 267 miles to put out fires. In August, it traveled 398 miles to put out fires. Which problem shows the total number of miles for both months?

```
 I I
 267
+398
 665
  ○
```

```
 I I
 276
+398
 674
  ○
```

```
  I
 267
+398
 655
  ○
```

```
  I
 267
+398
 565
  ○
```

4. Write and solve an addition story for 482 + 336.

_____

_____

_____

_____

_____

_____

Hundreds	Tens	Ones
☐	☐	
+		

Add. Look for the pattern.

Extend Your Thinking Write and solve the next addition problem that follows each pattern.

5.

Hundreds	Tens	Ones
2 ☐	0	9
+ 1	2	3

Hundreds	Tens	Ones
3 ☐	0	9
+ 2	2	3

Hundreds	Tens	Ones
4 ☐	0	9
+ 3	2	3

Hundreds	Tens	Ones
☐		
+		

6.

Hundreds	Tens	Ones
3 ☐	1	5
+ 4	2	7

Hundreds	Tens	Ones
4 ☐	1	5
+ 3	2	7

Hundreds	Tens	Ones
5 ☐	1	5
+ 2	2	7

Hundreds	Tens	Ones
☐		
+		

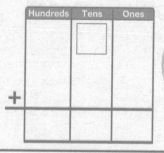

Look for the change in the addends and the sums.

Topic 8 | Lesson 3

Name _____

Solve & Share

159 people bought tickets for the game.

Then 272 more people bought tickets.

How many people bought tickets in all?

How can you use just paper and pencil to solve?

Do you need to regroup? Explain.

⭐ **TEKS 2.4C** Solve ... word problems involving addition ... within 1,000 using a variety of strategies based on place value, including algorithms. **Mathematical Process Standards** 2.1C, 2.1D, 2.1F.

Digital Resources at SavvasTexas.com

Solve   Learn   Glossary   Check   Tools   Games

Hundreds	Tens	Ones
☐	☐	
+		

Jan scored 115 points.
Tia scored 299 points.
How many points did they score in all?

First, add the ones.

Hundreds	Tens	Ones
	1	
1	1	5
2	9	9
+		4

Regroup 10 ones for 1 ten if you need to.

Then add the tens.

Regroup 10 tens for 1 hundred if you need to.

Hundreds	Tens	Ones
1	1	
1	1	5
2	9	9
+	1	4

Then add the hundreds.

Hundreds	Tens	Ones
1	1	
1	1	5
2	9	9
+ 4	1	4

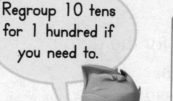

Sometimes you need to regroup ones, tens, or both. Sometimes you don't need to regroup at all!

So, 115 + 299 = 414.

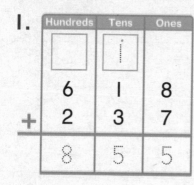

Guided Practice

Add. Use models if needed.

Do You Understand?

Show Me! For the problem above, how do you know you need to regroup?

1.

Hundreds	Tens	Ones
	1	
6	1	8
2	3	7
+ 8	5	5

2.

Hundreds	Tens	Ones
2	5	6
4	8	3
+		

3.

Hundreds	Tens	Ones
3	5	9
2	7	6
+		

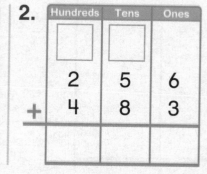

4.
$$425 + 148$$

5.
$$394 + 276$$

6.
$$347 + 242$$

Topic 8 | Lesson 4

Name _____

Add. Use models if needed.

7. 193
   + 246

8. 281
   + 406

9. 367
   + 423

10. 714
    + 138

11. 168
    + 471

12. 266
    + 596

13. 386
    + 354

14. 474
    + 513

15. 529
    + 164

16. 567
    + 162

17. 235
    + 196

18. 462
    + 263

19. 508
    + 247

20. 356
    + 232

21. 209
    + 549

Find the mistake.

22. **Extend Your Thinking** Melissa found the sum of 127 and 345 this way. Explain her mistake. What is the correct sum?

     127
   + 345

     462

Problem Solving Solve each problem.

23. There are 349 people on a boat. 255 people are on another boat. How many people are on both boats?

Hundreds	Tens	Ones
3	4	9
+ 2	5	5

_____ people

24. 163 students are in first grade. 217 students are in second grade. How many students are in both grades?

Hundreds	Tens	Ones
1	6	3
+ 2	1	7

_____ students

25. 222 grasshoppers are in a yard. Some ladybugs land in the yard. Now there are 598 insects in the yard. How many ladybugs landed in the yard?

222   ?

376 ○   222 ○

598 ○   572 ○

26. Extend Your Thinking Choose a three-digit number between 100 and 400. Add this number to 265. If you need to regroup, explain how you did it.

_____

_____

Hundreds	Tens	Ones
+		

_____

_____

Topic 8 | Lesson 4

Name _____

Another Look Use these steps to add 2 three-digit numbers.

Step 1: Add the ones. Regroup if you need to.
Step 2: Add the tens. Regroup if you need to.
Step 3: Add the hundreds.

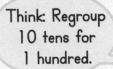
Think: Regroup 10 tens for 1 hundred.

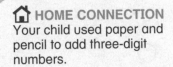
HOME CONNECTION
Your child used paper and pencil to add three-digit numbers.

HOME ACTIVITY Ask your child to show you how to find $294 + 581$.

$163 + 174 = $ _____?

Hundreds	Tens	Ones
1	1	
1	6	3
+ 1	7	4
3	3	7

Draw to regroup. Add.

Add.

1. $218 + 136 = $ _____?

Hundreds	Tens	Ones
	1	
2	1	8
+ 1	3	6
		4

2.

Hundreds	Tens	Ones
1	2	5
+ 2	4	2

3.

Hundreds	Tens	Ones
4	1	9
+ 2	5	6

4. An airplane made a total of 655 trips in two years. In the second year, the airplane made 326 trips.
How many trips did the airplane make in the first year?

192 ○

618 ○

329 ○

300 ○

5. Extend Your Thinking
Caitlin's paper shows how she added 345 and 271.
What mistake did she make?
What is the correct sum?

$$\begin{array}{r} 345 \\ +271 \\ \hline 516 \end{array}$$

_____

_____

_____

Add to find total distance. Use the map of the playground to find the distances from each activity to the next. You can use models to help.

6. From A to B to E

_____ + _____ = _____ feet

7. From D to A to C

_____ + _____ = _____ feet

8. From D to E to C

_____ + _____ = _____ feet

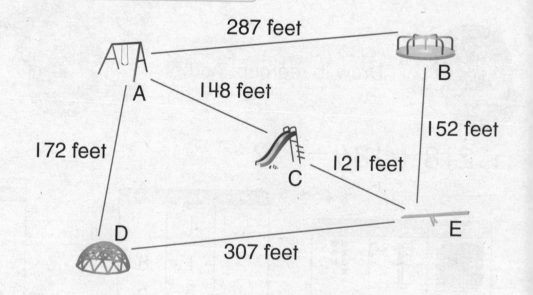

287 feet

A

148 feet

B

152 feet

172 feet

121 feet

C

D

307 feet

E

Topic 8 | Lesson 4

☆ Solve & Share ☆

Ami and Jorge enter their pumpkins in the Giant Pumpkin Contest. Ami's pumpkin weighs 335 pounds. Jorge's pumpkin weighs 254 pounds. How much more does Ami's pumpkin weigh than Jorge's pumpkin? Subtract any way you choose.

Lesson 8-5

Exploring Subtracting 3-Digit Numbers

⭐ TEKS 2.4C Solve ... word problems involving ... subtraction within 1,000 using a variety of strategies based on place value, including algorithms. **Mathematical Process Standards** 2.1A, 2.1C, 2.1D.

Digital Resources at SavvasTexas.com

Solve   Learn   Glossary   Check   Tools   Games

_____ − _____ = _____

Find 372 − 123.

I'll count back to find the answer.

I'll try to think of numbers that are easier to work with to help me.

One way to subtract is to count back.

Start at 372. Count back 1 hundred, then 2 tens, then 3 ones.

100 10 10 1 1 1

372, 272, 262, 252, 251, 250, 249

Another way to subtract is to use easier numbers.

$$372 - 122 \over 250$$

$$250 - 1 \over 249$$

123 is 122 + 1. So, I can take away 122. Then take away one more.

Both ways get the same answer!

So, $372 - 123 = 249$.

Do You Understand?

Show Me! How could you count back to find 434 − 241?

☆ **Guided Practice** ☆   Subtract any way you choose. Use models if needed. Show your work.

1. $485 - 138 = 347$

2. $342 - 154 = \underline{\quad}$

3. $321 - 115 = \underline{\quad}$

Name _____

☆ **Independent** ☆ **Practice** Subtract any way you choose. Show your work.

4. $598 - 361 =$ _____

5. $794 - 452 =$ _____

6. $871 - 355 =$ _____

7. $649 - 574 =$ _____

8. $423 - 297 =$ _____

9. $297 - 168 =$ _____

10. **Extend Your Thinking** Leo says that the difference of $526 - 232$ is greater than 200.
Is what Leo says reasonable? Why or why not?

_____

_____

_____

Sometimes it can help to use numbers that are close but easier to work with.

11. On Saturday, 28 fewer boys than girls played in soccer matches. If 214 girls played, how many boys played?

186 ○

166 ○

156 ○

136 ○

12. Felipe has 453 stamps in his collection. Emily has 732 stamps in her collection. How many more stamps does Emily have?

_____ stamps

13. Tia collected cans to raise money for school. She collected 569 cans on Monday. She collected some more cans on Tuesday. Now she has 731 cans. How many cans did Tia collect on Tuesday?

_____ cans

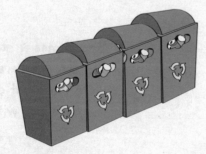

14. **Extend Your Thinking** Write a subtraction problem about recycling. Subtract 2 three-digit numbers. Solve the problem. Use pictures, numbers, or words.

Name _____

Another Look There are many ways to subtract.

Find $361 - 142$.

One way is to count back.

Start at 361 and count back 142.

Remember, 142 is 1 hundred, 4 tens, and 2 ones.

 **HOME CONNECTION**
Your child explored different ways to subtract 2 three-digit numbers with and without regrouping.

HOME ACTIVITY Ask your child to show you how to subtract $431 - 216$. Have your child explain every step of the subtraction.

```
 100  10   10   10   10    I    I
 ∩    ∩    ∩    ∩    ∩    ∩    ∩
361  261  251  241  231  221  220  219
```

So, $361 - 142 = $ __219__ .

Another way is to use easier numbers.

140 is easier to subtract than 142. $142 = 140 + 2$

Subtract 140.
Then subtract 2 more.

$$361 - 140 \over 221$$ $$221 - 2 \over 219$$

So, $361 - 142 = $ __219__ .

Subtract any way you choose.
Use models if needed. Show your work.

1. $412 - 166 = $ _____

2. $398 - 235 = $ _____

3. $753 - 308 = $ _____

4. Jimmy's hive has 528 bees. Julie's hive has 204 bees. How many more bees does Jimmy's hive have than Julie's?

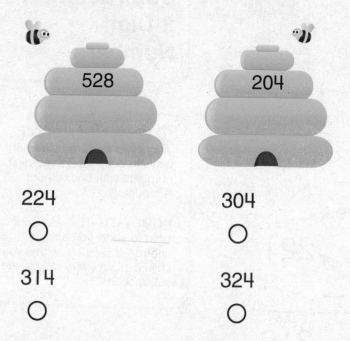

528

204

224
○

304
○

314
○

324
○

5. **Extend Your Thinking** Kelly cuts out 265 strips of paper for an art project. She glues some strips of paper to her piece of art.
Now she has 138 strips of paper left. How many strips of paper did Kelly use?

$$265 - \underline{\quad} = 138$$

_____ strips of paper

Mrs. Anderson gives star stickers to her class. She starts with 989 stickers in September. Find out how many she has left after December. Subtract any way you choose. Show your work.

6. In September, Mrs. Anderson gives away 190 stickers.

$$989 - 190 = \underline{\quad}$$

_____ stickers

7. In October and November, Mrs. Anderson gives away 586 stickers.

$$\underline{\quad} - \underline{\quad} = \underline{\quad}$$

_____ stickers

8. In December, Mrs. Anderson gives away 109 more stickers.

$$\underline{\quad} - \underline{\quad} = \underline{\quad}$$

_____ stickers

Name _____

Solve & Share

The red team and the blue team scored 630 points in all. Use a number card to show how many points the red team scored. How many points did the blue team score?

630

_____ + _____ = 630

⊕ **TEKS 2.4C** Solve ... word problems involving addition and subtraction within 1,000 using a variety of strategies based on place value, including algorithms. **Mathematical Process Standards** 2.1C, 2.1D, 2.1E.

Digital Resources at SavvasTexas.com

Solve Learn Glossary Check Tools Games

Find the missing part.

440 + ____ = 660

Count on or count back to find the missing part.

660

440 | ?

Count on from 440 to 660.

100   100   10   10
440, 540, 640, 650, 660

You counted on 220.

440 + 220 = 660

Count back from 660 to 440.

100   100   10   10
660, 560, 460, 450, 440

You counted back 220.

440 + 220 = 660

The missing part is 220!

660

440 | 220

Do You Understand?

Show Me! For the problem 440 + ____ = 660, would you choose counting on or counting back to solve the problem?

Guided Practice Count on or count back to find the missing part. Write the number.

1. 270 + 210 = 480

480

270 | 210

2. 350 + ____ = 610

610

350 |

Name _____

Count on or count back to find the missing part. Write the number.

3. ____ + 180 = 320

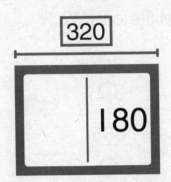
320
180

4. 250 + ____ = 800

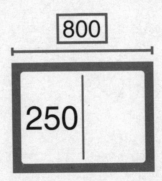
800
250

5. 360 + ____ = 720

720
360

6. ____ + 140 = 570

570
140

7. ____ + 180 = 830

830
180

8. 230 + ____ = 860

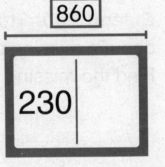
860
230

9. **Extend Your Thinking**
Find the missing part.
Tell the steps that you used.

____ + 340 = 750

_____

_____

_____

_____

10. Mrs. Hatcher has 260 flowers in her store. She wants 520 flowers in all. How many more flowers does she need?

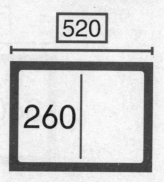

520

260

_____ more flowers

11. ⭐ Trent and Millie counted a total of 750 birds and 65 butterflies. Trent counted 380 of the birds. How many birds did Millie count?

360 ○   370 ○

470 ○   685 ○

12. **Extend Your Thinking** Write an addition story and a number sentence about a missing part. Use 400 as the whole and 130 as one part. Find the missing part.

_____

_____

_____

400

130

Name _____

Another Look You can count on by hundreds and by tens to find the missing part of 260 + ____ = 700.

First, count on by hundreds.   __4__ hundreds

260, __360__, __460__, __560__, __660__

100   200   300   400

Next, count on by tens.   __4__ tens

660, __670__, __680__, __690__, __700__

10   20   30   40

4 hundreds and 4 tens is 440. So, 260 + __440__ = 700.

700

260 | 440

🏠 **HOME CONNECTION**
Your child learned how to count on and count back to find the missing part of a three-digit number.

HOME ACTIVITY Give your child a number to represent the whole, such as 600, and a number to represent a part, such as 370. Then have your child count on or count back to find the missing part.

Count on or count back to find the missing part. Write the number.

1. 420 + ____ = 960

960

420 |

2. ____ + 190 = 630

630

190 |

3. 190 + ____ = 420

420

190 |

4. Clyde and Javier counted a total of 450 sheep.
Javier counted 210 sheep.
How many sheep did Clyde count?

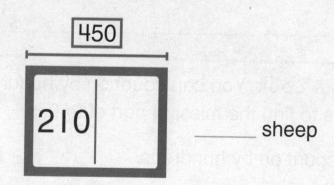

_____ sheep

5. Which weight is needed to balance the scale?
⭐

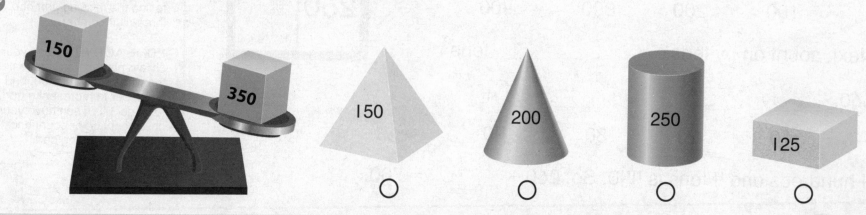

150 ○

200 ○

250 ○

125 ○

Extend Your Thinking Use the pictures to solve. Count on or count back.

Each box contains a number of paints.

Red 270   Blue 580   Yellow 350   Green 430   Holds 700

6. If Ms. Hoople packs the yellow paints in the orange box, how many more paints will that box hold?

_____ more paints

7. If Mr. Bromley packs the blue paints in the orange box, how many more paints will that box hold?

_____ more paints

8. Which two boxes together have enough paints to fit exactly into the orange box?

Name _____

Solve & Share

427 people are at the beach. 182 people are swimming.
How many people are not swimming?
Use place-value blocks to help. Draw your blocks below and solve.

⭐ TEKS 2.4C Solve ... word problems involving ... subtraction within 1,000 using a variety of strategies based on place value, including algorithms. **Mathematical Process Standards** 2.1C, 2.1F, 2.1G.

Hundreds	Tens	Ones

Hundreds	Tens	Ones

Digital Resources at SavvasTexas.com

Solve	Learn	Glossary	Check	Tools	Games

Use models to find 328 − 133.
First, subtract the ones.

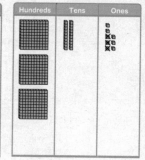

Hundreds	Tens	Ones
3	2	8
− 1	3	3
		5

Regroup 1 hundred as 10 tens.

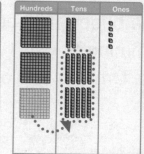

Hundreds	Tens	Ones
2	12	
3	2	8
− 1	3	3
		5

Subtract the tens and the hundreds.

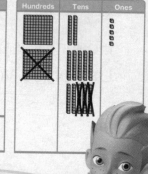

Hundreds	Tens	Ones
2	12	
3	2	8
− 1	3	3
1	9	5

So, 328 − 133 = 195.

Do You Understand?

Show Me! Do you need to regroup to subtract 759 − 328? Why or why not?

Guided Practice

Use models and your workmat. Subtract. Regroup if needed.

1.

Hundreds	Tens	Ones
4	12	
5	2	8
− 2	7	5
2	5	3

2.

Hundreds	Tens	Ones
3	6	4
− 1	2	7

3.

Hundreds	Tens	Ones
5	4	6
− 2	7	1

4.

Hundreds	Tens	Ones
4	6	2
− 1	8	1

5.

Hundreds	Tens	Ones
9	4	8
− 5	2	1

6.

Hundreds	Tens	Ones
7	3	0
− 2	1	4

Independent Practice

Use models and your workmat. Subtract. Regroup if needed.

7.

Hundreds	Tens	Ones
3	1	4
− 1	5	2

8.

Hundreds	Tens	Ones
6	5	3
− 4	1	9

9.

Hundreds	Tens	Ones
4	3	8
− 1	6	2

10.

Hundreds	Tens	Ones
6	3	2
− 4	8	0

11.

Hundreds	Tens	Ones
2	7	6
− 1	2	9

12.

Hundreds	Tens	Ones
5	4	9
− 3	1	6

13.

Hundreds	Tens	Ones
7	9	2
− 3	5	8

14.

Hundreds	Tens	Ones
3	0	6
− 1	7	4

15.

Hundreds	Tens	Ones
4	2	8
− 1	5	3

16.

Hundreds	Tens	Ones
9	2	7
− 6	8	2

17. Extend Your Thinking Find the missing numbers. Explain your steps for solving.

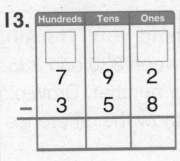

Hundreds	Tens	Ones
8	5	4
− 2	9	
		2

_____

_____

_____

_____

Problem Solving Solve the problems below.

18. Jeff has 517 baseball cards. He has 263 football cards. How many more baseball cards than football cards does he have?

Hundreds	Tens	Ones
−		

_____ more baseball cards

19. Luz has 258 toy cars. She gives 173 toy cars to friends. How many toy cars does Luz have left?

Hundreds	Tens	Ones
− 2	5	8
1	7	3

_____ toy cars

20. ⭐ There were 342 adults at the movie. There were 526 children at the movie. How many more children than adults were at the movie?

184 ○   264 ○

284 ○   868 ○

They were all at the movie at the same time.

21. Extend Your Thinking Choose a number between 330 and 336. Subtract 180 from your number. Draw place-value models to show the difference.

Another Look Follow these steps to subtract three-digit numbers.

$327 - 164 = $ _____

Step 1: Subtract the ones. Regroup if you need to.

Step 2: Subtract the tens. Regroup if you need to.

Step 3: Subtract the hundreds.

Think: Regroup 1 hundred for 10 tens.

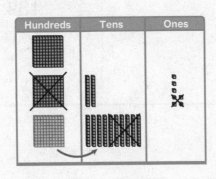

Hundreds	Tens	Ones

$327 - 164 = \underline{163}$

🏠 **HOME CONNECTION**
Your child used place-value models to subtract three-digit numbers.

HOME ACTIVITY Have your child draw place-value blocks to model 583 − 274.

Subtract to find the difference. Use the models to help.

1.

Hundreds	Tens	Ones

$549 - 295 = $ _____

2.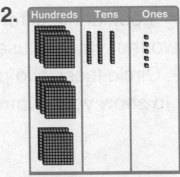

Hundreds	Tens	Ones

$835 - 516 = $ _____

Digital Resources at SavvasTexas.com

3. A farm has 319 animals. 136 of the animals are pigs. How many animals are not pigs?

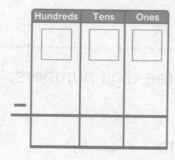

Hundreds	Tens	Ones
☐	☐	☐
−		

_____ animals are not pigs.

4. ★ One building is 332 feet tall. Another building is 208 feet tall. How many feet taller is the first building?

540 ○   136 ○

134 ○   124 ○

Solve the problems below.

5. Subtract to find the differences.

Hundreds	Tens	Ones
☐	☐	☐
4	3	7
− 1	6	4

Hundreds	Tens	Ones
☐	☐	☐
5	7	8
− 2	6	4

Hundreds	Tens	Ones
☐	☐	☐
3	8	1
− 1	9	0

Hundreds	Tens	Ones
☐	☐	☐
9	8	9
− 3	6	2

Hundreds	Tens	Ones
☐	☐	☐
6	2	3
− 3	7	1

6. Extend Your Thinking Look at the differences in each problem above. Find two that you can use to subtract and get a difference of 354. Circle those two problems. Then complete the workmat to show your subtraction.

Hundreds	Tens	Ones
☐	☐	☐
−		

Name _____

☆ ★ ☆
Solve & Share

The class made 547 keychains to sell.

There are 283 keychains left.

How many keychains has the class sold?

How can you use just paper and pencil to solve?

Do you need to regroup? Explain.

⭐ **TEKS 2.4C** Solve ... word problems involving ... subtraction within 1,000 using a variety of strategies based on place value, including algorithms. **Mathematical Process Standards** 2.1C, 2.1E, 2.1F.

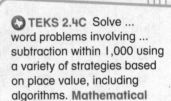

Digital Resources at SavvasTexas.com

Solve   Learn   Glossary   Check   Tools   Games

Hundreds	Tens	Ones
☐	☐	☐
−		

Ian has 849 stamps.
He uses 475 stamps.
How many stamps does
Ian have left?

First subtract the ones.

Hundreds	Tens	Ones
8	4	9
4	7	5
		4

Regroup 1 ten
for 10 ones if
you need to.

Regroup 1 hundred
for 10 tens if you
need to.

Then subtract the tens.

Hundreds	Tens	Ones
7	14	
8	4	9
4	7	5
	7	4

Then subtract the hundreds.

Hundreds	Tens	Ones
7	14	
8	4	9
4	7	5
3	7	4

So, 849 − 475 = 374.

Sometimes you need to
regroup tens or hundreds or
both. Sometimes you don't
need to regroup at all.

Do You Understand?

Show Me! Write a subtraction
problem where you don't need
to regroup. Tell why.

☆ Guided Practice ☆   Subtract. Use models if needed.

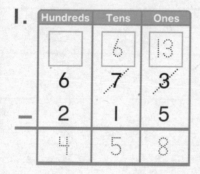

1.

Hundreds	Tens	Ones
	6	13
6	7	3
2	1	5
4	5	8

2.

Hundreds	Tens	Ones
5	6	9
1	8	7

3.

Hundreds	Tens	Ones
7	1	6
5	9	3

4. 481
  − 254

5. 365
  − 82

6. 835
  − 409

Topic 8 | Lesson 8

☆ **Independent** ☆
☆ **Practice** ☆
Subtract. Use models if needed.

7. 542
   − 361

8. 635
   − 108

9. 490
   − 63

10. 639
   − 485

11. 981
   − 276

12. 356
   − 234

13. 839
   − 568

14. 974
   − 257

15. 718
   − 36

16. 320
   − 112

17. 557
   − 363

18. 466
   − 265

19. 845
   − 527

20. 651
   − 522

21. 789
   − 495

22. **Extend Your Thinking** Jim subtracted 443 from 728 this way, but he made a mistake. What was his mistake? Explain.

$$
\begin{array}{r}
\overset{12}{7\!\!\!/28} \\
-\ 443 \\
\hline
385
\end{array}
$$

_____

_____

23. On Friday, 517 people saw a play. On Saturday, 384 people saw the play. How many more people saw the play on Friday than on Saturday?

$$517 - 384$$

_____ people

24. Bonnie had 563 marbles. She gave some of the marbles to her brother. She has 246 marbles left. How many marbles did she give to her brother?

$$563 - 246$$

_____ marbles

25. There are 627 grass seeds on the ground. 19 birds flew down. They ate 184 of the seeds. How many grass seeds are left?

608 ◯   543 ◯

443 ◯   184 ◯

Think: what information do I need to solve the problem?

26. Extend Your Thinking Write a story about 543 − 206. Then solve the problem.

$$543 - 206$$

Name _____

Another Look Use these steps to subtract three-digit numbers.

Step 1: Subtract the ones. Regroup if you need to.
Step 2: Subtract the tens. Regroup if you need to.
Step 3: Subtract the hundreds.

$$362 - 125$$

Hundreds	Tens	Ones
	5	12
3	6̸	2̸
− 1	2	5
2	3	7

So, $362 - 125 = 237$.

Think: Regroup 1 ten for 10 ones.

🏠 **HOME CONNECTION**
Your child used paper and pencil to subtract three-digit numbers.

HOME ACTIVITY Ask your child to show you how to subtract 586 − 237.

Subtract. Use models and your workmat if needed.

1.

Hundreds	Tens	Ones
4	2	9
− 1	7	4

2.

Hundreds	Tens	Ones
5	7	4
− 2	1	3

3.

Hundreds	Tens	Ones
7	8	8
− 2	6	9

Topic 8 | Lesson 8
Digital Resources at SavvasTexas.com
four hundred eleven **411**

4. There were 926 wild horses in a valley. Then 56 horses ran away, but 11 came back. How many horses are in the valley now?

○ 859   ○ 881   ○ 971   ○ 982

5. A local school held a charity coat drive for two months. The school collected 269 coats in the first month. 542 coats were collected in all. How many coats did the school collect in the second month?

_____ coats

6. Extend Your Thinking Use these numbers only once to finish the two subtraction problems. Then subtract.

2 5 7 1 4 6

Make the greatest difference.

```
  9 5 0
- □ □ □
_____
```

Make the least difference.

```
  9 5 0
- □ □ □
_____
```

Choose one player from each team. Write a subtraction problem using their scores. Then write how many more points the player from the A Team scored.

A Team Score	
Marco	745
Elena	916
Dekembi	692
Linda	885

B Team Score	
Jackie	452
Kalisha	325
Dante	581
Akmad	263

7. A Team
Player: _____

B Team
Player: _____

A Team
scored _____ more points.

Subtraction Problem

8. A Team
Player: _____

B Team
Player: _____

A Team
scored _____ more points.

Subtraction Problem

Solve & Share

Draw place-value blocks to show $418 - 302$.
Then write a math story for your picture and solve.

⭐ **TEKS 2.1G** Display, explain, and justify mathematical ideas ... using precise mathematical language ....
TEKS 2.4D Generate and solve problem situations ... **Mathematical Process Standards** 2.1B, 2.1D, 2.1F.

Digital Resources at SavvasTexas.com

Solve   Learn   Glossary   Check   Tools   Games

Analyze

Write a math story for 437 + 389.

You can start by drawing a strip diagram.

?

| 437 | 389 |

Plan

Write a story about your diagram.

Mrs. Glen's class collected 437 box tops. Mr. Harvey's class collected 389 box tops. How many box tops did the two classes collect in all?

Solve, Justify, and Evaluate

Solve your story.

$$
\begin{array}{r}
\overset{1\;1}{437} \quad \text{box tops} \\
+\ 389 \quad \text{box tops} \\
\hline
826 \quad \text{box tops in all}
\end{array}
$$

They collected 826 box tops in all.

Do You Understand?

Show Me! How does a strip diagram help you write an addition or subtraction story?

☆ Guided Practice ☆

Write a math story for the number sentence. Then solve.

1. 573 − 245 = _____

573

| 245 | ? |

573 people were at the zoo on Saturday. 245 people were there on Sunday. How many more people were at the zoo on Saturday?

2. 156 + 312 = _____

?

| 156 | 312 |

_____

_____

_____

Topic 8 | Lesson 9

Name _____

Write a math story for the number sentence. Then solve.

3. $201 - 142 =$ _____

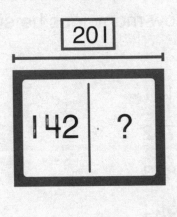

201

142 | ?

_____
_____
_____
_____

4. $562 + 319 =$ _____

?

562 | 319

_____
_____
_____
_____

5. $294 + 483 =$ _____

?

294 | 483

_____
_____
_____
_____

6. **Extend Your Thinking** Write a math story for the number sentence and solve.

$398 -$ _____ $= 159$ _____

_____

_____

7. Drew filled in this strip diagram to show 517 − 245. Write a story using the strip diagram. Solve the problem.

```
            517
    ┌─────────────────┐

    │  245  │    ?    │
    └─────────────────┘
```

_____

_____

_____

517 − 245 = _____

8. ⭐ Sean keeps track of how many laps he swims each month. He swam 381 laps in April and 492 laps in May. Which number sentence shows how many laps he swam in both months?

○ $492 − 381 = 111$

○ $381 + 381 = 762$

○ $492 + 381 = 873$

○ $492 + 492 = 984$

---

9. Extend Your Thinking Write an addition story and a subtraction story for the strip diagram. Then solve each problem.

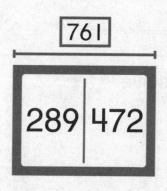

```
      761
  ┌───────────┐

  │ 289 │ 472 │
  └───────────┘
```

My addition story:

_____

_____

_____

My subtraction story:

_____

_____

_____

Name _____

Another Look You can draw place-value blocks to help you write a math story.

Write a math story for 423 − 312.

First draw place-value blocks to show 423. Then cross out blocks to show that you are subtracting 312.

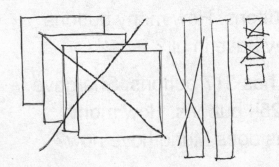

Last, write a story for your picture and solve the problem.

Sharon had 423 Pennies.
She put 312 pennies in her bank.
How Many pennies does she have left?
She has 111 pennies left.

🏠 **HOME CONNECTION**
Your child wrote addition and subtraction stories for number sentences such as 298 + 417 and 906 − 342.

HOME ACTIVITY Ask your child to write a number story for 374 + 608. Have your child solve the problem for his or her story.

Write a story and solve the problem. You can draw a picture of place-value blocks to help.

1. 647 − 429 = _____

_____

_____

_____

2. 584 + 413 = _____

_____

_____

_____

Solve each problem.

3. Algebra Use the strip diagram to complete the number sentences.

793

| 487 | 306 |

$487 + \underline{\quad} = 793$

$\underline{\quad} = 306 + 487$

$793 = 306 + \underline{\quad}$

4. Leo wrote a story for $317 + 254$. Which number story could he have written?

○ Maria has 317 buttons. John has 254 buttons. How many more buttons does Maria have than John?

○ Maria has 317 buttons. John has 254 buttons. How many buttons do they have in all?

○ Maria has 317 buttons. She gave John 254 buttons. How many buttons does Maria have now?

○ Maria has 317 buttons. John has 154 buttons. How many buttons do they have in all?

5. Extend Your Thinking Choose 2 three-digit numbers that are less than 400. Use your numbers to write an addition story and a subtraction story.

My addition story:

My subtraction story:

Name ______________________________

Solve & Share

Jody wants to bake 350 muffins.
She baked one batch of 160 muffins and one batch of 145 muffins.
How many more muffins does Jody need to bake?
Solve the problem. Find the hidden question.

Problem Solving

Lesson 8-10
Two-Step Problems

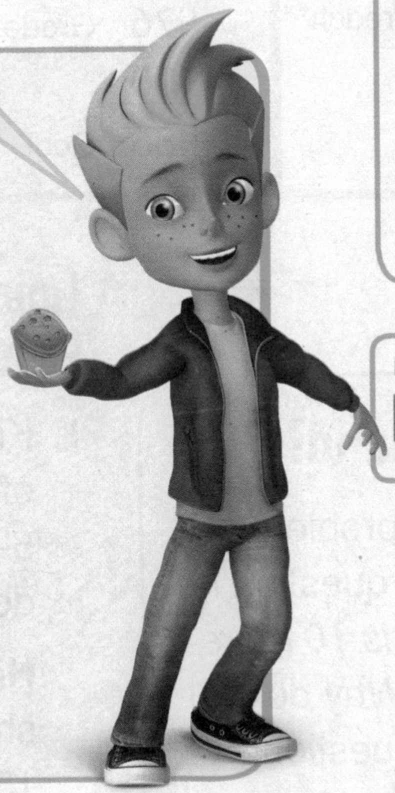

TEKS 2.1A Apply mathematics to problems arising in everyday life .... **TEKS 2.4C** Solve one-step and multi-step word problems involving addition and subtraction .... **Mathematical Process Standards** 2.1B, 2.1C, 2.1D.

Digital Resources at SavvasTexas.com

Solve | Learn | Glossary | Check | Tools | Games

Hidden Question	Step 1	Step 2

Analyze

Grade 2 wants to sell 10 more tickets to the school play than Grade 1.

Grade 1 sold 476 tickets. Grade 2 sold 439 tickets.

How many more tickets does Grade 2 have to sell to reach their goal?

Plan

How many tickets is 10 more than 476 tickets?

Hint: Add 10 to the number of tickets that Grade 1 sold.

$$\begin{array}{r} 476 \quad \text{Grade 1} \\ +\ 10 \\ \hline 486 \quad \text{Goal} \end{array}$$

Solve and Justify

The goal is to sell 486 tickets.

Now find how many more tickets Grade 2 has to sell.

$$\begin{array}{r} 486 \quad \text{Goal} \\ -\ 439 \quad \text{Already Sold} \\ \hline 47 \quad \text{Left to sell} \end{array}$$

Evaluate

You need to find the answer to the hint before you can solve the problem.

Do You Understand?

Show Me! In the problem above, the hidden question is *How many tickets is 10 more than 476 tickets?* Why do you think we call this question hidden? Explain.

Guided Practice

Solve each problem. Use the hidden question or hint to help you.

1. Kim had 455 shells. She sold 134 of the shells. She then bought 54 more shells. How many shells does Kim have now?

   Hidden Question: How many shells did Kim have after selling 134 shells?

   Step 1
   $$\begin{array}{r} 455 \\ -\ 134 \\ \hline 321 \end{array}$$

   Step 2
   $$\begin{array}{r} 321 \\ +\ 54 \\ \hline 375 \end{array}$$
   _____ shells

2. Cara had 561 pennies. She gave 235 of them to her brother and 125 to her sister. How many pennies does Cara have left?

   Hint: Add to find how many she gave away.

   Step 1
   $$+ \underline{\qquad}$$

   Step 2
   $$- \underline{\qquad}$$
   _____ pennies

Name _____

Write a hidden question or hint for Step 1. Then solve the problem.

Heights of Trees

River Birch	Laurel Oak	Elderberry	Buttonbush	Chinkapin
888 in.	750 in.	144 in.	240 in.	240 in.

3. How much taller is a River Birch than an Elderberry and a Chinkapin together?

Hint: _____

_____

_____

Step 1   **Step 2**

_____ inches taller

4. How much shorter is a River Birch than a Laurel Oak and a Buttonbush together?

Hidden Question: _____

_____

_____

Step 1   **Step 2**

_____ inches shorter

5. How much taller is a Laurel Oak than a Buttonbush and a Chinkapin together?

Hint: _____

_____

_____

Step 1   **Step 2**

_____ inches taller

6. Extend Your Thinking In Exercise 4, can you do Step 2 first and then do Step 1? Why or why not?

_____

_____

7. The garage door is 144 inches high. The truck is 112 inches high. There is a sign on top of the truck that is 27 inches high. Can the truck with the sign on it fit through the garage door? Explain your answer.

    Step 1   **Step 2**

_____

_____

_____

8. Tom earns $359. He spends $236 Monday through Friday. He spends $38 on Saturday. How much money does he have left?

Hidden Question: _____

_____

    Step 1   **Step 2**

9. Ted needs at least 223 inches of hose to water a new tree. He connects two shorter hoses to do the job. Which are the lengths of the two shorter hoses he uses?

  98 in. and 111 in.   145 in. and 95 in.
      ○   ○

  105 in. and 105 in.   25 in. and 123 in.
      ○   ○

10. Extend Your Thinking In Exercise 9, explain the two steps you took to solve the problem.

_____

_____

_____

Name _____

Another Look You need to use more than one step to solve many problems.

Read the problem. Follow the steps to solve.

Carl has 254 baseball cards.
He gives 145 to John and 56 to Amy.
How many cards does he have left?

> Think: You need to figure out how many baseball cards Carl has left.

Step I Add the number of cards he gives to John and the number of cards he gives to Amy.

$$145 + 56 = 201$$

> Think: Does the answer make sense?

Step 2 Subtract the number of cards Carl gave away from the number of cards he had.

$$254 - 201 = 53$$ 53 cards left

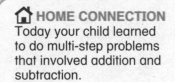

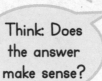

🏠 **HOME CONNECTION**
Today your child learned to do multi-step problems that involved addition and subtraction.

HOME ACTIVITY Ask your child to solve this problem: Suppose you have 45 minutes to get to bed. It takes 5 minutes to brush your teeth and 7 minutes to change your clothes. How much time do you have left to read a book?

Use two steps to solve each problem.

1. Mr. Wu buys a box of 300 nails. He uses 156 nails to build a deck. He uses 98 nails to build stairs between the deck and the ground. How many nails does he have left?

Step I $156 + \underline{\quad} = \underline{\quad}$

Step 2 $\underline{\quad} - \underline{\quad} = \underline{\quad}$

Mr. Wu has _____ nails left.

2. Pam runs 178 yards. Then she runs 107 yards. The race is 300 yards long. How many more yards must Pam run to finish the race? Write the hidden question. Then solve the problem.

_____

_____

_____ yards

3. Curt combines two jars of coins. He has at least 460 coins in all. How many coins are in each jar?

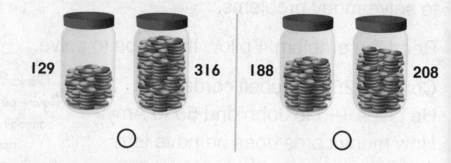

129   316   188   208
○   ○

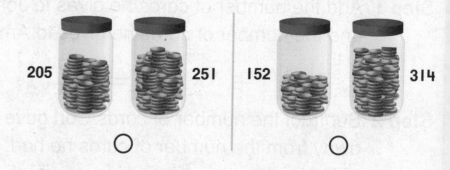

205   251   152   314
○   ○

Extend Your Thinking Jeff is at the store. Use the pictures and clues. Solve each problem.

4. Jeff took 426 steps. How many steps did he take between the guitar and the TV? _____ steps.

5. Jeff bought the guitar, the TV, and the radio. How much money did he spend in all? _____

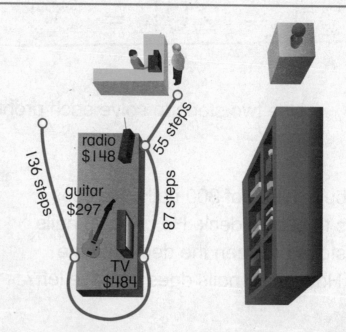

radio $148
136 steps
55 steps
guitar $297
87 steps
TV $484

Name _____

All aboard, problem solvers! **Connect** the numbers on the cars to **relate** addition and subtraction.

394 **520** **277** **160**

1. Write the greatest and the least numbers from the train.

_____ and _____

Find the sum.

_____ + _____ = _____

Use the addends and the sum from above to write a subtraction sentence.

_____ − _____ = _____

2. Choose two numbers from the train that have a sum where the number of tens is greater than the number of ones.

_____ + _____ = _____

3. Use mental math.

The train has gone 180 miles so far. How many more miles must it go to reach 325 miles?

_____ miles

4. Did you add or subtract to solve Exercise 3? Explain your thinking.

_____

_____

_____

What's the Rule?

1. Figure out each pattern. Write the rule. Write the number that comes next.

- 116 → 207 → 298 → 389 → ?

  The pattern rule is _____.

  The next number is _____.

- 567 → 458 → 349 → 240 → ?

  The pattern rule is _____.

  The next number is _____.

- 146 → 269 → 392 → 515 → ?

  The pattern rule is _____.

  The next number is _____.

- 987 → 765 → 543 → 321 → ?

  The pattern rule is _____.

  The next number is _____.

What's Wrong?

2. Reese got this problem wrong. Redo the problem to make it right.

$$
\begin{array}{r}
467 \\
+283 \\
\hline
640
\end{array}
\qquad +
$$

Arrow Math

3. Follow the arrows to change each number. Write the new number in the box. Keep on to the end of the row.

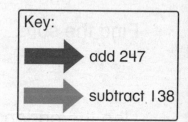

Key:
➡ add 247
➡ subtract 138

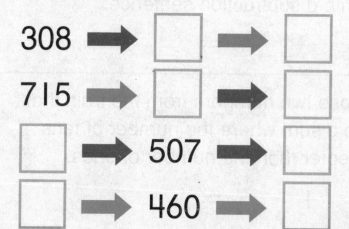

Set A

Find 245 + 134.

One way to add is to add the
hundreds, tens, and ones.
Then add all the sums.

$$
\begin{array}{ccc}
200 & 40 & 5 \\
+\,100 & +\,30 & +\,4 \\
\hline
300 & 70 & 9 \\
\end{array}
$$

245 + 134 = 379

Add any way you choose.
Use models if needed.

1. 141 + 562 = ____

2. 324 + 555 = ____

Set B

You can use mental math to add
three-digit numbers.

339 + 200 = ?

3 + 2 = 5

So, 339 + 200 = 539

Add using mental math.

3. 243 + 200 = ____

4. 578 + 300 = ____

You can use models to add three-digit numbers.

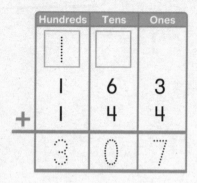
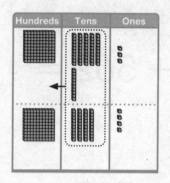

Add. Regroup if needed. Use models and your workmat to help you.

5.

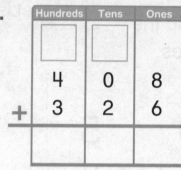

Hundreds	Tens	Ones
4	0	8
+ 3	2	6

6.

Hundreds	Tens	Ones
2	2	5
+ 3	6	1

Start with the ones to add three-digit numbers. Then add the tens and hundreds.

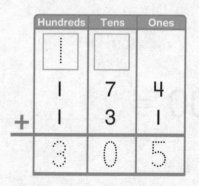

Add. Regroup and use models if needed.

7.

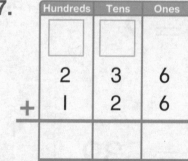

Hundreds	Tens	Ones
2	3	6
+ 1	2	6

8.

Hundreds	Tens	Ones
3	4	7
+ 2	6	1

One way to subtract is to use easier numbers.

$$564 \\ -155$$

$$564 \\ -154 \\ \overline{410}$$

155 is 154 + 1.
So, subtract 154 and take away 1 more.

$$564 - 155 = \underline{409}$$

Subtract any way you choose.
Use models if needed.

9. $873 - 312 = \underline{\hspace{2cm}}$

10. $911 - 408 = \underline{\hspace{2cm}}$

Set F

You can count on or count back to find a missing part.

$$250 + \underline{\hspace{1.5cm}} = 480$$

Count on from 250: 350, 450.
That's 200.
Count on from 450: 460, 470, 480.
That's 30.

$$200 + 30 = \underline{230}$$

$$250 + 230 = \underline{480}$$

Count on or count back to find the missing part. Write the number.

11. $470 + \underline{\hspace{1.5cm}} = 810$

12. $\underline{\hspace{1.5cm}} + 210 = 770$

You can use models to subtract three-digit numbers.

$$327 - 225 = ?$$

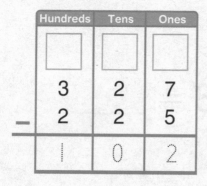

Hundreds	Tens	Ones
3	2	7
− 2	2	5
1	0	2

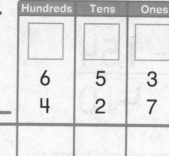

Use models and your workmat.
Subtract. Regroup if needed.

13.

Hundreds	Tens	Ones
6	5	3
− 4	2	7

14.

Hundreds	Tens	Ones
4	9	8
− 2	1	9

When you subtract three-digit numbers, start with the ones. Next subtract the tens, and then the hundreds.

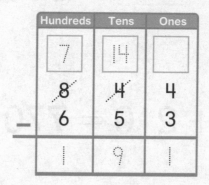

Hundreds	Tens	Ones
7	14	
8	4	4
− 6	5	3
1	9	1

Subtract. Regroup if needed.

15.

Hundreds	Tens	Ones
4	1	9
− 2	2	7

16.

Hundreds	Tens	Ones
7	3	1
− 4	4	6

Name _____

1. On Saturday, 786 people visited the zoo. On Sunday, 429 people visited.

   How many more people visited the zoo on Saturday than on Sunday?

   ○ 351

   ○ 357

   ○ 363

   ○ 367

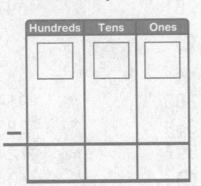

2. Ellen collected 405 cans to recycle. Beth collected 123 cans.

   How many cans did they both collect?

   ○ 628

   ○ 627

   ○ 528

   ○ 516

3. Jared had 139 baseball cards. He found more baseball cards. Now he has 439 baseball cards.

   How many baseball cards did Jared find?

   ○ 139

   ○ 200

   ○ 300

   ○ 578

4. Ms. Perna has 325 pieces of sea glass. She made a frame with 110 pieces. Then she put 60 pieces in a vase.

   How many pieces of sea glass does she have now?

   ○ 155

   ○ 215

   ○ 265

   ○ 495

5. Jim puts 640 books in 2 boxes.
Some books are in Box 1.
250 books are in Box 2.

How many books are in Box 1?

○ 250

○ 270

○ 350

○ 390

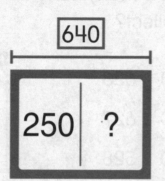

6. Rosa reads 283 pages. Pat reads
364 pages. Which shows the total
number of pages they read in all?

$$\begin{array}{r} 2\ 16 \\ 3\cancel{6}4 \\ -\ 283 \\ \hline 81 \end{array}$$
○

$$\begin{array}{r} 1 \\ 283 \\ +\ 364 \\ \hline 647 \end{array}$$
○

$$\begin{array}{r} 283 \\ +\ 364 \\ \hline 547 \end{array}$$
○

$$\begin{array}{r} 364 \\ -\ 283 \\ \hline 121 \end{array}$$
○

7. Bill's goal is to read 425 pages. He
reads 184 pages. Which shows how
many pages he still needs to read?

$$\begin{array}{r} 425 \\ -\ 184 \\ \hline 361 \end{array}$$
○

$$\begin{array}{r} 425 \\ +\ 184 \\ \hline 509 \end{array}$$
○

$$\begin{array}{r} 3\ 12 \\ \cancel{4}25 \\ -\ 184 \\ \hline 231 \end{array}$$
○

$$\begin{array}{r} 3\ 12 \\ \cancel{4}25 \\ -\ 184 \\ \hline 241 \end{array}$$
○

8. Ms. Tompkins drove 146 miles on Monday.
She drove 323 miles on Tuesday.

How many miles did she drive on both days?

○ 369

○ 388

○ 469

○ 489

9. Lisa picks apples.
She has 351 in her basket.
She uses 150 apples to make applesauce.
She uses 110 apples to make pies.

How many apples does she have left?

○ 611

○ 391

○ 191

○ 91

10. The Happy Horse Farm used 607 bales of hay during the winter. They used 295 bales of hay during the summer.

How many bales of hay did they use during those seasons?

○ 702

○ 802

○ 892

○ 902

11. Mrs. Mayer collected 479 postcards.
She gave away 183 postcards.
How many postcards did she keep?

○ 296

○ 316

○ 396

○ 662

12. The second graders read some books in January. They read 148 books in February. They read 299 books in all in both months.

How many books did the second graders read in January?

○ 447

○ 161

○ 152

○ 151

13. Write a math story and show your work for solving the problem.

$$283 + 165 = \underline{\hspace{1cm}}.$$

My addition story:

_____

_____

_____

_____

My work:

14. Write a math story and show your work for solving the problem.

$$576 - 218 = \underline{\hspace{1cm}}.$$

My subtraction story:

_____

_____

_____

_____

My work:

Glossary

add

When you add, you join groups together.

$$3 + 4 = 7$$

addend

the numbers you add together to find the whole

$$2 + 5 = 7$$

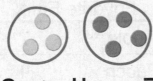

addends

addition sentence

plus

$$3 + 2 = 5$$

addend   addend   sum

after

424 comes after 423.

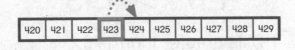

| 420 | 421 | 422 | 423 | 424 | 425 | 426 | 427 | 428 | 429 |

a.m.

7:10 AM

The half of the day from midnight to midday can be described as a.m.

area

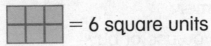 = 6 square units

The area is the measure of the space inside a plane shape.

bar graph

A bar graph uses bars to show data.

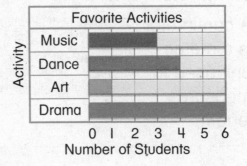

Favorite Activities

before

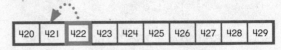

| 420 | 421 | 422 | 423 | 424 | 425 | 426 | 427 | 428 | 429 |

421 comes before 422.

borrow

When you borrow money or an item, it needs to be returned when you are done.

cents

1 cent (¢)   10 cents (¢)

centimeter (cm)

A centimeter is a metric unit used to measure length.

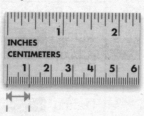

coins

1¢   5¢   10¢   25¢   50¢ $1.00

column

1	2	3	4	5
11	12	13	14	15
21	22	23	24	25
31	32	33	34	35

↑
column

compare

When you compare numbers, you find out if a number is greater than, less than, or equal to another number.

147 ⟩ 143

147 is greater than 143.

cone

A cone is a solid figure with a circle as its base and a curved surface that meets at a point.

consumer

When you use or buy something, you are a consumer.

cube

A cube is a solid figure with six faces that are matching squares.

cylinder

A cylinder is a solid figure with two matching circles as bases.

data

Favorite Fruit	
Apple	7
Peach	4
Orange	5

Data are information you collect.

decagon

A decagon is a polygon that has 10 sides.

decimal point

A decimal point separates dollars from cents.

$1.25

decimal point ↗

decrease

$$600 \longrightarrow 550$$

600 decreased by 50 is 550.

deposit

When you put money into a bank, you are making a deposit.

difference

the answer in a subtraction sentence

$$14 - 6 = 8$$

8 is the difference.

digits

Numbers have 1 or more digits. 43 has 2 digits.

dime

10 cents or 10¢

divide

You divide to separate a number of items into groups of equal size.

$$12 \div 3 = 4$$

divided by

$$18 \div 3 = 6$$

divided by

division sentence

$$4 \div 2 = 2$$

4 divided by 2 equals 2.

dodecagon

A dodecagon is a polygon that has 12 sides.

dollar

$1.00 or 100¢

dollar bill ($)   dollar coin

dollar sign

The dollar sign is the symbol that is placed before the numbers when you are writing an amount of money.

$$\$375$$

dollar sign

doubles

A doubles fact has two addends that are the same.

$$4 + 4 = 8$$

addend   addend   sum

edge

An edge is where two flat surfaces of a solid figure meet.

edge

eighths

When 1 whole is separated into 8 equal parts, the parts are called eighths.

equal parts

parts of a whole that are the same size.

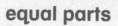

All 4 parts are equal.

equal share

2   2   2

An equal share is the same amount in each group.

equal to (=)

36 = 36

36 is equal to 36.

estimate

When you estimate, you make a good guess.

This table is about 3 feet long.

even

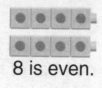

An even number can be shown as two equal parts.   8 is even.

expanded form

Expanded form shows the place value of each digit.

400 + 60 + 3 = 463

face

The flat surface of a solid figure that does not roll is called a face.

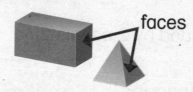

faces

fact family

a group of related addition and subtraction facts

2 + 4 = 6
4 + 2 = 6
6 − 2 = 4
6 − 4 = 2

flat surface

flat surfaces

foot (ft)

A foot is 12 inches.

fourths

When 1 whole is separated into 4 equal parts, the parts are called fourths.

fraction

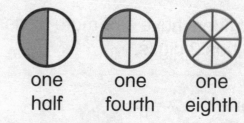

one half   one fourth   one eighth

A fraction names part of a whole or part of a set.

greater than (>)

5 is greater than 1.

$$5 > 1$$

greatest

the number or group with the greatest value

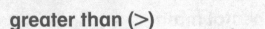

35 47 58 61

greatest

greatest value

The coin that has the greatest value is the one that is worth the most.

The quarter has the greatest value.

half-dollar

50 cents or 50¢

half past

Half past is 30 minutes past the hour.

It is half past 9.

halves

When 1 whole is separated into 2 equal parts, the parts are called halves.

height

Height is how tall something is.

hendecagon

A hendecagon is a polygon that has 11 sides.

heptagon

A heptagon is a polygon that has 7 sides.

hexagon

A hexagon is a polygon that has 6 sides.

hour

An hour is 60 minutes.

hundred

10 tens make 1 hundred.

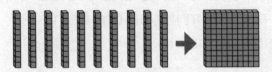

inch (in.)

An inch is a standard unit used to measure length.

increase

550 ⟶ 600

550 increased by 50 is 600.

input

The input is the number that you start with.

Input	Output
3	5
4	6
5	7

irresponsible

When you are given something to use for a certain amount of time and you do not return it, you are being irresponsible.

join

To join means to put together.

3 and 3 is 6 in all.

least

the number or group with the smallest value

35 47 58 61

least

least value

The dime has the least value.

lend

When you give someone money or an item that will be returned, you lend something to that person.

length

Length is the distance from one end to the other end of an object.

The length of the bat is about 1 yard.

less than (<)

2 is less than 6.

$$2 < 6$$

mental math

Mental math is math you do in your head.

Start at 23. Count on 33, 43.

$$23 + 20 = 43$$

meter (m)

A long step is about a meter. A meter is about 100 centimeters.

minute

There are 60 minutes in 1 hour.

multiplication sentence

$$4 \times 2 = 8$$

4 times 2 equals 8.

multiply

$$3 \times 2 = 6$$
$$2 + 2 + 2 = 6$$

To multiply 3×2 means to add 2 three times.

near doubles

An addition fact with near doubles has an addend that is one more than the other addend.

$$4 + 5 = 9$$

addend   addend

nearest centimeter

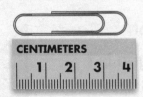

The closest centimeter to the measure is the nearest centimeter.

nearest inch

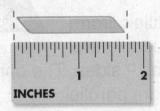

The closest inch to the measure is the nearest inch.

next ten

the following ten after a number

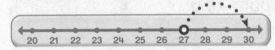

30 is the next ten after 27.

nickel

5 cents or 5¢

nonagon

A nonagon is a polygon that has 9 sides.

number line

A number line is a line that shows numbers in order from left to right.

number sentence

A number sentence has an operation symbol (+ or −) and an equal sign (=).

$$3 + 2 = 5 \qquad \begin{array}{r} 9 \\ -\ 2 \\ \hline 7 \end{array}$$

This is a horizontal number sentence.

This is a vertical number sentence.

number word

A number word shows a number using words. The number word for 23 is twenty-three.

octagon

An octagon is a polygon that has 8 sides.

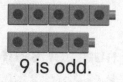

odd

An odd number cannot be divided into two equal parts.

9 is odd.

order

Numbers can be put in counting order from least to greatest or from greatest to least.

27 72 107 117 171

least

greatest

output

The output is the number you get after using the rule with an input.

Input	Output
3	5
4	6
5	7

parallelogram

A parallelogram is a quadrilateral that has 4 sides. The opposite sides are parallel.

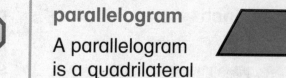

part

A part is a piece of a whole.

2 and 3 are parts of 5.

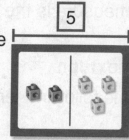

5

penny

I cent or I¢

pentagon

A pentagon is a polygon with 5 sides and 5 vertices.

pictograph

A pictograph uses pictures to show data.

Favorite Ball Games	
Baseball	
Soccer	
Tennis	

Each ⚲ = I student

plane shape

A plane shape is a flat shape.

circle   rectangle   square   triangle

p.m.

The half of the day from midday to midnight can be described as p.m.

7:10 PM

polygon

A polygon is a plane shape with 3 or more sides.

G8

Glossary

predict

When you predict, you say what you think will happen.

There is a pattern in this cube train.

You can predict that the next two cubes will be green and yellow.

producer

When you make something to sell, you are a producer.

product

The answer to a multiplication sentence is called the product.

$$4 \times 2 = 8$$

product

pyramid

A pyramid is a solid figure with a base that is a polygon and faces that are triangles that meet in a point.

quadrilateral

A quadrilateral is a polygon with 4 sides.

quarter

25 cents or 25¢

quarter past

15 minutes after the hour.

It is quarter past 4.

quarter to

15 minutes before the hour.

It is quarter to 4.

rectangular prism

A rectangular prism is a solid figure with bases that are rectangles.

regroup

10 ones can be regrouped as 1 ten.

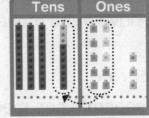

related

Addition facts and subtraction facts are related if they have the same numbers.

$$2 + 3 = 5$$
$$5 - 2 = 3$$

responsible

When you are given something to use for a certain amount of time and you return it when you are done, you are being responsible.

row

1	2	3	4	5
11	12	13	14	15
21	22	23	24	25
31	32	33	34	35

← row

save

If you save your money, you will have more money.

separate

To separate can mean to subtract, or to take something apart into two or more parts.

$$5 - 2 = 3$$

side

A side is a line segment that makes one part of a plane shape.

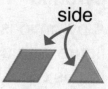
side

solid figures

Solid figures have length, width, and height.

These are all solid figures.

spend

If you spend your money, you will have less money.

sphere

A sphere is a solid figure that looks like a ball.

square units

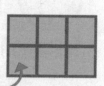

square unit

The area of the rectangle is 6 square units.

standard form

The standard form is a way to write a number using only digits.

436

subtract

When you subtract, you find out how many are left or which group has more.

$$5 - 3 = 2$$

subtraction sentence

$$12 - 4 = 8$$

difference

minus

sum

$$3 + 4 = 7$$

$$\begin{array}{r} 4 \\ + 3 \\ \hline 7 \end{array}$$

sum

sum →

symbol

A character or picture used to represent something is called a symbol.

The symbol will be ♀. Each ♀ represents 1 student.

tally mark

We use tally marks to keep track of information in an organized list.

Ways to Show 30¢			
Quarter	Dime	Nickel	Total
I		I	30¢
	III		30¢
	II	II	30¢
I		IIII	30¢
		卌 I	30¢

tens digit

how many groups of ten are in a number

2**3**8

↑
tens digit

thousand

10 hundreds make 1 thousand.

times

Another word for multiply is times.

times

$7 \times 3 = 21$

↑   ↑   ↑
factor   factor   product

trapezoid

A trapezoid is a plane shape with 4 sides, 4 angles, and 4 vertices. One pair of sides are parallel.

triangular prism

A triangular prism has two faces that are triangles and three other faces that are rectangles.

unequal

Unequal parts are parts that are not equal.

5 unequal parts

unit

You can use different units to measure objects.

About 12 inches. About 1 foot.

vertex

vertex

A vertex is a point where 2 sides or 3 or more edges meet. A cone also has a vertex.

whole

The two halves make one whole circle.

width

Width is the distance across an object.

withdrawal

When you take money out of the bank, you are making a withdrawal.

yard

A baseball bat is about a yard long.

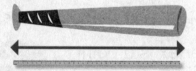